Vietnam War
Biographies

Volume 2: L–Z

Vietnam War
Biographies

Kevin Hillstrom
and Laurie Collier
Hillstrom

Diane Sawinski, Editor

AN IMPRINT OF THE GALE GROUP

DETROIT · SAN FRANCISCO · LONDON
BOSTON · WOODBRIDGE, CT

Vietnam War: Biographies

Kevin Hillstrom and Laurie Collier Hillstrom

Staff

Diane Sawinski and Allison McNeill, *U•X•L Senior Editors*
Carol DeKane Nagel, *U•X•L Managing Editor*
Thomas L. Romig, *U•X•L Publisher*

Sarah Tomasek, *Permissions Specialist*

Randy Bassett, *Image Database Supervisor*
Robert Duncan, *Imaging Specialist*
Pamela A. Reed, *Image Coordinator*
Dean Dauphinais, *Senior Image Editor*

Michelle DiMercurio, *Senior Art Director*

Mary Beth Trimper, *Manager, Composition and Electronic Prepress*
Evi Seoud, *Assistant Manager, Composition Purchasing and Electronic Prepress*

Rita Wimberley, *Senior Buyer*
Dorothy Maki, *Manufacturing Manager*

LM Design, *Typesetting*

Front cover photographs: Abbie Hoffman (reproduced by permission of New York Times Co./Archive Photos); Lyndon Johnson with troops (reproduced by permission of Corbis Corporation); Back cover photograph: Ngo Dinh Nhu (reproduced by permission of AP/Wide World Photos).

Library of Congress Cataloging-in-Publication Data

Hillstrom, Kevin, 1963-
 Vietnam War: biographies/Kevin Hillstrom and Laurie Collier Hillstrom; Diane Sawinski, editor.
  p. cm.
 Includes bibliographical references and index.
 ISBN 0-7876-4884-1 (set) - ISBN 0-7876-4885-X (vol. 1) - ISBN 0-7876-4886-8 (vol. 2)
 1. Vietnamese Conflict, 1961-1975-Biography-Juvenile literature. 2. United States-Biography-Juvenile literature. 3. Vietnam-Biography-Juvenile literature. [1. Vietnamese Conflict, 1961-1975-Biography. 2. United States-Biography.] I. Hillstrom, Laurie Collier, 1965- II. Sawinski, Diane M. III. Title.

DS557.5 .H55 2001
959.704'3'0922-dc21
[B]   00-056378

Printed in the United States of America

10 9 8 7 6 5 4 3 2

Contents

Volume 2: L-Z

Reader's Guide

Vietnam War: Biographies presents biographies of sixty men and women who participated in or were affected by the Vietnam War. These two volumes profile a diverse mix of personalities from both the United States and Vietnam, including politicians, military leaders, antiwar activists, journalists, authors, nurses, veterans, and civilians who got caught in the middle of the conflict.

Detailed biographies of major Vietnam War figures (such as Ho Chi Minh, Lyndon B. Johnson, Robert McNamara, Ngo Dinh Diem, and Richard M. Nixon) are included. But *Vietnam War: Biographies* also provides biographical information on lesser-known but nonetheless important and fascinating men and women of that era. Examples include Daniel Berrigan, a Catholic priest who went to prison for burning military draft files as a form of protest against the war; Jeremiah Denton, an American prisoner-of-war who blinked the word "torture" in Morse code during a televised interview with his North Vietnamese captors; Tim Page, a daring British combat photographer who produced some of the best known images of the war before being seriously wounded; Phan Thi Kim

Phuc, a nine-year-old Vietnamese girl who was photographed running naked down a country road after suffering terrible burns from a U.S.-ordered napalm attack in her village; and Jan Scruggs, an American veteran who led the drive to create the Vietnam Veterans Memorial in Washington, D.C.

Vietnam War: Biographies also features sidebars containing interesting facts, excerpts from memoirs, diaries, and speeches, and short biographies of people who are in some way connected with the leading figures of the era. Within each full-length biography, cross-references direct readers to other individuals profiled in the two-volume set. More than seventy black and white photographs enhance the text. In addition, each volume contains a timeline that lists significant dates and events of the Vietnam War era, a glossary, further readings, and a cumulative subject index.

Vietnam War Reference Library

Vietnam War: Biographies is only one component of the three-part U•X•L Vietnam War Reference Library. The other two titles in this set are:

- *Vietnam War: Almanac:* This work presents a comprehensive overview of the Vietnam War. The volume's sixteen chapters cover all aspects of the conflict, from the reasons behind American involvement, to the antiwar protests that rocked the nation, to the fall of Saigon to Communist forces in 1975. The chapters are arranged chronologically and explore such topics as Vietnam's struggles under French colonial rule, the introduction of U.S. combat troops in 1965, the Tet Offensive, and the lasting impact of the war on both the United States and Vietnam. Interspersed are four chapters that cover the growth of the American antiwar movement, the experiences of U.S. soldiers in Vietnam, Vietnam veterans in American society, and the effect of the war on Vietnam's land and people. The Almanac also contains "Words to Know" and "People to Know" sections, a timeline, research and activity ideas and a subject index.

- *Vietnam War: Primary Sources:* This title presents thirteen full or excerpted speeches and written works from the Vietnam War era. The volume includes excerpts from civil rights leader Martin Luther King, Jr.'s 1967 antiwar speech at Riverside Church in New York City; President Richard Nixon's 1969 "Silent Majority" speech; Le Ly Hayslip's memoir *When Heaven and Earth Changed Places,* about growing up in a war-torn Vietnamese village and becoming involved with the Viet Cong; and Admiral James Stockdale's memoir about his years in a Vietnamese prisoner-of-war camp, *In Love and War.* Each entry includes an introduction, things to remember while reading the excerpt, information on what happened after the work was published or the event took place, and other interesting facts. Photographs, source information, and an index supplement the work.

- A cumulative index of all three titles in the U•X•L Vietnam War Reference Library is also available.

Acknowledgments

The authors extend thanks to U•X•L Senior Editor Diane Sawinski and U•X•L Publisher Tom Romig at the Gale Group for their assistance throughout the production of this series.

Comments and Suggestions

We welcome your comments on *Vietnam War: Biographies* and suggestions for other topics in history to consider. Please write: Editors, *Vietnam War: Biographies,* U•X•L, 27500 Drake Rd., Farmington Hills, Michigan 48331-3535; call toll-free 800-877-4253; fax to 248-414-5043; or send e-mail via http://www.galegroup.com.

Vietnam War Timeline

1862   Under the Treaty of Saigon, Vietnam gives control of three eastern provinces to France.

1863   France makes Cambodia a French colony.

1883   Under the Treaty of Hue, France expands its control over all of Vietnam.

1887   France turns its holdings in Southeast Asia into one colony, called Indochina.

1893   France makes Laos a French colony.

1930   Ho Chi Minh creates the Indochinese Communist Party to oppose French colonial rule.

1940   Japan occupies Indochina during World War II.

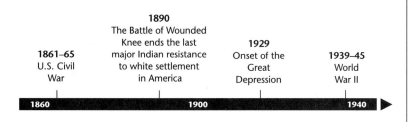

1890
The Battle of Wounded Knee ends the last major Indian resistance to white settlement in America

1861–65
U.S. Civil War

1929
Onset of the Great Depression

1939–45
World War II

1860   1900   1940

Ho Chi Minh.

1941 The Communist-led Vietnamese nationalist organization known as the Viet Minh is established.

March 1945 Emperor Bao Dai proclaims Vietnam an independent nation under Japan's protection.

April 1945 U.S. president Franklin Roosevelt dies; Harry S. Truman takes office.

August 1945 Japan surrenders to end World War II.

August 1945 Bao Dai is removed from power in the August Revolution.

September 1945 Ho Chi Minh establishes the Democratic Republic of Vietnam and declares himself president.

September 1945 U.S. Army Major A. Peter Dewey becomes the first American soldier to die in Vietnam.

March 1946 France declares Vietnam an independent state within the French Union.

November 1946 The First Indochina War begins with a Viet Minh attack on French forces in Hanoi.

1949 France creates the independent State of Vietnam under Bao Dai.

January 1950 Communist countries China, Yugoslavia, and the Soviet Union formally recognize the Democratic Republic of Vietnam under Ho Chi Minh.

February 1950 Democratic countries Great Britain and the United States formally recognize the State of Vietnam under Bao Dai.

May 1950 The United States begins providing military and economic aid to French forces in Vietnam.

June 1950 Truman sends U.S. troops into Korea to begin the Korean War.

1944
Anne Frank and family are captured by the Nazis after two years in hiding and taken to the concentration camp at Auschwitz

1946
The Cold War between the United States and the Soviet Union begins

1949
People's Republic of China proclaimed by Mao Tse-tung

1950
Korean War begins

1942   1946   1950

1952 Dwight Eisenhower becomes president of the United States.

1954 An estimated one million Vietnamese flee North Vietnam for South Vietnam. Many credit Edward Lansdale, a secret agent for the U.S. Central Intelligence Agency (CIA), as a key reason for this mass exodus.

March 1954 The Viet Minh set up a siege of the French outpost at Dien Bien Phu.

May 1954 Viet Minh forces defeat the French in the Battle of Dien Bien Phu.

June 1954 Bao Dai selects Ngo Dinh Diem as prime minister of the State of Vietnam.

July 1954 The Geneva Accords divide Vietnam into two sections: North Vietnam, led by Communists under Ho Chi Minh; and South Vietnam, led by a U.S.-supported government under Ngo Dinh Diem.

July 1954 Laos and Cambodia are granted full independence from France.

October 1954 French troops are withdrawn from Vietnam.

July 1955 Ngo Dinh Diem refuses to proceed with national elections required by the Geneva Accords.

September 1955 Cambodia gains independence from France; Norodom Sihanouk becomes prime minister.

October 1955 Diem takes control of the South Vietnamese government from Bao Dai and establishes the Republic of Vietnam.

1957 Communist rebels begin fighting for control of South Vietnam.

1959 Construction begins on the Ho Chi Minh Trail, a major supply and communications route for Communist forces.

1953 James Watson and Francis Crick decipher the structure of DNA

1954 Egypt and Britain conclude a pact on the Suez Canal, ending 72 years of British military occupation

1956 Soviet troops suppress a revolution in Hungary

1959 Ruth and Eliot Handler, owners of Mattel, unveil the Barbie Doll

1953   1956   1959

Robert McNamara.
Reproduced by permission of AP/Wide World Photos.

1960 Le Duan is elevated to secretary general of the Communist Party, making him one of the most powerful men in North Vietnam during the Vietnam War.

November 1960 Rebels try to overthrow the Diem government.

November 1960 John F. Kennedy becomes president of the United States.

November 1960 The National Liberation Front is established in North Vietnam to overthrow Diem and reunite the two parts of Vietnam.

1961 Kennedy offers military assistance to Diem and sends the first U.S. advisors to South Vietnam.

January 1963 The Battle of Ap Bac brings American public attention to Vietnam.

April 1963 Buddhists begin demonstrating against the Diem government.

June 1963 The suicide of a Buddhist monk draws international attention to the situation in Vietnam.

September 1963 President Kennedy sends military advisor Maxwell Taylor and Secretary of Defense Robert McNamara to Vietnam to conduct a study of the escalating situation between South Vietnam and the Viet Cong.

November 1963 Ngo Dinh Diem and other members of his government are assassinated; the Military Revolutionary Council takes control of South Vietnam.

November 1963 President Kennedy is assassinated; Lyndon Johnson takes office.

July 1964 Senator Barry Goldwater loses to Lyndon Johnson in one of the most lopsided presidential elections in American history.

August 1964 North Vietnamese patrol boats reportedly attack American warships in the Gulf of Tonkin.

Lyndon B. Johnson.
Reproduced by permission of AP/Wide World Photos.

1960
Theodore Maiman builds the first working laser

1961
CIA-backed invasion of Cuba at the Bay of Pigs

1962
Television satellite Telstar put into orbit by U.S.A.

| 1960 | 1961 | 1962 |

August 1964 The U.S. Congress passes the Gulf of Tonkin Resolution, which allows Johnson to use any means necessary to prevent North Vietnamese aggression.

November 1964 Johnson is reelected as president of the United States.

1965 Nguyen Thi Dinh is named deputy commander of the Communist-led National Liberation Front (NLF) armed forces, which is the highest combat position held by a woman during the Vietnam War.

February 1965 Viet Cong guerillas attack a U.S. base at Pleiku; the U.S. military retaliates with air attacks.

March 1965 The American bombing campaign known as Operation Rolling Thunder begins over North Vietnam.

March 1965 The first U.S. combat troops are sent to Vietnam.

March 1965 Faculty of the University of Michigan organize a teach-in to protest the war.

June 1965 Nguyen Cao Ky becomes premier of South Vietnam.

August 1965 Henry Cabot Lodge is appointed as American ambassador to South Vietnam.

November 1965 Antiwar demonstrations become widespread in the United States.

1966 U.S. national security advisor McGeorge Bundy resigns from office due to doubts about U.S. policy toward Vietnam.

1966 American prisoner-of-war Jeremiah Denton blinks "torture" in Morse code during a televised interview with his North Vietnamese captors.

January 1966 Senator J. William Fulbright arranges for the Senate Foreign Relations Committee to hold public hearings on American military involvement in Viet-

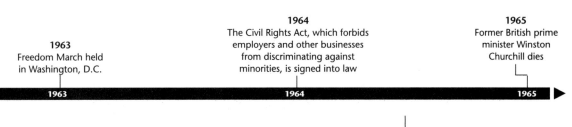

1963
Freedom March held in Washington, D.C.

1964
The Civil Rights Act, which forbids employers and other businesses from discriminating against minorities, is signed into law

1965
Former British prime minister Winston Churchill dies

1963   1964   1965

Martin Luther King, Jr.
Reproduced by permission of National Archives and Records.

Robert F. Kennedy.
Library of Congress.

nam. The hearings are widely credited with increasing public skepticism about the Johnson administration's handling of the Vietnam War.

February 1967 French journalist Bernard Fall is killed by a land mine while covering the war in Vietnam.

April 1967 Civil rights leader Martin Luther King, Jr., speaks out against the Vietnam War.

September 1967 Nguyen Van Thieu becomes president of South Vietnam.

October 1967 The March on the Pentagon draws 50,000 anti-war protesters to Washington, D.C.

October 1967 Navy pilot John McCain's fighter plane is shot down over Hanoi. He becomes a prisoner-of-war (POW) for more than five years in North Vietnam.

January 1968 The Siege of Khe Sanh begins.

January 1968 North Vietnamese forces, headed up by Vo Nguyen Giap, launch the Tet Offensive.

January 1968 The Battle for Hue begins.

February 1968 Clark Clifford replaces Robert McNamara as U.S. secretary of defense.

March 1968 U.S. troops kill hundreds of Vietnamese civilians in the My Lai Massacre.

March 1968 Johnson announces he will not seek reelection.

April 1968 Civil rights leader Martin Luther King, Jr., is assassinated.

May 1968 The United States and North Vietnam begin peace negotiations in Paris.

May 1968 Catholic priest Daniel Berrigan burns military draft files in Catonsville, Maryland, to protest the Vietnam War.

1966	1967	1967	1968
Cultural Revolution begins in China	Dr. Christiaan Barnard performs the first human heart transplant	*Rolling Stone* magazine begins publication	Ralph Lauren introduces his Polo line of clothing
1966	1967		1968

June 1968 U.S. senator and Democratic presidential candidate Robert F. Kennedy is assassinated.

June 1968 William Westmoreland is relieved of his command over U.S. troops in Vietnam.

August 1968 Antiwar protestors disrupt the Democratic National Convention in Chicago. Chicago police, under the leadership of Chicago mayor Richard J. Daley, are criticized for their use of violence to quiet angry protestors.

October 1968 Johnson announces an end to the bombing of North Vietnam.

November 1968 Richard M. Nixon is elected president of the United States.

January 1969 Former U.S. attorney general Ramsey Clark leaves office and becomes an outspoken member of the antiwar movement.

February 1969 Secret bombing of Cambodia begins.

April 1969 U.S. troop levels in Vietnam peak at 543,400.

June 1969 Nixon puts his "Vietnamization" policy into effect, reducing U.S. troop levels by 25,000.

September 1969 North Vietnamese leader Ho Chi Minh dies.

September 1969 The "Chicago Seven" trial begins, in which David Dellinger, Abbie Hoffman, Tom Hayden, and other prominent antiwar activists are charged with conspiracy for disrupting the Democratic National Convention.

April 1970 Lon Nol seizes power from Norodom Sihanouk in Cambodia.

April 1970 Nixon authorizes American troops to invade Cambodia.

William Westmoreland.
Reproduced by permission of Archive Photos.

Abbie Hoffman.
Library of Congress.

July 1969 U.S. astronaut Neil Armstrong becomes the first man to walk on the moon	**August 1969** Woodstock Music Fair attracts three hundred thousand people	**1970** Television and radio cigarette ads are banned in the U.S.	**1971** Greenpeace founded in Vancouver, Canada
1969		1970	1971

Bobby Seale.
Reproduced by permission of AP/Wide World Photos.

Vo Nguyen Giap.
Reproduced by permission of Archive Photos.

May 1970 The National Guard kills four student protestors during an antiwar demonstration at Kent State University in Ohio.

June 1970 U.S. troops withdraw from Cambodia.

October 1970 Antiwar groups hold the first Moratorium Day protests.

November 1970 Nixon makes his "Silent Majority" speech.

November 1970 The My Lai Massacre is revealed to the American people.

November 1970 Lt. William Calley is put on trial for his role in the My Lai Massacre.

December 1970 The U.S. Congress repeals the Tonkin Gulf Resolution.

February 1971 Daniel Ellsberg leaks the top-secret Pentagon Papers to reporter Neil Sheehan.

June 1971 The *New York Times* begins publishing the Pentagon Papers.

1972 Actress Jane Fonda makes a controversial visit to North Vietnam.

1972 American journalist Frances FitzGerald publishes *Fire in the Lake,* which looks at the war from a Vietnamese perspective.

1972 American journalist David Halberstam publishes *The Best and the Brightest,* about the U.S. officials who developed the government's policy toward Vietnam.

March 1972 North Vietnamese troops, under the leadership of Vo Nguyen Giap, begin the Easter Offensive.

June 1972 Republican agents associated with Nixon break into the Democratic presidential campaign headquarters at the Watergate Hotel in Washington, D.C.

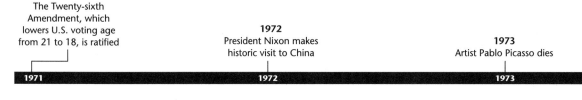

1971
The Twenty-sixth Amendment, which lowers U.S. voting age from 21 to 18, is ratified

1972
President Nixon makes historic visit to China

1973
Artist Pablo Picasso dies

1971   1972   1973

August 1972 The last U.S. combat troops withdraw from Vietnam.

November 1972 Nixon is reelected as president after defeating Democratic nominee George McGovern.

December 1972 U.S. warplanes begin the Christmas bombing campaign.

January 1973 The United States and North Vietnam sign the Paris Peace Accords.

February 1973 North Vietnam releases American prisoners of war (POWs).

June 1973 The U.S. Congress passes the Case-Church Amendment, prohibiting further American military involvement in Southeast Asia.

October 1973 Spiro T. Agnew resigns as vice president of the United States.

October 1973 North Vietnamese negotiator Le Duc Tho and U.S. secretary of state Henry Kissinger are awarded the Nobel Peace Prize.

November 1973 The U.S. Congress passes the War Powers Act over Nixon's veto, reducing the president's authority to commit U.S. military forces.

August 1974 Threatened with impeachment over the Watergate scandal, Nixon resigns from office; Gerald R. Ford becomes president of the United States.

September 1974 President Ford pardons Richard Nixon.

March 1975 North Vietnamese forces capture Hue, Da Nang, and other South Vietnamese cities.

March 1975 President Nguyen Van Thieu orders South Vietnamese forces to withdraw from the central provinces, causing the "Convoy of Tears."

1974
Anthropologists discover "Lucy,"
a hominid skeleton more than
three million years old

1975
Bill Gates organizes
Microsoft Corp.

1976
Viking I and *Viking II*
space probes land
on Mars

1974　　　　　　　　　　1975　　　　　　　　　　1976

Joan Baez.
Reproduced by permission of Jack Vartoogian.

April 1975 The U.S. embassy in Saigon is evacuated by military helicopters.

April 1975 North Vietnamese forces capture the South Vietnamese capital of Saigon to win the Vietnam War.

April 1975 Communist Khmer Rouge rebels capture the capital of Phnom Penh and take control of Cambodia.

May 1975 Khmer Rouge forces capture the U.S. merchant ship *Mayaguez.*

August 1975 The Communist-led Pathet Lao take control of Laos, removing prime minister Souvanna Phouma from rule.

1976 Vietnam veteran Ron Kovic publishes his memoir *Born on the Fourth of July.*

July 1976 Vietnam is reunited as one country under Communist rule, called the Socialist Republic of Vietnam. Pham Van Dong becomes premier of the newly formed country.

November 1976 Jimmy Carter is elected president of the United States.

1977 Carter pardons most Vietnam War draft evaders.

1977 Journalist Michael Herr publishes *Dispatches,* based on his experiences reporting on the war in Vietnam.

1978 Thousands of refugees known as "boat people" flee from Vietnam, creating an international crisis.

1978 Vietnam invades Cambodia and takes control of the government away from the violent Khmer Rouge.

1978 Veteran Bobby Muller cofounds the support organization Vietnam Veterans of America.

1979 China reacts to the Vietnamese invasion of Cambodia by invading northern Vietnam.

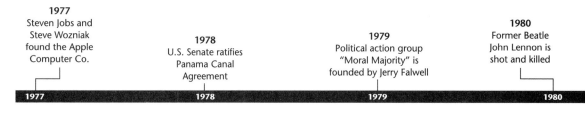

1977 Steven Jobs and Steve Wozniak found the Apple Computer Co.

1978 U.S. Senate ratifies Panama Canal Agreement

1979 Political action group "Moral Majority" is founded by Jerry Falwell

1980 Former Beatle John Lennon is shot and killed

1977   1978   1979   1980

1979	Vietnam veteran Jan Scruggs cofounds the Vietnam Veterans Memorial Fund (VVMF).

1979   Joan Baez forms a group called Humanitas to raise money for food and medical supplies for the many refugees from Vietnam, Cambodia, and Laos in refugee camps in northern Thailand.

1980   Ronald Reagan is elected president of the United States.

1980   U.S. Army nurse Lynda Van Devanter founds the Vietnam Veterans of America Women's Project to assist female veterans.

1982   The Vietnam Veterans Memorial, designed by Maya Lin, is dedicated in Washington, D.C.

1983   Photojournalist Tim Page publishes *Tim Page's Nam,* a collection of his best known images of the war.

1984   American Vietnam veterans reach an out-of-court settlement with chemical companies over health problems related to their wartime exposure to the poisonous herbicide Agent Orange.

1984   Diane Carlson Evans founds the Vietnam Women's Memorial Project to raise funds for a memorial for female veterans.

1986   Nguyen Van Linh becomes head of the Communist Party in Vietnam and introduces the *Doi Moi* economic reforms.

1986   *Platoon,* the award-winning film about a young American soldier in Vietnam, is released. It is directed by Vietnam veteran Oliver Stone.

1988   George Bush becomes president of the United States.

1988   Reporter Neil Sheehan publishes *A Bright Shining Lie: John Paul Vann and America in Vietnam.*

Lynda Van Devanter.
Reproduced by permission of AP/Wide World Photos.

Diane Carlson Evans.
Reproduced by permission of AP/Wide World Photos.

1981	1984	1986	1988
Acquired Immune Deficiency virus (AIDS) is identified	Olympic Games at Los Angeles, California, are boycotted by Soviet bloc countries	U.S. space shuttle *Challenger* explodes seconds after takeoff, killing seven astronauts including teacher Christa McAuliffe	Colin Powell becomes first black 4-star general in U.S. Army

| 1982 | 1984 | 1986 | 1988 |

Le Ly Hayslip.
Reproduced by permission of AP/Wide World Photos.

Nguyen Thi Binh.
Reproduced by permission of Corbis Corporation.

1989 Vietnam withdraws its troops from Cambodia.

1989 Le Ly Hayslip publishes *When Heaven and Earth Changed Places,* her memoir about growing up in South Vietnam during the Vietnam War.

1990 Tim O'Brien publishes *The Things They Carried,* which is regarded as the single greatest work of literature ever written about the American experience in Vietnam.

1992 Bill Clinton is elected president of the United States.

1993 The United Nations sponsors free elections in Cambodia; Norodom Sihanouk regains his position as king.

1993 The Vietnam Women's Memorial is dedicated in Washington, D.C.

1993 Nguyen Thi Binh, the second-ranking negotiator for the North Vietnamese side in the Paris peace talks, is elected vice president of Vietnam.

1994 President Clinton ends the economic embargo against trade with Vietnam.

1995 The United States restores full diplomatic relations with Vietnam.

1995 Former secretary of defense Robert McNamara publishes *In Retrospect,* in which he reveals his personal doubts about U.S. actions in Vietnam.

1998 Pol Pot, former leader of the Cambodian Communists known as the Khmer Rouge, dies under mysterious circumstances.

1990
Mikhail Gorbachev, president of the Soviet Union, is awarded the Nobel Peace Prize

1993
North American Free Trade Agreement (NAFTA) is signed

1997
U.S. diplomat Madeline Albright becomes the first woman secretary of state

1998
President Bill Clinton is impeached by the House of Representatives

1990   **1993**   **1996**   **1999**

Words to Know

A

ARVN: The South Vietnamese army, officially known as the Army of the Republic of South Vietnam. The ARVN fought on the same side as U.S. troops during the Vietnam War.

B

Buddhism: A religion based on the teaching of Gautama Buddha, in which followers seek moral purity and spiritual enlightenment.

C

Cambodia: Southeast Asian nation located on the western border of South Vietnam. During the Vietnam War, Cambodia experienced its own civil war between its pro-U.S. government forces and Communist rebels known as the Khmer Rouge.

Cold War: A period of intense rivalry between the United States and the Soviet Union as both nations competed to spread their political philosophies and influence around the world after the end of World War II. The climate of distrust and hostility between the two nations and their allies dominated international politics until the 1980s.

Colonialism: A practice in which one country assumes political control over another country. Most colonial powers established colonies in foreign lands in order to take possession of valuable natural resources and increase their own power. They often showed little concern for the rights and well-being of the native people.

Communism: A political system in which the government controls all resources and means of producing wealth. By eliminating private property, this system is designed to create an equal society with no social classes. However, Communist governments in practice often limit personal freedom and individual rights.

Coup d'etat: A sudden, decisive attempt to overthrow an existing government.

D

Dien Bien Phu: A French fort in northwestern Vietnam that was the site of a major battle in the Indochina War in 1954.

Domino Theory: A political theory that held that the fall of one country's government to communism usually triggered similar collapses in neighboring countries, as if the nations were dominoes falling in sequence.

E

Escalation: A policy of increasing the size, scope, and intensity of military activity.

G

Great Society: A set of social programs proposed by President Lyndon Johnson designed to end segregation and reduce poverty in the United States.

Guerrilla: A member of a native military force operating in small units in occupied territory to harass the enemy, often with surprise attacks.

H

Hanoi: The capital city of Communist North Vietnam. Also an unofficial shorthand way of referring to the North Vietnamese government.

I

Indochina: The name sometimes given to the peninsula between India and China in Southeast Asia. The term narrowly refers to Cambodia, Laos, and Vietnam, which were united under the name French Indochina during the colonial period, 1893-1954.

Indochina War: Later known as the First Indochina War (the Vietnam War became the Second Indochina War), this conflict took place between France and Communist-led Viet Minh forces in Vietnam, 1946-54.

K

Khmer Rouge: Communist-led rebel forces that fought for control of Cambodia during the Vietnam War years. The Khmer Rouge overthrew the U.S.-backed government of Lon Nol in 1975.

L

Laos: A Southeast Asian nation located on the western border of North Vietnam. During the Vietnam War, Laos experienced its own civil war between U.S.-backed forces and Communist rebels known as the Pathet Lao.

M

MIAs: Soldiers classified as "missing in action," meaning that their status is unknown to military leaders or that their bodies have not been recovered.

Military Revolutionary Council: A group of South Vietnamese military officers that overthrew President Ngo Dinh Diem and took control of South Vietnam's government in 1963.

N

Nationalism: A feeling of intense loyalty and devotion to a country or homeland. Some people argued that nationalism, rather than communism, was the main factor that caused the Viet Minh to fight the French for control of Vietnam.

North Vietnam: The Geneva Accords of 1954, which ended the First Indochina War, divided the nation of Vietnam into two sections. The northern section, which was led by a Communist government under Ho Chi Minh, was officially known as the Democratic Republic of Vietnam but was usually called North Vietnam.

NVA: The North Vietnamese Army, which assisted the Viet Cong guerilla fighters in trying to conquer South Vietnam. These forces opposed the United States in the Vietnam War.

O

Offensive: A sudden, aggressive attack by one side during a war.

P

Paris Peace Accords: A peace agreement, signed on January 25, 1973, between the United States and North Vietnam that ended direct American involvement in the Vietnam War.

Pentagon Papers: A set of secret U.S. Department of Defense documents that explained American military policy toward Vietnam from 1945 to 1968. They created a controversy when they were leaked to the national media in 1971.

Post-Traumatic Stress Syndrome (PTSS): A set of psychological problems that are caused by exposure to a dangerous or disturbing situation, such as combat. People who suffer from PTSS may have symptoms like depression, flashbacks, nightmares, and angry outbursts.

S

Saigon: The capital city of U.S.-supported South Vietnam. Also an unofficial shorthand way of referring to the South Vietnamese government.

Silent Majority: A term used by President Richard Nixon to describe the large number of American people he believed quietly supported his Vietnam War policies. In contrast, Nixon referred to the antiwar movement in the United States as a vocal minority.

Socialist Republic of Vietnam (SRV): The country created in 1976, after North Vietnam won the Vietnam War and reunited with South Vietnam.

South Vietnam: Created under the Geneva Accords of 1954, the southern section of Vietnam was known as the Republic of South Vietnam. It was led by a U.S.-supported government.

T

Tonkin Gulf Resolution: Passed by Congress after U.S. Navy ships supposedly came under attack in the Gulf of Tonkin, this resolution gave President Lyndon Johnson the authority to wage war against North Vietnam.

V

Veteran: A former member of the armed forces.

Veterans Administration: A U.S. government agency responsible for providing medical care, insurance, pensions, and other benefits to American veterans of Vietnam and other wars.

Viet Cong: Vietnamese Communist guerilla fighters who worked with the North Vietnamese Army to conquer South Vietnam.

Viet Minh: Communist-led nationalist group that worked to gain Vietnam's independence from French colonial rule.

Vietnamization: A policy proposed by President Richard Nixon that involved returning responsibility for the war to the South Vietnamese. It was intended to allow the United States to reduce its military involvement without allowing the country to fall to communism.

W

Watergate: A political scandal that forced U.S. President Richard Nixon to resign from office in 1974. In June 1972, Republican agents associated with Nixon's reelection campaign broke into the Democratic campaign headquarters in the Watergate Hotel in Washington, D.C., to gather secret information. Nixon and several members of his administration attempted to cover up the burglary.

Vietnam War
Biographies

Edward Lansdale

Born February 6, 1908
Dayton, Ohio
Died February 23, 1987
McLean, Virginia

U.S. intelligence agent in Vietnam

E dward Lansdale was a secret agent for the U.S. Central Intelligence Agency (CIA) who played an important role in South Vietnam during its first years of existence. During the 1950s he organized secret missions to hurt North Vietnam and strengthen South Vietnam's government. His efforts were so effective that he became known to some people as the "Father of South Vietnam." But as time passed, Lansdale's experiences in Vietnam turned sour. In 1963 he saw President Ngo Dinh Diem's (see entry) government fall in a military coup, and in later years his advice on conducting the war was ignored by American political leaders and generals.

Early life and education

Edward Geary Lansdale was born in Dayton, Ohio, on February 6, 1908. His parents were Henry and Sarah Frances (Philips) Lansdale. According to biographer Cecil Currey, "Lansdale grew up as a typical American boy of his time. He was a Boy Scout, had a paper route, worked on a bread route, fought and played with his brothers, sold the *Saturday Evening Post* on street corners . . . and made a B average in school."

"[Lansdale was] one of the greatest spies in history. [His] accomplishments were the stuff of legends."

Former CIA Director William Colby.

After graduating from high school in 1926, Lansdale enrolled in the University of California at Los Angeles (UCLA). In 1931 he left UCLA with a bachelor's degree and a second lieutenant of infantry ranking in the U.S. military reserves. During the remainder of the decade, Lansdale worked in the advertising industry and started a family with Helen Batcheller. They married in 1933 and eventually had two children (Batcheller died in 1972, and Lansdale married Patrocinio Yapcinco a year later).

When the United States became involved in World War II in 1941, Lansdale immediately applied to return to active military service. But when action on his application was delayed, he began to look for other ways to serve his country during the war. In 1942 he used political and military contacts to gain acceptance into the U.S. Office of Strategic Services (OSS), an agency whose responsibilities included intelligence-gathering and secret spy missions against America's enemies. In 1947 this agency became the Central Intelligence Agency (CIA).

In February 1943 Lansdale's request for a return to active service was finally granted. The Army made him a first lieutenant and assigned him to its Military Intelligence Service for "limited service." But as the war progressed, Lansdale spent most of his time working for the OSS. He transferred to the U.S. Air Force in 1947, after it became an independent branch of the U.S. armed forces, but he remained closely associated with the CIA.

Gains reputation as top American spy in Philippines

In 1950 Lansdale used his cover as an Air Force officer to undertake a CIA mission in the Philippines, where guerrillas known as Hukbalalhaps, or "Huks," wanted to overthrow the regime and institute a Communist government. But the United States fiercely opposed the Communist political philosophy. As a result, Lansdale was assigned to help defense minister Ramon Magsaysay and the Philippine government fend off the rebels and build a democratic government.

During the next few years, Lansdale launched a spectacularly successful campaign against the Huks. He worked with Magsaysay to introduce broad economic, social, and political reforms that helped the government "win the hearts and minds of the people." In addition, Lansdale employed psychological warfare techniques (actions designed to attack the mind or emotions of the enemy) that caused confusion and morale problems within the ranks of the Huks. At one point, the CIA agent even staged a series of fake vampire attacks that deeply frightened the superstitious Huks. By 1952 Lansdale's actions had helped neutralize the Huks and enabled Magsaysay to emerge as a strong and respected national leader of a blossoming democracy (Magsaysay's rule was cut short five years later when he died in a plane crash).

The CIA was so impressed with Lansdale's work in the Philippines that it decided to transfer him to South Vietnam, where another struggle against Communist rebels was just getting under way. South Vietnam had been created only a few months before by the Geneva Peace Accords, which ended French colonial rule in Vietnam. Under this treaty, Vietnam was temporarily divided into Communist-led North Vietnam and U.S.-supported South Vietnam. In addition, the agreement called for national elections to be held in 1956 so that the two sections of Vietnam could be united under one government. But South Vietnamese and American officials decided to ignore this part of the treaty because they feared that the Communists would be victorious and gain control over the entire country. This decision triggered hostilities between the two sides, which ultimately grew into the Vietnam War.

Lansdale's mission in Vietnam

Lansdale arrived in Vietnam in June 1954. Once he arrived in the capital city of Saigon, he immediately set up the Saigon Military Mission (SMM). This secret group of a dozen or so American soldiers and intelligence agents specialized in psychological warfare. Over the next several months, Lansdale and the other members of the SMM worked hard to give South Vietnam military, economic, and social advantages over North Vietnam.

One of Lansdale's key goals was to convince Vietnamese living in the North to relocate to the South. In order to accomplish this, he launched secret campaigns to frighten Northerners into leaving for the South. For example, Lansdale's agents spread rumors and counterfeit documents suggesting that North Vietnam's Communist leadership wanted to put many Vietnamese Catholics into huge prison camps. The SMM also recruited village chiefs and religious leaders to create what Stanley Karnow, author of *Vietnam: A History,* called "fake forecasts of doom under Communism." Finally, they distributed false information about a possible U.S. atomic bomb attack on North Vietnam.

An estimated one million Vietnamese—mostly Catholic—fled the North for the South during the mid-1950s. Many historians credit Lansdale's secret tactics as a key reason for this mass exodus. But he insisted that most people would have moved south anyway. "People just don't pull up their roots and transplant themselves because of slogans," Lansdale said in *Vietnam: A History.* "They honestly feared what might happen to them, and the emotion was strong enough to overcome their attachment to their land, their homes, and their ancestral graves. So the initiative was very much theirs—and we mainly made the transportation possible."

Lansdale also helped South Vietnamese President Ngo Dinh Diem strengthen his power. He trained Diem's forces in psychological warfare techniques, contributed to military strategy, and bribed local leaders to support the government. Diem respected and appreciated Lansdale for these efforts, and the two men soon became allies. As one member of the Saigon Military Mission told Cecil B. Currey in *Edward Lansdale: The Unquiet American,* "Diem trusted Lansdale about as much as he trusted any foreigner." This warm relationship with Diem reflected the agent's unusual ability to get along with Vietnamese people from every walk of life, from military officers to peasants.

As the months passed, however, Lansdale became angry about the widespread corruption, repression, and political fighting within Diem's government. The CIA agent warned Diem that if the government did not introduce reforms to correct these problems, it would lose the support of the South Vietnamese people. He expressed particular concern about Diem's habit of arresting political opponents. He told Diem that such actions "will only turn the talk into deep emotions of hatred and generate the formation of more clandestine [secret] organizations and plots to oppose you." But Diem

Fictional Treatments of Edward Lansdale

Two well-known novels of the 1950s featured major characters that were based at least in part on the life and career of Edward Lansdale. In 1955 British writer Graham Greene published *The Quiet American,* in which a Lansdale-like CIA agent named Alden Pyle resorts to ruthless and immoral actions to complete his mission against Communist forces in Vietnam. "In this . . . portrait," wrote Cecil Currey in *Edward Lansdale: The Unquiet American,* "[Pyle] blundered through the intrigue, treachery, and confusion of Vietnamese politics, leaving a trail of blood and suffering behind him." Today, Greene's book remains one of the most influential Vietnam War novels ever written.

A few years later a second book featuring a Lansdale-like character appeared. This book, *The Ugly American,* was written by Eugene Burdick, a professor of political science, and William Lederer, a former submarine captain who knew Lansdale in the Philippines. It featured the character of Colonel Edwin Barnum Hillandale, a brave American officer dedicated to keeping the Philippines out of the hands of Communist enemies. *The Ugly American* sold five million copies and spent more than a year on the best-seller lists.

The popularity of *The Ugly American* dramatically increased Lansdale's public visibility and gave him a reputation as one of the country's leading experts on guerrilla warfare, spying techniques, and Asian societies. But he resented the extra attention, especially after reporters started referring to him as "the Ugly American" in their stories. "[Lansdale] was well into his retirement before he ceased to care whether others identified him with Pyle or Hillandale," wrote Currey.

made little effort to correct his regime's growing political and military problems. Lansdale also detailed his concerns about Diem's repressive ways to U.S. officials in Washington, but his complaints had no impact on American policies. His frustration finally became so great that he requested a new assignment in 1956.

Lansdale returns to Vietnam

From 1957 to 1963, Lansdale worked for the U.S. Defense Department as deputy director of the Office of Special Operations, a department devoted to spying and other intelligence activities. In 1961, however, President John F. Kennedy

Former CIA Director William Colby.
Reproduced by permission of Archive Photos.

(see entry) sent Lansdale back to South Vietnam. The president shared Lansdale's belief that Diem needed to make reforms in order to win the loyalty of his nation's people. In addition, he was impressed with Lansdale's arguments that the best way to defeat the Communist threat in Vietnam was through the use of "counterinsurgency" techniques such as guerrilla-style warfare and pacification (the provision of aid and security to Vietnamese communities).

Upon returning to Saigon, Lansdale recommended increases in U.S. assistance to Diem. In January 1961, for example, he reported that "Vietnam is in a critical condition . . . requiring emergency treatment." But his efforts to breathe new life into Diem's fading regime failed. The president was murdered in a military coup in November 1963, and South Vietnam was wracked by political instability over the next several years.

Lansdale left South Vietnam after Diem's assassination, but he returned in 1965 as a special assistant to the U.S. ambassador. During that time, he repeatedly stated his beliefs that the United States could not win the Vietnam War without the support of the people or a military strategy that emphasized guerrilla warfare. But other U.S. officials ignored or criticized his recommendations, and he was unable to regain a position of real influence in Saigon. "He became an isolated and forlorn figure in his Saigon villa," wrote Glen Gendzel in *The Encyclopedia of the Vietnam War,* "and returned to the United States in 1968."

After submitting his resignation in 1968, Lansdale retired from public life. He settled in Virginia, where he died of heart disease in 1987. Today, he remains known as an important but shadowy figure in South Vietnam's early history, and as one of America's best-known intelligence agents. Lansdale was "one of the greatest spies in history," claimed former CIA Director William Colby. "[His] accomplishments were the stuff of legends."

Sources

Currey, Cecil B. *Edward Lansdale: The Unquiet American.* Boston: Houghton Mifflin, 1988.

Farrell, Barry. "The Ellsberg Mask." *Harper's,* October 1973.

Geyer, Georgie Anne. "Lansdale's Lament." *Washington Monthly,* June 1989.

Lansdale, Edward G. *In the Midst of Wars: An American's Mission to Southeast Asia.* New York: Harper and Row, 1972.

Lansdale, Edward G. "Two Steps to Get Us out of Vietnam." *Look,* March 4, 1969.

Le Duan

Born April 7, 1908
Quang Tri Province, Vietnam
Died July 10, 1986
Hanoi, Vietnam

North Vietnamese political leader

Le Duan published ten books and more than a hundred articles outlining his Communist philosophy during his lifetime.

Le Duan.
Reproduced by permission of Archive Photos.

Le Duan was one of the leaders of the Communist Party in Vietnam for nearly thirty years. He first joined the Communist rebels as a young man during their fight for independence from French rule. In 1930 he joined Ho Chi Minh (see entry) and other future North Vietnamese leaders in forming the Indochinese Communist Party. Le Duan rose through the ranks to become secretary general of the party, which had become known as the Vietnamese Workers' Party, in 1957. During the Vietnam War, he convinced Ho Chi Minh to support the South Vietnamese guerrilla fighters known as the Viet Cong. Le Duan remained in charge of the Vietnamese Communist Party until his death in 1986, although some younger members had begun to view his ideas as outdated by that time.

Keeps identity and background secret

Le Duan was born on April 7, 1908, in Quang Tri province in central Vietnam. Little is known about his early life. In fact, even his true identity is uncertain. He adopted the name Le Duan when he began his career as a revolutionary leader. Le Duan often claimed that he grew up in poverty in a rural village. But historians suspect that he actually came from a middle-class family, since it was clear that he had received a good education in French-speaking schools.

After completing his education, Le Duan took a job as a clerk for a railway company. At this time, Vietnam was a colony of France. Le Duan's job brought him into contact with Vietnamese Communists who wanted to gain Vietnam's independence from French rule. He eagerly joined other railway workers in demonstrations against the French colonial government. By the mid-1920s French forces began to crack down on protestors. Fearing for his safety, Le Duan fled to China, where he joined a growing number of Vietnamese Communists. In 1928 he joined the Revolutionary Youth League led by future North Vietnamese leader Ho Chi Minh. Two years later, Le Duan became a founding member of the Indochinese Communist Party.

After returning to Vietnam in 1931, Le Duan was arrested for his political activities against the French colonial government. He was sentenced to twenty years in prison, but he was released in 1936 when a more tolerant government came to power in France. Le Duan then continued his revolutionary activities, mostly in the southern provinces of Vietnam. In 1939 he was elected to the central committee that led the Communist Party. But the following year French forces once again began arresting their political opponents. Le Duan spent the next five years in a French prison on Con Son island. While in captivity, he met a number of fellow Communist revolutionaries and exchanged ideas and strategies with them.

Favors an active role in reuniting North and South

In the meantime, France suffered a series of military defeats during World War II (1939–45) and surrendered to Germany. Unable to protect its colonies in Indochina, the French government allowed Japan to occupy Vietnam and build military bases there. Ho Chi Minh and the Vietnamese Communists known as the Viet Minh viewed the Japanese occupation as an opportunity to break free from French rule. In 1945 the Allied Forces (which mainly consisted of the United States, Great Britain, and the Soviet Union) defeated both Germany and Japan to win World War II. A short time later, Ho Chi Minh declared Vietnam's independence from both the French and the Japanese.

But it soon became clear that France was not willing to give up control of its former colony. In 1946 a new war began between the French and the Viet Minh. Le Duan was released from prison in 1945 and went to Hanoi, where he served in the Communist Party leadership. In 1950 he was sent to the southern provinces of Vietnam as the main representative of the Communists. He did not play a major role in the war against the French, but he did build a political following in the South that would become important later.

In 1954 the Viet Minh defeated the French after nine years of fighting. The Geneva Peace Accords, which formally ended the war, divided Vietnam into two parts: Communist-led North Vietnam under Ho Chi Minh, and U.S.-supported South Vietnam under Ngo Dinh Diem (see entry). The peace agreement also provided for nationwide free elections to be held in 1956 to reunite the two parts of the country under one government. But American leaders worried that free elections would bring power to the Communists. They felt that a Communist government in Vietnam would increase the strength of China and the Soviet Union and threaten the security of the United States. As a result, Diem and his American advisors refused to hold the elections.

North Vietnamese leaders became angry when Diem failed to hold the elections as scheduled. They were determined to reunite the country, by force if necessary. Le Duan remained in South Vietnam after the peace agreement was signed. He organized opposition to the Diem government among his political followers. Le Duan believed that the Communist Party should take an active role in reuniting the two parts of Vietnam. He argued that North Vietnam should use a combination of political and military strategies to overcome resistance in the South. In 1956 Le Duan explained his views in an influential pamphlet called *The Path of Revolution in the South*.

Elected leader of the Communist Party

Later that year, Le Duan returned to Hanoi and became acting secretary general of the Vietnamese Workers' Party, which was the new name of the Indochinese Communist Party. Ho Chi Minh held the official title, but he left the actual job to Le Duan. Le Duan replaced Truong Chinh, whose attempts to combine North Vietnam's family farms into large, government-run collectives had resulted in peasant revolts. Le Duan had more success in mobilizing the farmers and increasing food production, but his methods sometimes included intimidation and violence.

In 1960 Le Duan was formally elevated to secretary general of the Communist Party. This position made him one of the most powerful men in North Vietnam during the Vietnam War. One of his main contributions to the war effort was to convince Ho Chi Minh and other party leaders to support the South Vietnamese Communists known as the Viet Cong. The Viet Cong fought against the Diem government using tactics of guerilla warfare. As Diem became more and more unpopular among the people, the Viet Cong gained control of large areas of the South Vietnamese countryside. Le Duan believed that the Viet Cong could eventually take over South Vietnam.

But the United States began sending money, weapons, and military advisors to help South Vietnam defend itself against North Vietnam and the Viet Cong. In 1965 President Lyndon Johnson (see entry) sent American combat troops to join the fight on the side of South Vietnam. But deepening U.S. involvement in the war failed to defeat the Communists. Instead, the war turned into a bloody stalemate. As the conflict dragged on, Ho Chi Minh became ill and faded from public view. When Ho died in 1969, Le Duan became the main political figure in North Vietnam. He continued to lead the Communist Party through the remainder of the Vietnam War.

Encounters problems in peacetime

In 1975 North Vietnam captured the South Vietnamese capital of Saigon to win the Vietnam War. After winning the war, Le Duan and the Communist leaders of North Vietnam reunited the two halves of the country to form the Socialist Republic of Vietnam. Then they introduced a series of changes designed to transform Vietnam into a socialist society. For example, the government took control of all farmland and business activities and placed restrictions on the lives of the

Vietnamese people. These changes created terrible hardships for the Vietnamese. Before long, hundreds of thousands of Vietnamese people decided that they could not live under the new government and began fleeing the country as refugees.

Over the next few years, the economic situation in Vietnam continued to deteriorate. Le Duan and the other Communist Party leaders struggled to lead the reunited country during peacetime. By the 1980s the situation had become so desperate that the Communist government was forced to make a series of economic reforms. These reforms restored some private property and free-market business incentives in Vietnam. During this time, Le Duan's health began to fail. He traveled to Moscow several times to receive treatment for liver disease. On July 10, 1986, the Communist Party newspaper reported that he had died.

During his thirty years as secretary general of the Communist Party in Vietnam, Le Duan developed a reputation as a rigid and secretive man. He published ten books and more than a hundred articles outlining his Communist philosophy during his lifetime. Upon his death, younger and more progressive members of the party discarded many of his ideas in an attempt to breathe new life into the Vietnamese economy and society.

Sources

Contemporary Newsmakers. Detroit: Gale Research, 1986.

Le Duan. *On the Right of Collective Mastery.* 1980.

Le Duan. *The Vietnamese Revolution: Fundamental Problems, Essential Tasks.* 1971.

Le Duc Tho

Born October 14, 1911
Dich Le, Vietnam
Died in 1990
Hanoi, Vietnam

North Vietnamese political leader

L e Duc Tho was the main negotiator for the Communist government of North Vietnam. He squared off against Henry Kissinger (see entry), the U.S. secretary of defense, in a series of peace talks between 1968 and 1973. The two men finally reached an agreement in January 1973 that ended U.S. involvement in the Vietnam War. They even shared the Nobel Peace Prize for their efforts. But as it turned out, the Paris Peace Agreement did not end the Vietnam War. North Vietnam and South Vietnam both violated the treaty, and the fighting continued for two more years.

A young revolutionary

Le Duc Tho was born October 14, 1911, in the village of Dich Le in Nam Ha province in northern Vietnam. His name at birth was Phan Dinh Khai. He adopted the name Le Duc Tho years later in order to hide his true identity from his political enemies. At the time of his birth, Vietnam was a colony of France known as French Indochina. Tho's father was a civil servant in the French colonial government.

"Once the Paris accord on Vietnam is respected, the arms are silenced, and a real peace is established in South Vietnam, I will be able to consider accepting [the Nobel Peace Prize]."

Le Duc Tho.
Reproduced by permission of Corbis Corporation.

By the time he reached his late teens, Tho had begun organizing demonstrations against French rule and actively promoting Vietnamese independence. In 1930 he helped form the Indochinese Communist Party with other young revolutionaries, including the future leader of North Vietnam, Ho Chi Minh (see entry). Later that year, Tho was arrested for his opposition to the French colonial government. He spent the next six years doing hard labor in Con Son prison.

Upon his release from prison in 1936, Tho resumed his political activities. He was arrested again in 1939 and spent some time in Son La prison camp. While there, he wrote a poem expressing his feelings about a foreign power controlling his country: "Rage grips me against those barbaric imperialists [cruel people who seek to extend their power over others], / So many years their heels have crushed our country. / A thousand thousand oppressions." Some sources say that Tho escaped to China in 1941 and helped Ho Chi Minh form the Viet Minh, a Communist-led Vietnamese nationalist group. But other sources say that Tho was released in 1944.

Fights for Vietnamese independence

During World War II (1939–45), France was forced to give up some of its control over Vietnam. When the war ended in 1945, the Viet Minh launched a successful revolution to regain control of their country. That September, Ho Chi Minh formally declared Vietnam's independence. But it soon became clear that France was not willing to give up its former colony. War erupted between the French and the Viet Minh in late 1946. During this conflict, which became known as the Indochina War, Tho became a leader of the Communist Party. In 1948 he took charge of Viet Minh resistance to the French government in the southern part of Vietnam.

After nine years of war, the Viet Minh defeated the French in 1954. The Geneva Accords, which ended the Indochina War, divided Vietnam into two sections. The northern section, which was led by a Communist government under Ho Chi Minh, was officially known as the Democratic Republic of Vietnam but was usually called North Vietnam. The southern section, which was led by a U.S.-supported government under Ngo Dinh Diem (see entry), was known as the Republic of South Vietnam.

The peace agreement also provided for nationwide free elections to be held in 1956, with a goal of reuniting the two sections of Vietnam under one government. But U.S. government officials worried that holding free elections in Vietnam would bring power to the Communists who had led the nation's war for independence from France. They felt that a Communist government in Vietnam would increase the power of the Soviet Union and threaten the security of the United States. As a result, the U.S. government and South Vietnamese President Diem refused to hold the elections.

North Vietnamese leaders grew angry when the South Vietnamese government failed to hold the required elections. The Communists were determined to overthrow Diem and reunite the country, by force if necessary. Within a short time, a new war began between the two sections of Vietnam. One of North Vietnam's main weapons in the Vietnam War was a group of guerrilla fighters known as the Viet Cong that operated in the South Vietnamese countryside. The Viet Cong mingled with the villagers and tried to convince them to support the Communist efforts to overthrow Diem's government. The U.S. government sent money, weapons, and military advisors to help South Vietnam defend itself against North Vietnam and the Viet Cong.

Tho's exact role in the early years of the Vietnam War is not known. It is clear that he strongly supported North Vietnam's efforts to reunite the country under a Communist government. Some sources say that he returned to South Vietnam in the late 1950s or early 1960s and supervised Viet Cong operations from a secret base in the jungle. American involvement in the conflict increased steadily during this time. In 1965 President Lyndon Johnson (see entry) authorized U.S. bombing missions over North Vietnam and sent American combat troops to South Vietnam. But deepening U.S. involvement failed to defeat the Communists. Instead, the war turned into a bloody stalemate.

Negotiations proceed at a slow pace

In 1968 the United States and North Vietnam agreed to open peace negotiations in Paris, France. At first, Xuan Thuy was the chief negotiator for the North Vietnamese side.

Nguyen Thi Binh (1927–)

Nguyen Thi Binh, often referred to as Madame Binh, was the second-ranking negotiator for the North Vietnamese side in the Paris peace talks. While Le Duc Tho represented the Communist government of North Vietnam, Madame Binh represented the National Liberation Front (NLF), an organization of revolutionaries in South Vietnam. The NLF—which included a military arm, the guerrilla fighters known as the People's Revolutionary Army or Viet Cong—fought with North Vietnam to overthrow the South Vietnamese government and reunite the two parts of the country.

Nguyen Thi Binh was born near Saigon in 1927. She was the granddaughter of Phan Chau Trinh, a famous early leader in the struggle to gain Vietnam's independence from France. Although she was educated in French schools, Madame Binh joined the fight against the French colonial government as a teenager. By the time she reached her twenties, she was the leader of a student resistance movement. She was arrested in 1950 for participating in demonstrations and spent the next three years in prison.

Released from prison after the Viet Minh defeated the French in 1954, Madame Binh continued her political activities. She became an outspoken opponent of American involvement in the struggle for political control over Vietnam. In 1960 she joined the NLF and was elected to the organization's leadership committee. She also served as vice president of the South Vietnam Women's Union for Liberation, another group dedicated to ending American involvement and reuniting Vietnam under one government.

Over the next several years, Madame Binh served as a diplomat for the NLF. She traveled all over the world to attend meetings and conferences, including Moscow and Beijing. During her travels, she gave numerous interviews about her cause. She was eventually recognized as the main spokesperson for the NLF. In 1969 the NLF formed a political arm known as the People's Revolutionary Government (PRG). The PRG was intended to be an alternative government of South Vietnam. It opposed the U.S.-supported government led by President Nguyen Van Thieu (see entry).

Tho showed up several weeks later. His official title was "special advisor," but it soon became clear that he held the real power to negotiate for the Communists. The Americans, led by Secretary of Defense Henry Kissinger, viewed Tho as a tough, serious adversary in the peace talks. He was always

Nguyen Thi Binh. *Reproduced by permission of Corbis Corporation.*

When representatives of the United States and North Vietnam began meeting in Paris to discuss a peaceful settlement of the conflict, Madame Binh represented the NLF/PRG. Henry Kissinger (see entry), the American negotiator, resented her presence at the peace talks. He believed that the Viet Cong was not a legitimate political group and should not be allowed to participate. Kissinger also disliked Madame Binh personally and felt that she complicated the bargaining process by making ridiculous proposals. "Their demands are absurd," he complained. "They want us to withdraw and on the way out to overthrow the Saigon government." For her part, Madame Binh considered Kissinger to be self-centered and "vain."

During the negotiations, Madame Binh worked to reduce President Thieu's hold on political power in South Vietnam. She also tried to secure the release of political prisoners in the South. When the two sides reached a final agreement in 1973, she criticized the deal for its handling of the issue of prisoners but eventually signed it. After North Vietnam won the war in 1975 and established a Communist government over all of Vietnam, Madame Binh became the minister of education. It was the highest position held by a woman and one of the highest held by a member of the PRG in the new government. She also continued to travel and represent her country at events around the world. In 1993 she was elected vice president of Vietnam.

polite, but he was also strongly dedicated to his cause and unwilling to compromise on certain demands. Tho "was in no hurry," Michael Maclear wrote in *The Ten Thousand Day War.* "He would smile at Kissinger, never saying yes, never quite saying no."

Kissinger's initial position in the negotiations was that both American and Communist forces should be withdrawn from South Vietnam. Once this occurred, then the two sides could discuss various plans for the country's political future. But Tho refused to go along with this plan. Instead, he insisted that North Vietnam would continue fighting until the U.S. troops were withdrawn. He also demanded that the South Vietnamese government, which by this time was led by Nguyen Van Thieu (see entry), be replaced by a coalition government that included Communist representatives. With such a wide gap between the two sides, the negotiators made little progress and eventually broke off their talks.

In August 1969 Tho and Kissinger began meeting secretly in hopes of negotiating a settlement. Their talks continued off and on for more than two years. As the war dragged on, the American people became bitterly divided over U.S. involvement, and antiwar demonstrations took place across the country. In the meantime, the Communist countries of China and the Soviet Union began to reduce their support for North Vietnam. These factors made both sides more willing to reach a compromise.

In January 1972 President Richard Nixon (see entry) told the American people about the secret negotiations. Feeling that an agreement was near, North Vietnam launched the Spring Offensive in March. The Communists used this attack to move additional troops into South Vietnam and improve their bargaining position. But Nixon responded by ordering large-scale bombing raids over North Vietnam. In October 1972 Tho and Kissinger returned to Paris and reached a preliminary agreement. But the deal fell apart when South Vietnamese President Thieu objected to it. Determined to force the Communists' hand, Nixon then ordered the heaviest bombing raids of the war over North Vietnamese cities. These attacks, which took place in late December, became known as the "Christmas bombings."

The Paris Peace Agreements

On January 25, 1973, Tho and Kissinger announced that they had reached a final agreement to end U.S. involvement in the Vietnam War. It was signed by the governments of

the United States, North Vietnam, and South Vietnam two days later.

Under the terms of the agreement, the United States agreed to withdraw its troops from Vietnam within sixty days. Kissinger also agreed to allow some Communist forces to remain in the South. In exchange, North Vietnam agreed to let President Thieu remain in power. But the agreement also established a National Council of Reconciliation—which would include representatives from both North and South Vietnam—to organize elections and form a new government. Finally, the peace agreement provided for the return of all American soldiers held by North Vietnam as prisoners of war.

When the Paris Peace Agreements were signed, both sides claimed that they had come out on top. Tho called the agreement "a very great victory for the Vietnamese people . . . and all the peace-loving peoples of the world, including the American people who displayed their solidarity and gave

A view of the 1973 Paris Peace Conference, including Le Duc Tho (foreground) and Henry Kissinger (background).
Reproduced by permission of Corbis Corporation.

devoted support to the just struggle of our people." But some observers pointed out that very little had changed between this agreement and the agreements that had been considered years earlier. In addition, some people criticized the agreement because it left the political future of South Vietnam uncertain. After all, that had been the main issue the two sides had been fighting to decide.

Refuses to accept the Nobel Peace Prize

As many people expected, the peace in Vietnam did not last long. The last American troops withdrew from the country in early 1973. Almost immediately, the South Vietnamese forces under President Thieu began clashing with the Communist forces that remained in the countryside. Each side blamed the other for breaking the treaty. In June 1973 Tho and Kissinger met again and issued a joint statement urging both sides to comply with the terms of the peace agreement. Still, the fighting continued.

On October 16, 1973, Tho and Kissinger received the Nobel Peace Prize for their efforts in ending the Vietnam War. The decision to give the award to the two negotiators created a great deal of controversy, especially since the agreement had not actually led to peace in Vietnam. In fact, some observers sarcastically called it the "Nobel War Prize." In recognition of the crisis that still gripped his country, Tho refused to accept the honor. "Once the Paris accord on Vietnam is respected, the arms are silenced, and a real peace is established in South Vietnam, I will be able to consider accepting this award," he said in a statement to the award committee.

In 1975 Tho secretly traveled to South Vietnam with North Vietnamese General Van Tien Dung. The two men helped plan a major Communist offensive designed to overthrow Thieu's government. When the attack took place, North Vietnamese forces rolled across the South, capturing city after city. In April 1975 the Communists took control of Saigon to win the Vietnam War. Over the next year, they established a single Communist government over all of Vietnam. Tho remained active in the Communist Party until 1986, when he resigned during a power struggle over economic reforms. He died in Hanoi in 1990.

Sources

Dillard, Walter Scott. *Sixty Days to Peace.* 1982.

Goodman, Allan E. *The Lost Peace: America's Search for a Negotiated Settlement of the Vietnam War.* 1978.

Maclear, Michael. *The Ten Thousand Day War: Vietnam, 1945–1975.* New York: Avon, 1981.

Porter, Gareth. *A Peace Denied: The United States, Vietnam, and the Paris Agreement.* Bloomington: Indiana University Press, 1975.

Le Ly Hayslip

Born 1949
Ky La, Vietnam

Vietnamese writer and humanitarian

"In May 1970, I stepped
from the . . . airliner
that had taken me
from the hell my
country had become to
the heaven I hoped
America would be."

L e Ly Hayslip is best known as the author of *When Heaven and Earth Changed Places,* a memoir about her experiences growing up in a South Vietnamese village during the Vietnam War. When she was a teenager, Hayslip became involved with the Communist guerrilla fighters known as the Viet Cong. She spent several years carrying messages and setting booby traps to help the Viet Cong in their fight against American and South Vietnamese government forces. When it became clear that her life was in danger from both sides, Hayslip moved to Saigon for several years. In 1970 she escaped to the United States. Since then, she has established a humanitarian organization to help the American and Vietnamese people come to terms with the war.

Childhood in a war-torn country

Phung Thi Le Ly Hayslip was born in 1949 in the small village of Ky La, near Danang in central Vietnam. She was the sixth child born into a close-knit peasant family that earned a living growing rice. At the time of Hayslip's birth, Vietnam was a colony of France known as French Indochina. But Vietnamese Communist rebels, known as the Viet Minh, were fighting to gain Vietnam's independence from France.

In 1954 the Viet Minh forces finally defeated the French. The Geneva Accords, which marked the end of the war, divided Vietnam into two sections. The northern section, which was led by a Communist government under Ho Chi Minh (see entry), was officially known as the Democratic Republic of Vietnam but was usually called North Vietnam. The southern section, which was led by a U.S.-supported government under Ngo Dinh Diem (see entry), was known as the Republic of South Vietnam. Hayslip's village became a part of South Vietnam.

The peace agreement also provided for nationwide free elections to be held in 1956, with a goal of reuniting the two parts of Vietnam under one government. But U.S. government officials worried that holding free elections in Vietnam would bring power to the Communists who had led the nation's war for independence from France. They felt that a Communist government in Vietnam would increase the power of the Soviet Union and threaten the security of the United States. As a result, the U.S. government and South Vietnamese President Diem refused to hold the elections.

North Vietnamese leaders grew angry when the South Vietnamese government failed to hold the required elections. The Communists were determined to reunite the country, by force if necessary. Within a short time, a new war began between North and South Vietnam. One of North Vietnam's main weapons in the war was a group of South Vietnamese guerrilla fighters known as the Viet Cong. The Viet Cong mingled with the villagers and tried to convince them to support the Communist efforts to overthrow Diem's government and reunite the country.

Joins the Viet Cong

By the early 1960s the Viet Cong and the South Vietnamese government forces were struggling to win the loyalty of the people of South Vietnam. Like many other villagers, Hayslip and her family became caught in the middle. In fact, the war divided her family. One of her brothers went to North Vietnam to join the Communist forces, while one of her sisters married a policeman who provided security for South Vietnamese government officials.

The conflict disrupted the lives of the South Vietnamese peasants and caused them a great deal of hardship. During the day, government troops would come to Hayslip's village and build fortifications to keep out the Viet Cong. These troops questioned the peasants about their knowledge of the Viet Cong and sometimes put people in prison. But at night, the Viet Cong secretly controlled her village. They used a combination of propaganda (information designed to promote their cause and reduce support for the opposing cause) and terrorism to gain the peasants' support.

"Everything I knew about the war I learned as a teenaged girl from the North Vietnamese cadre [a group of trained revolutionaries] leaders in the swamps outside Ky La," Hayslip explained in *When Heaven and Earth Changed Places*. "During these midnight meetings, we peasants assumed everything we heard was true because what the Viet Cong said matched, in one way or another, the beliefs we already had." For example, the Viet Cong told the villagers that they were fighting for Vietnam's independence and freedom from foreign control. They said that the United States—which sent money, weapons, equipment, and military advisors to help South Vietnam defend itself against North Vietnam and the Viet Cong— was only trying to return their country to the status of a colony.

By the time she was twelve years old, Hayslip had become an active member of the Viet Cong children's army. For the next two years, she carried information, stood guard, and stole supplies for the guerrilla fighters. Hayslip also helped the Viet Cong set booby traps for South Vietnamese and American soldiers. Throughout this time, she was frequently arrested and questioned by the government troops. Sometimes the South Vietnamese officers beat and tortured her in an attempt to gain information about the Viet Cong.

After a while, the Viet Cong began to suspect that Hayslip was actually a government spy. Despite the help she had provided the guerrilla fighters, the Viet Cong sentenced her to death for betraying their secrets. But the Viet Cong agents who were supposed to kill her instead raped her and let her go. Since sex outside of marriage goes against traditional Vietnamese values, this action disgraced her in the eyes of her village.

When Hayslip was fourteen, her mother took her to the South Vietnamese capital of Saigon. They hoped that living in the city would help keep Hayslip safe from the Viet Cong. In Saigon, Hayslip worked as a maid, a waitress, and a hospital attendant. She also sold stolen goods on the streets to American soldiers. But she still was not free from the Viet Cong. They sent a message to her father saying that they wanted Hayslip to plant a bomb for them in Saigon. Her father ended up committing suicide in order to protect her from being drawn back into the Viet Cong.

Escapes to the United States

Hayslip remained in Saigon for five years. During this time, the United States continued to increase its military involvement in Vietnam. In 1965 President Lyndon Johnson (see entry) sent American combat troops into the country and launched large-scale bombing missions in the countryside. Hayslip had her first child at sixteen and struggled to take care of him. Over time, she decided that her best hope for raising a family in safety was to move to the United States. In the late 1960s Hayslip met a middle-aged American construction engineer, Ed Munro, who was working in Saigon. He agreed to marry her and bring her to the United States.

"In May 1970, I stepped from the Pan Am airliner that had taken me from the hell my country had become to the heaven I hoped America would be," Hayslip recalled in her book *Child of War, Woman of Peace*. "I was twenty years old with two sons, both by different fathers. I didn't speak much English, and my manners were better suited to peasant villages and Saigon street corners than a suburb of San Diego, which was to be my new home—a place stranger to a Vietnamese farm girl than the dark side of the moon."

Hayslip's first husband died of the lung disease emphysema three years after they settled in California. She then married an American veteran of the Vietnam War, Steve Butler. But Butler developed drinking problems and eventually committed suicide. From this point on, Hayslip struggled to raise her three young sons alone in a strange country. She worked as a housekeeper, a factory worker, and a restaurant manager over the years. She also learned English and gradually became more confident. "Steadily, diligently [persistently], she set about securing a life for her children, for her extended family—and then for other Vietnamese," Frances McCue wrote in the *New York Times Book Review*.

In 1988 Hayslip founded the East Meets West Foundation. This humanitarian aid organization was designed to help heal the physical and emotional wounds that remained on both sides from the Vietnam War. The foundation sent American veterans to Vietnam to build schools and hospitals. Hayslip encouraged veterans to make "another 'tour of duty' in service to humanity and yourself—to heal the wounds that may linger in your spirit and help the Vietnamese people, who, like war victims anywhere, are the spiritual partners of your journey."

Tells her life story in two books

In 1989 Hayslip published *When Heaven and Earth Changed Places: A Vietnamese Woman's Journey from War to Peace*. This book tells the story of her childhood in war-torn Vietnam. It also includes diary entries from a return visit she made to her homeland in 1986, when she was reunited with her mother and several other surviving family members. *When Heaven and Earth Changed Places* was praised by critics for giving American readers a Vietnamese person's perspective on the war. "I do not believe anyone who reads it will ever be able to think about the Vietnam war in quite the same way again," Arnold R. Isaacs wrote in the *Washington Post Book World*.

Some reviewers expressed surprise that the overall message of Hayslip's book was one of hope and forgiveness. After all, she had lost her father, brother, and a hundred family friends and distant relatives in the war. But instead of taking sides or placing blame, she wrote with sympathy for everyone involved in the war. "We all did what we had to do," she stated in her book. "By mingling our blood and tears on the earth, god has made us brothers and sisters."

In 1993 Hayslip published a sequel to her memoir called *Child of War, Woman of Peace*. This book begins with her arrival in the United States in 1970. It describes her struggles to adapt to a new culture and to raise her sons alone. Although it was not as highly acclaimed as her first book, *Child of War, Woman of Peace* was praised for contributing to the understanding of immigrants in the United States. Hayslip's two memoirs formed the basis for a major motion picture, *Heaven and Earth,* directed by Vietnam veteran Oliver Stone (see entry).

Sources

FitzGerald, Frances. *Fire in the Lake: The Vietnamese and the Americans in Vietnam.* Boston: Little, Brown, 1987.

Hayslip, Le Ly, with Jay Wurts. *When Heaven and Earth Changed Places: A Vietnamese Woman's Journey from War to Peace.* New York: Doubleday, 1989.

Hayslip, Le Ly, with James Hayslip. *Child of War, Woman of Peace.* New York: Anchor Books, 1993.

Isaacs, Arnold R. Review of *When Heaven and Earth Changed Places. Washington Post Book World,* July 16, 1989.

McCue, Frances. Review of *Child of War, Woman of Peace. New York Times Book Review,* April 11, 1993.

Maya Lin

Born October 5, 1959
Athens, Ohio

American architect and artist who designed the Vietnam Veterans Memorial

> "I felt a memorial should be honest about the reality of war, and be for the people who gave their lives."

Maya Lin.
Reproduced by permission of AP/Wide World Photos.

As a twenty-one-year-old architecture student at Yale University, Maya Lin won a competition to design the Vietnam Veterans Memorial in Washington, D.C. Her winning design—a long, V-shaped wall of polished black marble engraved with the names of the American soldiers killed in Vietnam—created a great deal of controversy at first. But soon after the memorial was dedicated in 1982, the American people embraced it as a powerful and moving tribute to the fallen soldiers. Since then, it has become the most visited site in Washington, D.C.

An artistic and studious young woman

Maya Ying Lin was born on October 5, 1959, in Athens, Ohio. She was raised in a household that was full of art and literature. Both of her parents, Henry Huan Lin and Julia Chang Lin, came from prominent Chinese families. They immigrated to the United States in the late 1940s, after a Communist government came to power in China. When Lin's parents met, they both worked as professors at Ohio University in Athens. Henry Lin was an artist and taught art history, while Julia Lin was a poet and taught literature.

As a girl, Maya Lin loved to work with her hands, making pottery, ceramics, and sculptures. She also enjoyed walking in the woods near her home and connecting with nature. She was an excellent student, but she sometimes had trouble fitting in with other people her age. She had no interest in the high school social scene and preferred to spend her time reading or studying mathematics. Lin became valedictorian of her high school class, and she was accepted into prestigious Yale University upon graduation in 1977.

Lin has described Yale as the first place she ever felt truly comfortable and at home. She enjoyed the challenging academic environment, as well as the beautiful campus in New Haven, Connecticut. During her first two years at Yale, she took a variety of liberal arts courses. When she needed a break from her studies, she often walked through an old cemetery near the center of town. "I've always been intrigued with death, and man's reaction to it," she commented in a *New York Times* interview.

In her junior year Lin decided to concentrate her studies on architecture (the design of buildings). She had always considered herself to be an artist, and she viewed architecture as art on a large scale. She spent one semester studying in Europe, where she visited some of the best-known examples of architecture in Paris, London, and Athens, Greece. Back in the United States for her senior year, one of her professors told her about a competition to design a memorial to the Americans who had died in the Vietnam War.

The Vietnam Veterans Memorial

The Vietnam War was a conflict between the Communist nation of North Vietnam and the U.S.-supported nation of South Vietnam. North Vietnam wanted to overthrow the South Vietnamese government and reunite the two countries under one Communist government. But U.S. government officials felt that a Communist government in Vietnam would increase the power of the Soviet Union and threaten the security of the United States. In the late 1950s and early 1960s the U.S. government sent money, weapons, and military advisors to help South Vietnam defend itself. In 1965 President Lyndon Johnson (see entry) sent American combat troops to join the fight on the side of South Vietnam.

But deepening U.S. involvement in the war failed to defeat the Communists. Instead, the war turned into a bloody stalemate. The American public became bitterly divided about how to proceed in Vietnam, and antiwar demonstrations took place across the country. By the time American troops were withdrawn in 1973, more than 58,000 Americans had lost their lives in Vietnam.

Since U.S. involvement in the Vietnam War had caused so much controversy, the Americans who fought and died there received very little recognition afterward. One veteran, Jan Scruggs (see entry), was determined to change this situation. He came up with the idea of building a memorial to honor those who had died in Vietnam and to help heal the wounds the war had created in American society. In the late 1970s Scruggs formed an organization of fellow veterans, the Vietnam Veterans Memorial Fund (VVMF), and started raising money for a memorial.

Rather than hiring an artist to design the memorial, the VVMF decided to hold a contest to select a design. They believed that a contest would raise public awareness and support for the memorial. The instructions they provided to contest entrants said only that the design should incorporate the names of all 58,000 Americans who were killed in Vietnam, and that it should be in harmony with the natural surroundings of its site in Washington, D.C.

Lin enters the contest

When Lin first heard about the contest, she did not know much about the Vietnam War. But she felt that this worked to her advantage, because her design would not be influenced by politics. Lin did know something about memorials and their meaning. She had always liked to visit peaceful cemeteries, and she had also taken a course on memorial design at Yale.

Lin's idea for her design came to her as she visited the memorial site in Washington, D.C., with a group of fellow students. She thought about the pain suffered by the families and friends of the dead soldiers. She visualized this pain as a scar in the earth that would never quite heal. She decided that her design would feature two stone walls, set down into the ground, engraved with the names of the Americans who were killed in Vietnam. "I felt a memorial should be honest about the reality of war, and be for the people who gave their lives," she noted in *To Heal a Nation*.

Upon returning to Yale, Lin showed sketches of her design to her professor and classmates. Her professor suggested that she make the two walls meet at an angle. Lin also decided to arrange the names chronologically, in the order in which the soldiers died, rather than alphabetically. This way, the names of the first and last Americans killed would meet in the middle. "The war's beginning and end meet," she explained in *Always to Remember*. "The war is complete, coming full circle." Finally, she decided to construct the walls out of black marble. She knew that this shiny material would reflect a mirror image of the sky and trees, as well as the people looking at it.

Design creates controversy

When Lin sent her entry to the VVMF, it joined 1,400 other design proposals from around the United States. These designs were reviewed by a panel of important architects and landscape designers. The judges kept coming back to Lin's design, which they found simple and direct, yet also powerful and strangely haunting. They finally selected her entry as the design for the Vietnam Veterans Memorial. Lin received a $20,000 prize for winning the contest.

Lin became an instant celebrity. Reporters around the country all wanted to interview the twenty-one-year-old Yale student who had beaten out many prominent American artists in the contest to design the Vietnam Veterans Memorial. Several major art critics praised her design, and Scruggs and other members of the VVMF expressed their support as well.

But within a short time, Lin's design became the subject of controversy. A number of prominent people began speaking out against it. Some people felt that it was too different from other war memorials, which usually consisted of patriotic statues. Other people claimed that Lin was too young to understand the Vietnam War and how it had divided the American people. Finally, a few people resorted to racism in their criticism of her design. They resented the fact that a person of Asian heritage had designed the memorial to American soldiers who had died in Southeast Asia.

Lin was shocked and disappointed by the criticism of her design. The controversy also upset Scruggs and other people who believed that Lin's design offered a powerful tribute to the Americans who lost their lives in Vietnam. But opponents continued to fight it, and conservative lawmakers successfully blocked its construction. Work on the memorial began only after the two sides agreed on a compromise. Under the terms of this agreement, a statue of three young American soldiers and an American flag would be added to the site near Lin's memorial. Lin objected to the installation of the statue, which was designed by sculptor Frederick Hart. But the VVMF members convinced her that her memorial might never be built without the inclusion of the statue.

After earning her bachelor's degree from Yale in 1981, Lin moved to Washington, D.C., to work with the architectural firm VVMF had hired to turn her design into reality. Although she had much less experience than the other architects working on the project, she continued to exercise control over her design. In fact, she had a say in everything from the alignment of the walls to the type style used for the lettering. The Vietnam Veterans Memorial was dedicated in a special ceremony on Veterans Day in 1982.

Once the Vietnam Veterans Memorial was dedicated, the controversy over Lin's design faded away. It was replaced by a widespread recognition that the memorial was a powerful tribute to those who died while serving their country. In fact, the memorial became known as a place where those who had lost friends and loved ones could go to grieve and remember in a special way. Many visitors noted that the wall's design made them feel close to the people they had lost in Vietnam. They valued the opportunity to touch the names and to leave pictures, letters, flowers, and other items at the wall in memory of friends and family.

Continues producing architecture and sculpture

In 1983 Lin returned to Yale. She earned her master's degree in architecture in 1986. The following year, the university presented her with an honorary doctorate as one of its most distinguished graduates. Then in 1988 she received the

Presidential Design Award for the Vietnam Veterans Memorial. During this time, Lin moved to New York City and set up a studio to work on her architectural designs and sculpture. She designed several homes and sold her sculptures in prominent art galleries.

For several years after she completed the Vietnam Veterans Memorial, Lin resisted the idea of working on another memorial. But in 1988 the Southern Poverty Law Center in Montgomery, Alabama, asked her to design a memorial to the people who died in the civil rights movement of the 1960s. Surprised that no memorial had been built to recognize this important period in American history, she accepted the commission.

On her way to inspect the site, Lin read the famous words of Martin Luther King, Jr.: "We will not be satisfied until justice rolls down like waters, and righteousness like a mighty stream." She decided that her design would include flowing water. Her design for the Civil Rights Memorial featured a huge granite disk placed on its side, like a table. The edge of the disk was engraved with a time line of people and events in the civil rights movement. Immediately behind the disk was a black granite wall with water gently cascading down its face. Visitors were encouraged to walk around the disk, touch the names, and remember the activists who helped create a new era of equality in American society.

Lin has continued to be in demand as an architect, monument designer, and sculptor. In 1989 she designed an open-air peace chapel at Juniata College in Pennsylvania. The following year, she completed a project called the Women's Table, which honors the contributions of women at Yale. In 1994 she designed a huge, futuristic clock for the ceiling of Penn Station in New York City. One year later, director Freida Lee Mock traced Lin's remarkable career in an Academy Award-winning documentary film, *Maya Lin: A Strong Clear Vision.*

Sources

Ashabranner, Brent. *Always to Remember: The Story of the Vietnam Veterans Memorial.* New York: Putnam, 1988.

Ezell, Edward Clinton. *Reflections on the Wall: The Vietnam Memorial.* Harrisburg, PA: Stackpole Books, 1987.

Malone, Mary. *Maya Lin: Architect and Artist.* Springfield, NJ: Enslow, 1995.

Mock, Freida Lee. *Maya Lin: A Strong Clear Vision.* PBS, 1995 (documentary film).

Scruggs, Jan C., and Joel L. Swerdlow. *To Heal a Nation: The Vietnam Veterans Memorial.* New York: Harper and Row, 1985.

Henry Cabot Lodge

Born July 5, 1902
Nahant, Massachusetts
Died February 27, 1985
Beverly, Massachusetts

American diplomat and U.S. ambassador
to South Vietnam in the mid-1960s

Henry Cabot Lodge served as America's ambassador to South Vietnam from mid-1963 to mid-1964, and again from mid-1965 through 1967. During his first stay in Saigon, Lodge helped convince the U.S. government to support the coup that removed President Ngo Dinh Diem (see entry) from power. After resuming his ambassadorial duties in 1965, Lodge's low opinion of the South Vietnamese government remained unchanged. But his strong anti-Communist beliefs made him a firm supporter of continued U.S. military involvement in Vietnam.

Member of a prominent political family

Henry Cabot Lodge was born on July 5, 1902, in Nahant, Massachusetts. He was raised in one of New England's most distinguished and powerful Republican families. In addition, his grandfather—and namesake—Henry Cabot Lodge (1850–1924) had been a U.S. senator and one of President Theodore Roosevelt's closest friends and political allies.

After earning a degree from Harvard University, Lodge worked in the newspaper business for several years, dividing

"We are launched on a course from which there is no respectable turning back . . . ."

Henry Cabot Lodge.
Courtesy of the Library of Congress.

237

his time between the *Boston Evening Transcript* and the *New York Herald Tribune.* In 1932 the young Republican won election into the Massachusetts legislature. He served two terms from 1933 to 1936 before moving on to the U.S. Senate.

Upon joining the Senate, Lodge became known as one of the Republican Party's steadiest conservatives. In 1942 he won reelection to the Senate, but two years later he resigned in order to serve in the U.S. Army in World War II. He was stationed in Europe until the war ended in 1945. When Lodge returned to America, he quickly regained his seat in the U.S. Senate. But in 1953 he lost his first election, falling to future president John F. Kennedy (see entry), a Democrat.

After losing his Senate seat, Lodge served his country as ambassador to the United Nations (UN) for much of the 1950s. Appointed U.S. representative to the UN by President Dwight Eisenhower in 1953, he remained in that position until 1960. At that time, Republican presidential candidate Richard M. Nixon (see entry) chose him as his vice-presidential running mate. Nixon's decision to select Lodge was widely praised. The Massachusetts Republican was known as a well-spoken and knowledgeable politician whose firm anti-Communist beliefs would appeal to voters. But once again, John F. Kennedy foiled Lodge's political ambitions. Kennedy and vice-presidential running mate Lyndon B. Johnson (see entry) narrowly defeated Nixon and Lodge to win the White House.

The November 1960 election defeat disappointed Lodge, but it did not hurt his career. In fact, his reputation remained so strong that in 1963 President Kennedy asked him to take over as America's ambassador to South Vietnam. Lodge accepted the position, which gave him considerable power over the flow of American aid to President Ngo Dinh Diem's (see entry) regime.

Ambassador to South Vietnam

When Lodge arrived in South Vietnam in August 1963, its government was engaged in a struggle for political survival. The nation had been created nine years earlier, after Vietnam defeated its old French colonial rulers to gain independence. But the 1954 Geneva peace agreement that ended the French-Vietnamese conflict created two countries within Vietnam.

Lodge's Message Supporting a Military Coup

When Lodge became U.S. ambassador to South Vietnam in mid-1963, he quickly determined that the Saigon government headed by President Ngo Dinh Diem (see entry) was doomed to fail. For this reason, Lodge urged the Kennedy administration not to oppose a proposed military coup that would remove Diem from power. On October 25, 1963, Lodge sent a message to U.S. National Security Advisor McGeorge Bundy (see entry) in which he explained his belief that a coup might help the South resist North Vietnam and its Viet Cong allies. Following is an excerpt from that message:

We should not thwart [stop] a coup for two reasons. First, it seems at least an even bet that the next government would not bungle and stumble as much as the present one has. Secondly, it is extremely unwise in the long range for us to pour cold water on attempts at a coup, particularly when they are just in their beginning stages. We should remember that this is the only way in which the people in Vietnam can possibly get a change of government. Whenever we thwart attempts at a coup, as we have done in the past, we are incurring very long lasting resentments, we are assuming an undue responsibility for keeping the incumbents in office, and in general are setting ourselves in judgment over the affairs of Vietnam. Merely to keep in touch with this situation and a policy merely limited to 'not thwarting' are courses both of which entail some risks but these are lesser risks than either thwarting all coups while they are stillborn [still being considered] or our not being informed of what is happening . . . . In judging proposed coups, we must consider the effect on the war effort. Certainly a succession of fights for control of the Government of Vietnam would interfere with the war effort. It must also be said that the war effort has been interfered with already by the incompetence of the present government and the uproar which this has caused.

One week later, a group of South Vietnamese military generals executed Diem and seized power over the country. But the generals proved unable to maintain their hold over the country. Instead, the coup ushered in a period of even greater political instability in Saigon, as nine different governments took power over the following two years.

North Vietnam was headed by a Communist government under revolutionary leader Ho Chi Minh (see entry). South Vietnam, meanwhile, was led by a U.S.-supported government under Diem.

The Geneva agreement provided for nationwide free elections to be held in 1956 so that the two sections of Vietnam could be united under one government. But U.S. and

South Vietnamese officials refused to hold the elections because they feared that the results would give the Communists control over the entire country. When the South refused to hold elections, North Vietnam and its allies in the South—known as the Viet Cong—launched a guerrilla war against Diem's government. The United States responded by sending money, weapons, and advisors to aid in South Vietnam's defense. Despite this assistance, however, some American analysts expressed concern that Communist guerrilla activities and Diem's unpopularity among his own people might soon push the South to the point of collapse.

Lodge conducted an intensive study of the situation in South Vietnam when he took over as ambassador. He quickly decided that President Diem's corrupt and repressive government would never be able to gain widespread support from the South Vietnamese people. In fact, Lodge adopted such a negative view of the Diem government that he joined some other U.S. officials in calling for a change in leadership in Saigon. "We are launched on a course from which there is no respectable turning back: the overthrow of the Diem government," Lodge declared in an August 29, 1963, cable to U.S. secretary of state Dean Rusk (see entry).

In the fall of 1963 Lodge was secretly contacted by several South Vietnamese military officers. Aware of America's unhappiness with Diem's administration, they asked Lodge if the United States would support a coup (pronounced koo; a military overthrow of the government). Lodge urged President Kennedy to support the coup, and after several weeks of uncertainty, the Kennedy administration extended a promise not to interfere with the generals' scheme. On November 1, the military plotters successfully seized power from Diem. They executed Diem—an action that reportedly upset the Kennedy administration—and installed a new government.

Lodge expressed regret about Diem's death. But he also maintained that the coup was the only practical alternative available to the United States and the South Vietnamese generals. "In this country, it rarely occurs to anyone that an election is an efficient or appropriate way to get anything important accomplished," Lodge remarked in a February 1964 report. "The traditional way of doing important things here is by well-planned, well-thought-out use of force."

Supporter of limited U.S. involvement in Vietnam

In the months following Diem's removal, Lodge repeatedly expressed support for decisive military action against North Vietnam. He encouraged President Lyndon Johnson (who succeeded Kennedy after his assassination in November 1963) to authorize air strikes against North Vietnam. The ambassador argued that an effective bombing campaign would raise spirits in the South and hurt morale in the North. Lodge also favored "covert operations"—secret spying and sabotage missions—into North Vietnam.

Still, Lodge urged the Johnson administration to limit its involvement in the war. He thought that America should help the South develop military strategy and create programs to increase popular support among the peasants. He also approved of U.S. military and financial aid packages to South Vietnam. But he believed that the United States should not take on the primary responsibility for actually fighting the war. He warned against sending American ground troops into Vietnam. The ambassador worried that such a step might drag U.S. forces too deeply into the war or trigger a military response from the Communist governments in China or the Soviet Union.

In June 1964 Lodge resigned as ambassador to South Vietnam in order to work on the presidential campaign of Republican Governor William Scranton of Pennsylvania. He was replaced by General Maxwell Taylor (see entry). But Scranton failed to get the Republican nomination, and Lodge resumed his duties as ambassador in June 1965.

Returns to Vietnam

When Lodge returned to Saigon as U.S. ambassador, he worked on "pacification" programs designed to increase popular support for the South Vietnamese government among ordinary citizens. In addition, he lobbied the Johnson administration to increase the level of bombing against North Vietnam. But Lodge privately expressed little confidence in the nation's future. He continued to hold a very low opinion of South Vietnam's political and military leadership. Moreover, he argued that U.S. military strategy in Vietnam was too impatient and did not pay enough attention to political and economic issues in the country. "We could have done something [else] that cost less, took longer and would have had lasting results," he insisted in *The Ten Thousand Day War.*

Lodge stepped down as ambassador to South Vietnam in 1967, but he remained active in international politics. He served briefly as ambassador to West Germany (now part of the united Federal Republic of Germany) and also represented the United States as "ambassador-at-large." In March 1968 Lodge and other respected advisors—collectively known as the "Wise Men"—counseled President Johnson to scale back U.S. military operations in Vietnam. Moreover, they urged Johnson to find a way to gracefully withdraw from the war, which had become a source of tremendous pain and anger in communities all across the United States. Johnson reluctantly followed their advice and called a halt to the three-year-long Rolling Thunder bombing campaign against North Vietnam. One year later, President Richard Nixon made Lodge the head U.S. representative in peace talks with North Vietnamese negotiators. But the talks failed to produce an agreement, and the United States remained in Vietnam for another four years before a treaty was finally reached.

In 1970 Lodge was named special U.S. envoy (diplomatic representative) to the Vatican, the government of the Roman Catholic Church in Italy. He served his country in that capacity until 1977, when he retired to his home in Massachusetts. Lodge died on February 27, 1985.

Sources

Blair, Anne E. *Lodge in Vietnam: A Patriot Abroad.* New Haven, CT: Yale University Press, 1995.

Hammer, Ellen J. *A Death in November: America in Vietnam, 1963.* New York: Dutton, 1987.

Lodge, Henry Cabot. *As It Was: An Inside View of Politics and Power in the '50s and '60s.* New York: Norton, 1976.

Lodge, Henry Cabot. *The Storm Has Many Eyes: A Personal Narrative.* New York: Norton, 1973.

Maclear, Michael. *The Ten Thousand Day War.* New York: St. Martin's Press, 1979.

Miller, William J. *Henry Cabot Lodge.* New York: Heineman, 1967.

Prochnau, William. *Once Upon a Distant War: David Halberstam, Neil Sheehan, Peter Arnett—Young War Correspondents and Their Early Vietnam Battles.* New York: Times Books, 1995.

Lon Nol

Born November 13, 1913
Veng Province, Cambodia
November 17, 1985
Fullerton, California

President of Cambodia, 1970–1975

Lon Nol.
Reproduced by permission of AP/Wide World Photos.

L on Nol was the president of Cambodia—the country along Vietnam's southwestern border—during the Vietnam War. Cambodia was increasingly drawn into the conflict between Communist North Vietnam and U.S.-supported South Vietnam during his rule. In fact, the United States launched a military invasion of Cambodia just one month after he took control of the government from Prince Norodom Sihanouk (see entry). Lon Nol struggled to maintain his hold on power over the next few years as a group of Cambodian Communist rebels, known as the Khmer Rouge, gained strength and took over large areas of the country. He finally fled from his homeland in April 1975, when the Khmer Rouge captured the capital city of Phnom Penh.

Cambodia is drawn into the Vietnam War

Lon Nol was born on November 13, 1913, in Prey Veng province in southern Cambodia, near the Vietnam border. At the time of his birth, all of Indochina—including Cambodia and Vietnam—was under the colonial rule of France. As the son of a government official, Lon Nol was educated at a French school in Saigon, Vietnam, along with other future Cambodian leaders like Prince Norodom Sihanouk and Sisowath Sirik Matak. Upon completing his education in 1934, Lon Nol began rising through the government ranks in French-ruled Cambodia. In 1951 he became chief of the national police force.

In the early 1950s, though, France's long years of colonial rule in Indochina came to an end. In 1954 a group of Communist-led Vietnamese nationalists known as the Viet Minh defeated the French after nine years of war. The agreement that ended this war divided Vietnam into two sections, Communist-led North Vietnam and U.S.-supported South Vietnam. At the same time, France granted independence to all of its colonies in Indochina, including Cambodia. Prince Norodom Sihanouk—who had been named king of Cambodia by the French in 1941 but then had fought for Cambodian independence—gave up his throne in order to become president of Cambodia in 1955.

Over the next few years, Lon Nol became one of Sihanouk's most trusted advisors. The president rewarded his loyalty by giving him a series of important posts in the government, including defense minister and premier. In the meantime, however, Cambodia was increasingly threatened by a new war that had broken out in Vietnam. This war pitted North Vietnam and its secret allies, the South Vietnamese Communists known as the Viet Cong, against South Vietnam. North Vietnam wanted to overthrow the South Vietnamese government and reunite the two countries under one Communist government. But U.S. government officials worried that a Communist government in Vietnam would encourage other countries in Indochina to adopt communism. They felt that this would increase the power of China and the Soviet Union and threaten the security of the United States.

In the late 1950s and early 1960s the U.S. government sent money, weapons, and military advisors to help South Vietnam defend itself against North Vietnam and the Viet Cong. Sihanouk declared that Cambodia would remain neutral, or refuse to take sides, in the conflict. In 1965 President Lyndon Johnson (see entry) sent American combat troops to join the fight on the side of South Vietnam. At this point, Sihanouk began to worry that increased U.S. involvement would expand the war into Cambodia. He decided to cut off diplomatic ties with the United States. Before long, Sihanouk's fears came true.

The intense fighting with American troops encouraged the Viet Cong and North Vietnamese forces to move their base of operations across the border into eastern Cambodia.

Lon Nol takes control of the government

Lon Nol opposed the Vietnamese presence in Cambodia, but Sihanouk reluctantly allowed the Communist forces to enter the country. By the late 1960s the war in Vietnam had caused severe economic hardship and growing unrest in Cambodia. A group of Cambodian Communists known as the Khmer Rouge, under the command of a mysterious man named Pol Pot (see entry), began plotting an armed revolution against Sihanouk's government. To increase his hold on power, Sihanouk reorganized the government and made Lon Nol the prime minister. Together, they began working to remove the Vietnamese Communists from Cambodia.

In 1969 Sihanouk reestablished ties with the United States and allowed American forces to begin bombing Viet Cong and North Vietnamese bases along the border. But the bombing only forced the Vietnamese Communists to move deeper into Cambodian territory. In addition, it caused suffering among the Cambodian people and convinced thousands of peasants that the government could not protect them. Many of these people switched their support to the Khmer Rouge. Lon Nol urged Sihanouk to increase the size of the Cambodian army in order to fight the North Vietnamese and crush the Khmer Rouge rebellion, but Sihanouk continued to insist that Cambodia remain neutral.

In March 1970, while Sihanouk was visiting France, a group of leaders who were unhappy with his government made plans to overthrow him. Prime Minister Lon Nol and Deputy Prime Minister Sisowath Sirik Matak were among those involved in the plan. The Cambodian National Assembly voted to remove Sihanouk from power and make Lon Nol the new head of the government. Knowing that Lon Nol wanted to force the Vietnamese Communists out of Cambodia, U.S. officials backed him as the country's new leader. Shortly after taking power, Lon Nol approved pogroms (organized massacres) of ethnic Vietnamese living in Cambodia. In the meantime, Sihanouk met with Vietnamese and Cambodian Communist leaders in China. He agreed to support his former enemies, the Khmer Rouge, in their efforts to overthrow Lon Nol's government.

On April 30, 1970, U.S. and South Vietnamese combat forces launched an invasion of Cambodia. This ground attack was intended to wipe out the Viet Cong and North Vietnamese bases inside the border. American officials did not notify Lon Nol about the invasion in advance, but he agreed to endorse it in return for military and economic aid from the United States. During the invasion, South Vietnamese forces destroyed villages and murdered Cambodian civilians (people not involved in the military) in revenge for the earlier pogroms. The invasion also pushed the Vietnamese Communist forces further into Cambodia, where they captured the ancient city of Angkor.

When the American invasion ended a month later, the situation in Cambodia was worse than it had ever been. People from villages along the border fled from the fighting and streamed into the capital city of Phnom Penh as refugees, creating terrible economic hardships. In addition, the Khmer Rouge continued to increase its size and popularity. In fact, with Sihanouk's support, it began to emerge as a legitimate political alternative to Lon Nol's government.

Cambodia falls to the Khmer Rouge

Over the next year, Cambodia's military forces suffered a string of defeats to the Khmer Rouge and the North Vietnamese Army. As a result, Lon Nol's government became even weaker and less popular. In February 1971 Lon Nol suffered a stroke and went to Hawaii for two months of medical treatment. He temporarily resigned as president and turned power over to Sisowath Sirik Matak. That October, Lon Nol declared a state of emergency and resumed full control over the government. He also took a series of steps to silence the opposition to his rule, including placing tight controls on the media and limiting the rights of citizens. In March 1972 Lon Nol named himself president, prime minister, and head of the armed forces of Cambodia.

Throughout this time of crisis, Lon Nol proved to be a poor and indecisive leader. Always a deeply religious and superstitious man, he began to rely on advice from astrologers when making important decisions. After U.S. forces withdrew from

Vietnam in 1973, Lon Nol demanded that the Vietnamese Communists leave Cambodia. He did not seem to realize how weak his position became without American support. At this point, the North Vietnamese Army had defeated his military in a long series of battles. In addition, the Khmer Rouge rebels controlled more than 75 percent of the countryside of Cambodia and held the loyalty of nearly half of the civilian population.

Lon Nol struggled to maintain his hold on power as fighting continued over the next two years. The Khmer Rouge eventually controlled all of Cambodia except the capital of Phnom Penh. Realizing that defeat was near, Lon Nol fled from the country on April 1, 1975. Two weeks later, the Khmer Rouge captured Phnom Penh and took control of Cambodia. On April 30, North Vietnamese forces captured the South Vietnamese capital of Saigon to win the Vietnam War. To complete the string of Communist victories in Indochina, a group of Communist rebels known as the Pathet Lao also seized power in neighboring Laos.

Immediately after taking power, the Khmer Rouge launched a brutal program designed to transform Cambodia into a simple farming society. They renamed the nation Democratic Kampuchea and called the beginning of their rule Year Zero. They drove people out of cities and towns into the countryside. They abolished money, prohibited religious practice, eliminated private property, ended all formal education, and forbade the publication of newspapers. Worst of all, the Khmer Rouge murdered hundreds of thousands of Cambodian citizens in an effort to rid the country of "intellectuals" who opposed their rule. Some people were killed simply because they wore eyeglasses. Many others were herded into forced labor camps, where they died of starvation or disease. Historians estimate that as many as two million Cambodians—or one-fourth of the overall population—died under the Khmer Rouge.

During this time, Cambodia was still involved in disputes with Vietnam over national borders and leadership of Indochina. In December 1978 the Vietnamese government sent troops into Cambodia to overthrow the Khmer Rouge. By January 1979 Vietnam's invasion forces had captured Phnom Penh. They immediately put an end to the brutal policies of the Khmer Rouge. They also established a new, pro-Vietnamese government under Prime Minister Hun Sen.

Even though the Vietnamese invasion of Cambodia had removed the violent Khmer Rouge from power, many countries around the world criticized Vietnam's actions. For example, the United States and other countries formed an economic embargo to punish Vietnam. The U.S. government also provided support to Cambodian rebels fighting against the Hun Sen government, including the Khmer Rouge.

Despite the international reaction, Vietnam continued its occupation of Cambodia for ten years. During this time, former President Lon Nol settled in the United States, where he continued to suffer from health problems. He died on November 17, 1985, in Fullerton, California. The Vietnamese Army withdrew from Cambodia in 1989, but political instability and violence continued to plague the country through the 1990s.

Sources

Chandler, David P. *The Tragedy of Cambodian History: Politics, War, and Revolution since 1945*. New Haven, CT: Yale University Press, 1991.

Isaacs, Arnold. *Without Honor: Defeat in Vietnam and Cambodia*. Baltimore: Johns Hopkins University Press, 1983.

Kamm, Henry. *Cambodia: Report from a Stricken Land*. New York: Arcade Publishing, 1998.

Kirk, Donald. *Wider War: The Struggle for Cambodia, Thailand, and Laos*. New York: Praeger, 1971.

Ponchaud, Francois. *Cambodia: Year Zero*. New York: Holt, Rinehart, and Winston, 1977.

Graham Martin

Born in 1912
Mars Hill, North Carolina
Died in 1990

U.S. ambassador to South Vietnam, 1973–1975

G raham Martin served as U.S. ambassador to South Vietnam during the final years of the Vietnam War. A strong supporter of President Nguyen Van Thieu (see entry), Martin waged a fierce but unsuccessful campaign to increase U.S. military aid for South Vietnam. Martin's ambassadorship to South Vietnam ended in April 1975, when North Vietnamese forces captured the capital city of Saigon to end the war. Since then, his handling of the evacuation of American and Vietnamese personnel from Saigon during the war's final days has become a topic of controversy and debate.

Works as diplomat around the world

Graham A. Martin first made his mark in the world as a newspaperman, but he eventually entered the world of international politics. During the 1940s and 1950s he became a prominent American diplomat, and in 1963 he was named U.S. ambassador to Thailand. He held this post for four years. In 1969 President Richard Nixon (see entry) appointed him ambassador to Italy. Martin served the Nixon administration in Italy for four years before the president asked him to take the same position in South Vietnam.

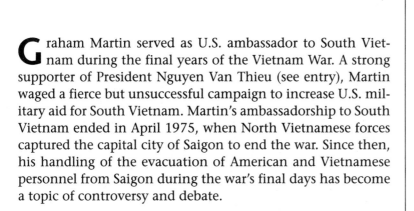

"[Martin] was manipulative . . . [and] out-and-out lying [about the situation in South Vietnam]."

Former U.S. Information Agency official Alan Carter

Graham Martin.
Reproduced by permission of AP/Wide World Photos.

Martin succeeded Ellsworth Bunker as U.S. ambassador to South Vietnam in 1973. He arrived in Saigon shortly after the signing of the 1973 Paris Peace Accords. This treaty paved the way for the withdrawal of American military forces from Vietnam after nearly eight years of war. The departure of U.S. troops from Vietnam was very troubling to South Vietnamese President Nguyen Van Thieu and other members of his regime. Despite U.S. promises of continued military aid, they worried that the American withdrawal meant that they would have to fend off future threats from North Vietnam by themselves. One of Martin's main jobs, then, was to reassure Thieu that the United States would provide military assistance to his government for as long as necessary.

A defender of the South Vietnamese government

Martin worked hard over the next two years on behalf of Thieu's government. He hated the Communist political philosophy of North Vietnam, and he was convinced—as were many other Americans—that a Communist victory over South Vietnam would be a disaster for the Vietnamese people and America's international prestige. As a result, he spent much of his time trying to convince war-weary American lawmakers that the South deserved increased U.S. support.

But Martin's desire to help Thieu became so great that he delivered misleading or false information about the situation in South Vietnam. "Over a long period of time [Martin] practiced a brand of deception designed to try to manipulate Congress," charged former U.S. Information Agency official Alan Carter in *The Bad War*. "That's not the role of an American ambassador. He was manipulative . . . [and] out-and-out lying [about the situation in South Vietnam]." Many Vietnam War historians have also faulted Martin for his performance during this period. "Like scores of previous U.S. officials in South Vietnam, he insisted the government forces were making progress in their war," wrote Robert Schulzinger in *A Time for War*. "Martin [also] rejected any criticism of the South as Communist propaganda. A true believer in the cause, he questioned the judgement, motives, and patriotism of anyone who doubted the capacity of the South Vietnamese government."

South Vietnam begins to crumble

Violent conflicts between North and South Vietnam continued to flare throughout 1973 and 1974. In early March 1975 North Vietnam launched a major military offensive into the South in hopes of winning the war once and for all. As the North Vietnamese Army (NVA) marched southward, the South Vietnamese Army (ARVN) unexpectedly collapsed. As a result, the Communists were able to capture city after city without bloodshed. Many of the South Vietnamese people, meanwhile, fled in panic. Fearful that the Communists would turn their guns on them, these refugees clogged roadways and boats in their desperate efforts to escape the advancing NVA.

Meanwhile, Martin traveled to the United States in order to lobby Congress for increased military aid to the South. While in Washington, D.C., however, he underwent surgery on his jaw. The operation delayed his return to Saigon until late March. By this time, the entire country of South Vietnam seemed to be on the verge of collapse.

On March 30 the city of Da Nang fell to the rapidly advancing North Vietnamese forces when battered ARVN troops broke into a chaotic retreat. The loss of this major city signaled that South Vietnam was in serious trouble. But Martin was one of few people who did not see the defeat as an absolute catastrophe for the South. In fact, he insisted that "despite journalistic accounts, what happened here [in Da Nang] was a planned military withdrawal." He went on to describe the situation in the rest of South Vietnam as "reasonably stable."

Saigon is surrounded

By mid-April 1975 Communist forces had advanced to within forty miles of Saigon, South Vietnam's capital. On April 17 President Gerald Ford issued an emergency request for $722 million in military assistance to the South. Martin and other officials who supported this request hoped that it would allow South Vietnam to stay alive and persuade the North to negotiate a truce that would leave the nation somewhat independent from the Communists. But U.S. lawmakers rejected the request. They believed that additional military aid would not be able to save South Vietnam, and they knew that the Amer-

In April 1975, President Gerald Ford ordered an immediate emergency evacuation of all American personnel from Saigon.
Reproduced by permission of Archive Photos.

ican public was tired of the Vietnam War. These factors convinced Congress to keep the United States on the sidelines during South Vietnam's last days of existence.

On April 21 President Thieu resigned from office. He was replaced by his elderly vice president, Tran Van Huong. Around this same time, U.S. Major General Homer Smith organized a major evacuation of American and Vietnamese personnel out of Saigon's Tan Son Nhut air base. For the next week, hundreds of men and women were evacuated through this operation. But Martin remained hopeful that Saigon could somehow be saved, so he decided to hold off on issuing his own evacuation orders. As a result, hundreds of American and Vietnamese people associated with the U.S. embassy remained in the city.

By April 26 NVA forces had surrounded the capital. A day later, Communist troops launched artillery attacks and air raids against Tan Son Nhut air base, Saigon's main airport. The air raid was carried out by captured American jets that were flown by South Vietnamese pilots who had defected to the North. This attack ruined the runways and made it impossible for fixed-wing aircraft to land. From this point forward, all people fleeing Saigon would have to get out by boat or helicopter.

Orders the final evacuation

By the last days of April it was clear that Saigon was going to fall to the NVA within a matter of days. But Martin—who came down with pneumonia during this time—refused to believe that South Vietnam was entering its final days of existence. On April 28, in fact, he sent a cable to Washington in which he predicted that the United States could maintain a presence in Saigon for "a year or more." He also continued to hold off on giving a final evacuation order, even though

Operation Babylift

When North Vietnamese forces closed in on Saigon in April 1975, American and South Vietnamese officials organized an operation to rescue hundreds of Vietnamese orphans so they could be adopted in the United States and Australia. This effort—called "Operation Babylift"—called for hundreds of children to be flown out of the city on American military planes.

The first flight of Operation Babylift took place on April 4. At that time, a giant American transport plane known as a C-5A was loaded up with 243 Vietnamese children and several American women to watch over them. As it turned out, not all of the youngsters on the plane were orphans. In fact, many were the children of terrified parents who worried that the Communists would murder them if they remained in Saigon.

Unfortunately, the first flight of Operation Babylift ended in tragedy. Shortly after takeoff, a pressure door at the rear of the plane came loose. The plane subsequently spun out of control and crashed into a swamp a short distance from the airport. A total of 178 children were killed in the fiery crash. "Americans saw it all on television," noted Robert Schulzinger, author of *A Time for War.* "For many of them the plane crash symbolized much of the horror and futility of the American involvement in Vietnam."

the city was crumbling all around him. He later explained that he believed that the evacuation order would set off a panic throughout Saigon. But when President Ford heard about the NVA attack on the air base, he personally ordered an immediate emergency evacuation of all American personnel from Saigon, including Martin and the rest of the embassy personnel.

When Martin received Ford's instructions, he reluctantly ordered the evacuation to begin. At 10:51 A.M. on April 29, Armed Forces Radio began playing the song "White Christmas." This song was the signal to begin the final helicopter evacuation out of Saigon. Throughout the rest of the day, hundreds of Americans and their South Vietnamese friends and coworkers gathered at the U.S. embassy to be airlifted out of Saigon. Embassy officials also worked to destroy U.S. records about the war. But they did not have enough time

The Last Americans Killed in Vietnam

On April 27, 1975, North Vietnamese rockets and artillery slammed into the Tan Son Nhut air base outside of Saigon. The attack killed two Marines: Corporal Charles McMahon, Jr., of Woburn, Massachusetts, and Lance Corporal Darwin Judge of Marshalltown, Iowa. Two days later, two Marine chopper pilots—Captain William C. Nystul of Coronado, California, and First Lieutenant Michael Shea of El Paso, Texas—died when their helicopter crashed into the South China Sea during evacuation operations. These soldiers were the last four Americans killed in action during the Vietnam War.

to burn all the files, so many of these records eventually fell into the hands of the Communists. The North Vietnamese later used these files, which included information on Vietnamese citizens who had helped the Americans during the war, to imprison thousands of people.

Final hours in Saigon

When the people of Saigon realized that the last Americans were fleeing the city, panic erupted in the streets. Some South Vietnamese helicopter pilots flew out to the South China Sea, where a fleet of U.S. warships was waiting to transport the evacuees. American Navy personnel were forced to push a dozen or so South Vietnamese helicopters off the ships and into the sea to keep the decks clear for incoming U.S. helicopters. Thousands of Vietnamese civilians, meanwhile, crowded onto barges and boats to escape the city.

The helicopter lift out of Saigon lasted for about twenty-one hours. About 5,000 people, including 4,100 Vietnamese and 900 Americans, were evacuated from the roof of the embassy during this time. Ambassador Martin was one of the very last to leave. As he was herded onto the helicopter, he clutched the American flag that had flown over the embassy's walls in his hands.

At 8 A.M. on April 30, Ford ordered the evacuation ended. As a result, approximately 420 Vietnamese men and women who had helped the Americans during the war were left behind on the embassy roof. Trapped in the city, they had no choice but to await the arrival of the Communists. One day later, the NVA captured Saigon and renamed it Ho Chi Minh City, after Communist leader Ho Chi Minh (see entry), who had led North Vietnam until his death in 1969. The fall of Saigon marked the end of the Vietnam War.

Retires from public life

Upon returning to the United States, Martin served as a special assistant to Secretary of State Henry Kissinger (see entry). In 1977 he retired from government service and settled in Winston-Salem, North Carolina. In 1978 the Federal Bureau of Investigation (FBI) launched an inquiry into Martin's handling of the embassy files in Saigon, but no charges were ever brought against the former ambassador. Martin died in March 1990.

On April 29, 1975, hundreds of Americans and their South Vietnamese friends and coworkers gathered at the U.S. embassy to be airlifted out of Saigon.
Reproduced by permission of AP/Wide World Photos.

Sources

Church, George J. "Saigon: The Final Ten Days." *Time,* April 24, 1995.

Engelmann, Larry. *Tears before the Rain: An Oral History of the Fall of South Vietnam.* New York: Oxford University Press, 1990.

"Graham Martin: Our Man in Saigon." *Time,* April 21, 1975.

Schulzinger, Robert D. *A Time for War: The United States and Vietnam, 1941–1975.* New York: Oxford University Press, 1997.

Snepp, Frank. *Decent Interval: An Insider's Account of Saigon's Indecent End.* New York: Random House, 1977.

Summers, Harry G., Jr. "Final Days of South Vietnam." *American History,* April 1995.

Willenson, Kim. *The Bad War: An Oral History of the Vietnam War.* New York: New American Library, 1987.

John McCain

Born August 29, 1936
Panama Canal Zone, Panama

U.S. senator from Arizona, 1987-present;
U.S. Navy pilot who spent more than five years
as a prisoner of war (POW) in North Vietnam

John S. McCain is one of the best-known American veterans to serve in the Vietnam War. A fighter pilot with the U.S. Navy during the war, he was shot down over North Vietnam in 1967 while on a bombing mission. After ejecting from his plane, he was captured by Communist forces. He spent the next five-and-a-half years as a prisoner of war (POW) before gaining his release in 1973. After returning to the United States, he became a U.S. senator representing the state of Arizona. In 2000 he launched a campaign to win the Republican nomination for the presidency. McCain's war hero status and reputation for honesty made him a strong candidate, but he eventually lost the nomination to Texas Governor George W. Bush.

Member of a famous military family

John Sidney McCain III was born August 29, 1936, in Panama, to John S. McCain, Jr., an American naval officer, and Roberta (Wright) McCain. As McCain grew up, he realized that he was a member of one of America's most prominent military families. In fact, his father and grandfather were the first father-and-son admirals in the history of the U.S. Navy.

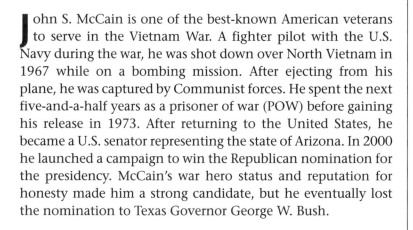

"From the moment I regained my freedom I was intent on not letting Vietnam, or at the least the most difficult memories of my time there, intrude on my future happiness."

John McCain.
Reproduced by permission of AP/Wide World Photos.

257

McCain's paternal grandfather, John S. McCain, Sr., commanded U.S. naval carriers in the Pacific during World War II. McCain's father, meanwhile, was a highly regarded officer who later commanded all American forces in the Pacific during the Vietnam War.

As a youngster, McCain was known for his fearless but rebellious nature. After graduating from Episcopal High School in Alexandria, Virginia, in 1954, he reluctantly enrolled in the U.S. Naval Academy in Annapolis, Maryland. McCain had mixed feelings about pursuing a navy career, but he knew that his family expected him to continue its tradition of naval service.

After arriving at the academy, McCain quickly emerged as a leader among his fellow midshipmen (students). But he also gained a reputation as a rowdy rule-breaker. In fact, he accumulated so many demerits (marks against his record) for various infractions that his student ranking plummeted. He eventually graduated fifth from the bottom of his class of 795 students in 1958.

After graduating, McCain entered the U.S. Navy, where he trained as a fighter pilot. In 1965 he married Carol Shepp and adopted her two sons, Doug and Andrew. They later had a daughter together named Sidney Ann.

Goes to Vietnam

As McCain's navy career progressed, he followed the growing war in Vietnam with great interest. This war pitted the U.S.-supported nation of South Vietnam against the Communist nation of North Vietnam and its guerrilla allies—known as the Viet Cong—who operated in the South. The war began in the mid-1950s, when Communists first initiated efforts to take over South Vietnam and unite it with the North under one Communist government. But the United States strongly opposed the Communist maneuvers because of fears that a takeover might trigger Communist aggression in other parts of the world. As a result, the United States provided military and financial aid to South Vietnam in the late 1950s and early 1960s.

In 1965 the United States escalated its involvement in the Vietnam War. It sent thousands of American combat troops into the South and executed hundreds of air raids against Communist targets. But deepening U.S. involvement in the war failed to defeat the joint Viet Cong-North Vietnamese forces. Instead, the war settled into a bloody stalemate that eventually claimed the lives of more than 58,000 U.S. soldiers and caused bitter internal divisions across America.

McCain was sent to Vietnam in 1967, when American involvement in the war was reaching its height. He was assigned to the aircraft carrier *Forrestal* off the coast of North Vietnam. Over the next few months, he flew numerous combat missions against North Vietnamese positions. On July 29, 1967, however, he was nearly killed in a disastrous accident on the deck of the *Forrestal.* That day, a rocket from another aircraft accidentally came loose and struck the fuel tank of McCain's plane just as he was preparing to fly off the flight deck. The rocket triggered a deadly blaze that quickly spread across the deck. McCain barely escaped the flames, which quickly reached several other airplanes. Within a matter of minutes, the fire detonated several other powerful bombs and destroyed dozens of airplanes on the carrier. The massive fire did $72 million of damage to the ship, not including aircraft destroyed. It also claimed the lives of 134 servicemen, making it the worst military accident of the Vietnam War.

Shot down over Hanoi

The fire forced the *Forrestal* to undergo massive repairs. Eager to continue flying, McCain transferred to the *Oriskany,* another U.S. aircraft career that was in need of additional combat pilots.

On October 26, 1967, McCain took off from the *Oriskany* on his twenty-third bombing mission in Vietnam. He was part of a group of fighters that had been ordered to bomb power plants in the North Vietnamese capital city of Hanoi. While flying above Hanoi, however, a North Vietnamese anti-aircraft missile destroyed the right wing of McCain's plane. As his plane spun out of control, McCain was forced to eject. He landed in a lake, where a crowd of Vietnamese dragged him out of the water, beat him, stabbed him with a bayonet, and turned him over to authorities.

McCain was taken to a prison known as the "Hanoi Hilton," where North Vietnam kept many American POWs. He

This photo claims to show the capture of John McCain by a group of Vietnamese after his plane was shot down. *Reproduced by permission of AP/Wide World Photos.*

was thrown in a prison cell with two broken arms, a broken shoulder, and a shattered knee. Over the next several days, his captors demanded that he provide them with military information, but he refused to cooperate. When McCain's interrogators asked him for the names of fellow American pilots, he gave them the names of the starting offensive line of the Green Bay Packers football team.

McCain received no medical care for his injuries for nine days. At that time, however, his captors learned that his father was a high-ranking officer with the U.S. Navy. They treated his wounds and allowed fellow POWs to help McCain, but the delay in treatment had a serious negative impact. He never regained full use of either of his arms or his broken leg.

After seven months of captivity, McCain was offered an early release from prison. The opportunity to go home was tempting, but he refused it. Instead, he obeyed the American prisoner of war code of conduct, which states that prisoners should only accept release in the order in which they are captured. By the time of McCain's imprisonment, more than a hundred other American POWs had already been captured. McCain knew that accepting early release would hurt the morale of his fellow prisoners and give the North Vietnamese a propaganda tool (a psychological weapon to hurt enemy morale) to use against the United States.

McCain's refusal to accept release ahead of his fellow prisoners infuriated his captors. They beat him for a week until he signed a statement confessing that he was a war criminal. While he is not blamed for signing the confession because of the torture he endured, McCain continues to express deep regret about it. "It's the only blemish [on my war record]," he told Robert Timberg in *The Nightingale's Song*. "It's something I'll never get over."

Over the next few years, McCain endured long months of solitary confinement in which he was not allowed to communicate with anyone. He also lost a third of his body weight because of malnutrition. In addition, he was beaten so many times for his defiant attitude that most of his teeth were broken off at the gum line. Finally, McCain's captors hung him up by his broken arms for hours at a time and tortured him in a number of other ways. But despite the physical and emotional trauma of his ordeal, McCain refused to give up his hope of eventually regaining his freedom.

McCain's POW ordeal ends

McCain and the rest of the American POWs held in Hanoi were finally released in March 1973, after the United States and North Vietnam agreed on a treaty that called for the withdrawal of American forces from Vietnam. "When the American prisoners were released in 1973, we were flown first to Clark Air Force Base in the Philippines," McCain recalled in *People Weekly*. "I have often maintained that I left Vietnam behind me when I arrived at Clark. That is an exaggeration. But from the moment I regained my freedom I was intent on not letting Vietnam, or at the least the most difficult memories of my time there, intrude on my future happiness. Looking back in anger at any experience is self-destructive, and I am grateful to have avoided it."

After receiving medical treatment in the Philippines, McCain returned to America, where he received a hero's welcome. In recognition of his bravery and sacrifice in service to his country, McCain received many of the nation's highest military awards, including the Silver Star, the Bronze Star, the Legion of Merit, the Purple Heart, and the Distinguished Flying Cross.

McCain then resumed his military career. He enrolled in the National War College in Washington, D.C., in 1973–74, then returned to flying as a training squadron commander. He was promoted to captain in 1977, the same year that the Navy named him their liaison (official representative) to the U.S. Senate. Around this time, however, McCain's marriage began to crumble, in part because he engaged in a number of extramarital affairs. In January 1980 McCain and his first wife divorced after a long separation. Five months later, he married Cindy Hensley, with whom he eventually had four children.

Enters the world of politics

McCain retired from the Navy in 1981 after twenty-two years of military service. He moved to Phoenix, Arizona, where he became involved in the state's strong Republican Party. In 1982 he won a seat in the U.S. House of Representatives as a Republican. He was reelected by a comfortable margin in 1984.

In 1986 McCain replaced Barry Goldwater (see entry) as one of Arizona's two U.S. senators after Goldwater decided to retire. Soon after assuming his Senate duties, McCain was named as one of the notorious "Keating Five." This was a group of five senators who were charged with improperly working on behalf of Charles Keating, the owner of a savings and loan institution that went bankrupt because of his irresponsible actions. The Senate Ethics Committee investigated the matter and determined that McCain was not guilty of any wrongdoing. But they criticized him for exercising "poor judgment" in his dealings with Keating. This scandal deeply embarrassed McCain, and he continues to regard it as the biggest stain on his political career.

During the late 1980s and early 1990s McCain put the Keating scandal behind him. Over time, he instead became better known for his conservative voting record and his strong sense of honor and patriotism. By the mid-1990s he had emerged as a crusader for campaign finance reform, a strong advocate for American military veterans, a supporter of increased defense spending, and a tough opponent of the tobacco industry.

During this period McCain also became an outspoken supporter of reestablishing trade and diplomatic relations with Vietnam. "I've made my peace with Vietnam and with the Vietnamese," explained McCain, who has made eight visits to Vietnam since the war ended. "There are Vietnamese whom I will never be able to forgive for their cruelty to us [American POWs]. The Vietnamese people will someday be free, but they are not yet. And our opposition to a regime that denies its people basic human rights was and is honorable. But I choose to use the opportunities afforded by normal relations to help Vietnam find a better future than its hard, war-torn past." In 1995, twenty years after the Vietnam War ended, the United States and Vietnam finally reestablished diplomatic ties.

Makes strong bid for the presidency

In September 1999 McCain announced his intention to run for the Republican Party's nomination for president in the year 2000. At the same time, he published a memoir called *Faith of My Fathers.* In this book McCain talked about the military careers of himself, his father, and his grandfather. The book, which includes an emotional account of McCain's experiences as a Vietnam POW, became a best-seller and helped McCain's campaign tremendously.

McCain waged a spirited campaign for the Republican nomination in late 1999 and early 2000. His personal history, his reputation for honesty and toughness, and his calls to clean up American politics all appealed to American voters. Ultimately, however, he lost the nomination to Texas Governor George W. Bush, a son of former president George H. Bush.

Sources

Alter, Jonathan. "White Tornado: John McCain's History as a POW Is Only Part of His Story." *Newsweek,* November 15, 1999.

McCain, John, with Mark Salter. *Faith of My Fathers: A Family Memoir.* New York: Random House, 1999.

McCain, John. "How the POWs Fought Back." *U.S. News and World Report.* May 14, 1973.

McCain, John. "I've Made My Peace with Vietnam." *People Weekly,* May 1, 2000.

Simon, Roger. "A Trip Back to His Future." *U.S. News and World Report,* May 8, 2000.

Timberg, Robert. *John McCain: An American Odyssey.* New York: Simon and Schuster, 1999.

Timberg, Robert. *The Nightingale's Song.* New York: Simon and Schuster, 1995.

George McGovern

Born July 19, 1922
Avon, South Dakota

U.S. senator from South Dakota, 1962–1980;
Democratic presidential nominee in 1972

South Dakota Democratic Senator George McGovern was one of the earliest and harshest critics of American military involvement in South Vietnam. His censure of U.S. policy in Vietnam began in early 1965 and remained strong throughout the war. In 1972 McGovern won the Democratic Party's nomination for the presidency. Over the next several months, he vowed to immediately pull out of Vietnam if he defeated President Richard Nixon (see entry) in the general election. But Nixon soundly thrashed his challenger in the November election, winning forty-nine states.

"Freedom is worth fighting for, but it cannot be achieved through an alliance with unpopular forces abroad that deny freedom."

Political beliefs shaped by religion and war

George Stanley McGovern was born on July 19, 1922, in the small farming community of Avon, South Dakota. His parents were Joseph McGovern, a Methodist minister, and Frances (McLean) McGovern; he had three siblings. When he was six years old, George and his family moved to Mitchell, South Dakota, where he spent the remainder of his youth.

George McGovern.
Reproduced by permission of Archive Photos.

265

McGovern was a shy and studious boy who was deeply influenced by his family's religious convictions. During high school, however, he conquered his shyness and became a leading member of the school debate team. In 1940 he graduated from high school and enrolled in Dakota Wesleyan College, which was located in Mitchell.

In 1943 McGovern married Eleanore Stegeberg, with whom he had five children. A short time later, McGovern received his induction notice to make himself available for military duty. He joined the Army Air Corps, and in February 1944 he was sent to Europe to fight in World War II. Over the next several months he flew thirty-five bombing missions over the war-torn continent. He was an excellent pilot and earned several medals for his performance, including the Distinguished Flying Cross. But McGovern's exposure to the war's terrible violence and destruction had a huge impact on him emotionally. By the time the war ended in 1945, he had developed a deep hatred for war and an interest in political leaders who emphasized messages of peace.

In 1946 McGovern returned to Dakota Wesleyan and earned his bachelor's degree. He then enrolled in Garrett Theological Seminary in Evanston, Illinois, in order to pursue a career as a minister. His religious faith remained strong during this time, but he eventually decided that the ministry was not for him. In 1947 he enrolled at Northwestern University, also in Evanston, where he became increasingly involved in liberal politics. He graduated two years later with a master's degree.

Growing interest in politics

In 1949 McGovern returned to Mitchell and joined the faculty of Dakota Wesleyan as a professor of history and political science. During this time, he began to consider a possible career in politics. His liberal political beliefs made the Republican Party unattractive to him, so he allied himself with South Dakota's Democratic Party.

When McGovern first joined the Democrats, the state organization was in terrible shape. Disorganized and ignored by South Dakota's largely conservative population, the party had practically disappeared from public view. But McGovern single-handledly revived the state party over the next few years, and in 1956 he defeated a Republican to win a seat in the U.S. House of Representatives. McGovern's victory made him the first Democrat to represent South Dakota in Congress in twenty years.

After winning reelection in 1958, McGovern set his sights on winning one of South Dakota's U.S. Senate seats. He lost in 1960, but he benefited from the election of John F. Kennedy (see entry) to the presidency that year. McGovern was a close friend and political ally of both the new president and his brother, Robert F. Kennedy (see entry). After assuming office, President Kennedy put McGovern in charge of his administration's Food for Peace Program. McGovern received high praise for his directorship of the program, which worked to provide aid to nations around the world suffering from starvation and malnutrition.

Wins place in the Senate

In 1962 McGovern left Food for Peace to run for the U.S. Senate again. McGovern's political beliefs were more liberal than those of the average South Dakota voter, but his reputation for integrity and hard work lifted him to victory. He defeated Republican nominee Joe Bottum in the fall election, becoming the first Democratic senator from South Dakota since 1936.

McGovern served in the U.S. Senate for the next eighteen years, winning reelection four times. During that time, he came to be regarded as one of the Senate's most liberal members. This reputation developed quite rapidly, mostly because of his early criticism of growing U.S. involvement in Vietnam.

Once a colony of France, Vietnam had won its freedom in 1954 after an eight-year war with the French. But the country had been divided into two sections by the 1954 Geneva peace agreement. North Vietnam was headed by a Communist government under revolutionary leader Ho Chi Minh (see entry). South Vietnam, meanwhile, was led by a U.S.-supported government under President Ngo Dinh Diem (see entry).

The Geneva agreement provided for nationwide free elections to be held in 1956 so that the two sections of Vietnam could be united under one government. But U.S. and South Vietnamese officials refused to hold the elections because they believed that the results would give the Communists control over the entire country. When the South refused to hold elections, Communist guerrillas known as Viet Cong took up arms against Diem's government. The United States responded by sending money, weapons, and advisors to aid in South Vietnam's defense. By 1963, when McGovern assumed his Senate seat, this assistance was expanding at a very rapid rate.

Leading Senate critic of the Vietnam War

In 1964 McGovern reluctantly voted in support of the Tonkin Gulf Resolution, which gave President Lyndon Johnson (see entry) broad freedom to increase American military involvement in Vietnam. But in 1965, when Johnson began sending U.S. ground troops to fight in the conflict, McGovern emerged as a vocal critic of the administration's Vietnam policies.

The South Dakota senator charged that the United States should not be helping South Vietnam's government because of its history of repression (the denial of basic rights) and violence toward its own people. McGovern also argued that the conflict in Vietnam was a civil war that should be settled by its own people. Finally, he warned that U.S. involvement in the conflict would cost billions of dollars and thousands of American lives, with no guarantee of victory. "We are being pulled step by step into a jungle quicksand that may claim our sons and that may claim sons of Asia for years to come," McGovern declared in an April 1967 Senate speech. "Freedom is worth fighting for, but it cannot be achieved through an alliance with unpopular forces abroad that deny freedom."

In 1968 McGovern entered the race for the Democratic presidential nomination after the leading candidate—and his good friend—Robert Kennedy was assassinated in California. Democratic voters ignored his late entry into the race, turning instead to Hubert Humphrey, who had been vice president in the Johnson administration. But Humphrey was handily beaten by Republican nominee Richard Nixon, who told voters he had a secret plan to get American out of Vietnam with its pride intact.

McGovern's and Nixon's Vietnam policies

After assuming office in January 1969, Nixon launched a gradual withdrawal of American troops from Vietnam. But he also expanded U.S. military operations into the neighboring countries of Cambodia and Laos and ordered heavy bombing of North Vietnam. The president's policies infuriated McGovern, who called the war "a moral and political disaster—a terrible cancer eating away at the soul of our nation."

In 1970 McGovern and Republican Senator Mark Hatfield of Oregon introduced a Senate bill calling for the withdrawal of all U.S. troops from South Vietnam by the end of the year. McGovern argued passionately for the bill. "Every senator in this chamber is partly responsible for sending 50,000 young Americans to an early grave, and in one sense this chamber literally reeks of blood," he said in a September 1 speech in the Senate chambers. "Every senator here is partly responsible for that human wreckage at Walter Reed [military hospital] and all across the land—young boys without legs, without arms, or genitals, or faces, or hopes. If we don't end this damnable war those young men will some day curse us for our pitiful willingness to let the executive [president] carry the burden that the constitution places on us." But the bill went down in defeat.

In 1972 McGovern won the Democratic nomination for the presidency. The candidate took liberal positions on a wide range of social and economic issues. But his major emphasis was on ending the war in Vietnam. "In 1968, Americans voted to bring our sons home from Vietnam in peace—and since then, 20,000 have come home in coffins," McGovern stated in accepting his party's nomination. "I have no secret plan for peace. I have a public plan. As one whose heart has ached for ten years over the agony of Vietnam, I will halt the senseless bombing of Indochina on Inauguration Day [the day that the president is sworn into office] . . . . Within ninety days of my inauguration every American soldier and every American prisoner will be out of the jungle and out of their cells and back home in America where they belong."

Nixon defeats McGovern for the presidency

McGovern hoped that the American public's great weariness with the Vietnam War would help lift him to victory over President Nixon in the fall 1972 elections. But McGovern's campaign encountered numerous problems. He was forced to replace vice-presidential nominee Tom Eagleton with Sargent Shriver after reporters learned that Eagleton had a history of mental depression. Several of McGovern's economic proposals were widely ridiculed, and his liberal reputation turned off large groups of voters. And most importantly, a majority of Americans decided that Nixon was keeping his promise to gradually get America out of Vietnam. This belief doomed McGovern, who based much of his campaign on the war.

Nixon ended up defeating McGovern by one of the largest margins in American history. Nixon won forty-nine states (including McGovern's home state of South Dakota) and 61 percent of the popular vote. McGovern won only 38 percent of the vote and carried only Massachusetts and the District of Columbia.

After his defeat, McGovern returned to the U.S. Senate. In 1974 he managed to turn back a challenge from Republican candidate Leo Thorsness—a former prisoner of war in Vietnam—and keep his seat. He spent the next six years championing a variety of liberal causes, including programs to combat poverty and hunger in America and elsewhere. In 1980, though, South Dakota's conservative population finally voted McGovern out of office, replacing him with Republican Jim Abdnor.

Fighter for social causes

In 1984 McGovern made a final bid for the presidency. But he failed to generate any meaningful support for his campaign, and he withdrew from the race in March. McGovern remained retired from political office after that, but he continued to work on behalf of social causes in which he believed.

In 1994 McGovern's daughter Terry lost a long battle with alcoholism. She froze to death one winter night after drinking herself into unconsciousness. This tragedy devastated McGovern and his family, who had spent years trying to help Terry triumph over her dependency. The family responded to her death by establishing the McGovern Family Foundation, an organization dedicated to helping people with alcoholism. In 1996 McGovern published a critically acclaimed memoir called *Terry: My Daughter's Life-and-Death Struggle with Alcoholism.*

McGovern also maintained his lifelong activism on behalf of poor and hungry people worldwide during the 1990s. In 1998 he was named the United States' Permanent Representative to the Food and Agricultural Organization (FAO), a United Nations organization that works to combat world poverty and hunger.

Sources

Anson, Robert S. *McGovern: A Biography.* New York, 1972.

Kimball, Jeffrey. *Nixon's Vietnam War.* Lawrence: University Press of Kansas, 1998.

McGovern, George. *Grassroots: The Autobiography of George McGovern.* New York: Random House, 1977.

McGovern, George. *Vietnam, Four American Perspectives: Lectures.* West Lafayette, IN: Purdue University Press, 1990.

White, Theodore H. *The Making of the President, 1972.* New York: Bantam, 1973.

Robert McNamara

Born June 9, 1916
San Francisco, California

U.S. secretary of defense, 1961–1968

"I could see no good way to win—or end—an increasingly costly and destructive war."

R obert McNamara is one of the most controversial figures of the entire Vietnam War. As U.S. secretary of defense during both the Kennedy and Johnson administrations, he played a major part in shaping U.S. policy toward Vietnam. In fact, some people referred to the conflict in Vietnam as "McNamara's War" because of his role as primary architect and manager of the American war effort. As the war dragged on, McNamara lost confidence in an eventual U.S. victory and became tormented by doubts about the conflict. But he did not share these concerns with the American public. Instead, he publicly defended U.S. actions in Vietnam for another two years before leaving the government in early 1968.

Special advisor to U.S. military

Robert Strange McNamara was born June 9, 1916, in San Francisco, California. His parents were Robert James McNamara, a manager for a shoe company, and Clara Nell (Strange) McNamara. McNamara grew up in Piedmont, California, before attending college at the University of California, Berkeley. After earning a bachelor's degree in 1937, he moved on to Harvard University. He graduated from Harvard with a master's degree in business administration in 1939.

McNamara worked for a short time at a San Francisco accounting firm before returning to Harvard in 1940 as an assistant professor of business administration. When the United States entered World War II one year later, he volunteered for military service. The Navy turned down his application because of his poor eyesight, but McNamara still found a way to contribute to the war effort. In 1942 he taught special courses to U.S. Army Air Force officers (the Air Force did not become a separate branch of the military until July 1947). In addition, he helped the Air Force set up systems to keep track of their materials and personnel.

In 1943 the Army sent McNamara to England, where he helped develop and manage Air Force bombing operations. He remained in this special advisory role until April 1946, when he was released from active military service with the rank of lieutenant colonel.

High-ranking Ford executive

After returning to the United States, McNamara joined with eight other Air Force management experts who decided to form a business consulting company. A short time later, the Ford Motor Company hired this group—known collectively as the "Whiz Kids"—to reverse its declining business fortunes. After studying the company, McNamara's group delivered a set of recommendations designed to improve Ford's efficiency and financial performance. Ford's leadership was especially impressed by McNamara's insights. As a result, the company offered McNamara a management position within the company.

McNamara accepted the offer and became a manager for the automaker. Over the next few years, he rose rapidly through the corporate ranks, becoming known as a brilliant administrator with a good instinct for anticipating the American public's changing car-buying tastes. By 1957 he was vice president in charge of all of Ford's car and truck divisions and a member of its board of directors. On November 9, 1960, McNamara was named president of Ford Motor Company. This promotion made him the first non-member of the Ford family ever to serve as the company's president.

Joins Kennedy administration

McNamara's term as president of the Ford Motor Company ended five weeks later, when John F. Kennedy (see entry)—who would be taking over as president of the United States in January 1961—asked him to join his administration as secretary of defense. McNamara's national reputation as a talented manager and statistical genius had made a deep impression on Kennedy. He believed that McNamara's abilities made him ideally suited to oversee America's vast military forces.

After McNamara was sworn in as secretary of defense on January 21, 1961, he immediately began making changes designed to improve the efficiency and strength of the armed forces. Relying on reports from civilian financial and statistical analysts who studied all aspects of U.S. military performance, McNamara reorganized the budgets and management practices of the Army, Navy, and Air Force. He also shut down military bases that were no longer needed and refused to spend money on weapons systems he did not like. His actions angered some American military leaders but pleased many lawmakers, government officials, and newspaper editors.

During McNamara's first few years as secretary of defense, he and other Kennedy administration officials became increasingly concerned about a growing war in Vietnam. This conflict pitted the Communist nation of North Vietnam and its allies, the South Vietnamese Communists known as the Viet Cong, against the U.S.-supported nation of South Vietnam.

American involvement in Vietnam's affairs had actually begun in the 1950s. At that time, the United States began sending military and financial aid to South Vietnam to help it establish a strong economy and a democratic government. During the early 1960s, however, America became gravely concerned that South Vietnam was on the verge of being conquered by North Vietnam and its Viet Cong allies. Most American officials believed that if the South were overrun by the Communists, other nations would become more vulnerable to a Communist takeover. This concern convinced McNamara and the Kennedy administration to launch a major U.S. military buildup in Vietnam during the early 1960s.

McNamara and the Vietnam War

In November 1963 Kennedy was assassinated, and Vice President Lyndon B. Johnson (see entry) became president. Under Johnson, U.S. military involvement in Vietnam escalated rapidly. "Between January 28 and July 28, 1965, President Johnson made the fateful choices that locked the United States onto a path of massive military intervention in Vietnam," recalled McNamara in his memoir *In Retrospect*. This intervention, he added, "ultimately destroyed his presidency and polarized [divided] America like nothing since the Civil War. During this fateful period, Johnson initiated bombing of North Vietnam and committed U.S. ground forces . . . . All of this occurred without adequate public disclosure or debate, planting the seeds of an eventually debilitating [crippling] credibility gap."

When the United States first sent ground troops into Vietnam in early 1965, McNamara was highly confident that America would win a swift and easy victory over the Communists. He thought that by using statistical analysis and other management techniques to direct the powerful U.S. military, America would methodically roll over the enemy. By the end of the year, though, McNamara realized that the Viet Cong and North Vietnamese were willing to absorb tremendous punishment in order to reunite the country under Communist rule. In addition, he lost faith in South Vietnam's ability to govern itself without continued military and financial support from America.

In early 1966 McNamara urged Johnson to negotiate a peaceful end to the war. He warned the president that the war was turning into a bloody stalemate that might last for years. "I could see no good way to win—or end—an increasingly costly and destructive war," he explained in *In Retrospect*. "It became clear then . . . that military force—especially when wielded [controlled] by an outside power—just cannot bring order in a country that cannot govern itself."

As McNamara wrestled with his growing doubts about the war, American families, neighborhoods, and communities became bitterly divided over U.S. involvement in Vietnam. But even as antiwar protests flared across the country, McNamara refused to confess his doubts about the war to the American public. Instead, he repeatedly assured the public that the United States was on its way to victory. In fact, McNamara

McNamara Recalls the Suicide of Norman Morrison

In late 1965 an American man named Norman R. Morrison set himself on fire in front of the Pentagon, the United States' central military headquarters, in order to protest U.S. policies in Vietnam. Morrison was a member of the Quaker religious group, which holds strong beliefs that violence in any form is unacceptable. His decision to commit suicide by self-immolation (setting oneself on fire) shocked the nation. Some historians believe that his action contributed to Robert McNamara's change of heart toward the war.

In the following excerpt from McNamara's memoir *In Retrospect: The Tragedy and Lessons of Vietnam,* the former secretary of defense recalls Morrison's suicide and its impact on the McNamara family:

Antiwar protest had been sporadic and limited through the fall of 1965 and had not compelled attention. Then came the afternoon of November 2, 1965. At twilight that day, a young Quaker named Norman R. Morrison, father of three and an officer of the Stoney Run Friends Meeting in Baltimore, burned himself to death within forty feet of my Pentagon window. When he set himself on fire, he was holding his one-year-old daughter in his arms. Bystanders screamed, "Save the child!" and he flung her out of his arms. She survived.

Morrison's death was a tragedy not only for his family but also for me and the country. It was an outcry against the killing that was destroying the lives of so many Vietnamese and American youth.

I reacted to the horror of his action by bottling up my emotions and avoided talking about them with anyone—even my family. I knew [my wife] Marg and our

defended U.S. military strategy in Vietnam throughout 1966 and 1967, even after he had lost all faith in its effectiveness. He also continued to send tens of thousands of American soldiers into the conflict. His actions during this period made him a major target of antiwar protestors.

McNamara repeatedly clashed with U.S. military leaders over Vietnam strategy and tactics during this period as well. American military commanders believed that they could defeat the Communists if Johnson approved a massive escalation of bombing attacks against North Vietnam. But McNamara argued that increased bombing would not stop the Communists. He charged that the bombing strategy would only create higher civilian casualties and greater damage to the battered Vietnamese countryside.

Norman Morrison. *Reproduced by permission of AP/Wide World Photos.*

three children shared many of Morrison's feelings about the war, as did the wives

and children of several of my cabinet colleagues. And I believed I understood and shared some of his thoughts. There was much Marg and I and the children should have talked about, yet at moments like this I often turn inward instead—it is a grave weakness. The episode created tension at home that only deepened as dissent and criticism of the war continued to grow.

Thirty years after Morrison committed suicide, his widow, Anne Morrison Welsh, read *In Retrospect*. Much of the public reaction to McNamara's memoir was negative, but Welsh released a public statement in support of the former defense secretary: "I am grateful to Robert McNamara for his courageous and honest reappraisal of the Vietnam War and his involvement in it. I hope his book will contribute to the healing process."

Leaves the Johnson administration

By late 1967 it was clear to President Johnson and other members of his administration that McNamara no longer believed in the war. "Two months before he left he felt he was a murderer and didn't know how to extricate [remove] himself," Johnson told biographer Doris Kearns in *Lyndon Johnson and the American Dream*. "I was afraid he might have a nervous breakdown." As a result, Johnson decided to replace McNamara as secretary of defense.

McNamara resigned in February 1968 to serve as president of the World Bank, an organization that lends money to poor nations for economic, educational, and social programs. In his memoir, McNamara claimed that he was not on the verge of "emotional and physical collapse" when he resigned.

Instead, he stated that he left the Johnson administration because of differences over Vietnam policy. "The fact is I had come to the conclusion, and had told [Johnson] point-blank, that we could not achieve our objective in Vietnam through any reasonable military means, and we therefore should seek a lesser political objective through negotations. President Johnson was not ready to accept that. It was becoming clear to both of us that I would not change my judgment, nor would he change his. Something had to give."

In any case, McNamara was an unhappy and disillusioned man when he left the Johnson White House. A Johnson aide named Harry McPherson told Stanley Karnow, author of *Vietnam: A History,* about a farewell luncheon that McNamara attended in February 1968: "He reeled off the familiar statistics—how we had dropped more bombs on Vietnam than all of Europe during World War II. Then his voice broke, and there were tears in his eyes as he spoke of the futility, the crushing futility, of the air war. The rest of us sat silently—I for one with my mouth open, listening to the secretary of defense talk that way about a campaign for which he had, ultimately, been responsible. I was pretty shocked."

McNamara served as president of the World Bank from 1968 to 1981. During his presidency, the organization flourished and dramatically increased the size and scope of its funding operations. After leaving the World Bank, McNamara devoted his time to several issues that concerned him, including world poverty, nuclear arms policy, and environmental pollution.

In Retrospect creates controversy

In 1995 McNamara published a memoir in which he tried to explain his actions during the Vietnam War. In this book, called *In Retrospect: The Tragedy and Lessons of Vietnam,* McNamara insisted that he and other U.S. officials of the Vietnam era "acted according to what we thought were the principles and traditions of this nation. We made our decisions in light of those values. Yet we were wrong, terribly wrong . . . . I truly believe that we made an error not of values and intentions but of judgement and capabilities." In *In Retrospect,* McNamara blamed the U.S. defeat in Vietnam on American ignorance of Vietnamese history and culture and errors in military strategy. "The foundations of our decision making were gravely flawed," he wrote.

The publication of *In Retrospect* triggered a new storm of debate about the war and McNamara's role in it. For many Americans, the book's appearance rekindled dark memories of a bloody and unsuccessful war that bitterly divided the nation. "As Mr. McNamara confesses the guilt he feels at being an early architect of the war, he isn't getting much absolution [forgiveness]," noted an April 16, 1995, editorial in the *Detroit Free Press*. "Those who still think Vietnam was a cause that should have been fought and could have been won are enraged by his restrospective judgment of it as a futile, unnecessary conflict. Those who opposed the war when it was being waged tend to have a bitter, I-told-you-so reaction to his memoir."

But reaction to McNamara's book was not entirely negative. In fact, some reviewers and readers called the memoir a courageous work that expressed great sadness about the American and Vietnamese lives that were lost in the conflict. But many Americans—including Vietnam veterans, former antiwar protestors, U.S. lawmakers, and journalists who covered the

Former enemies Robert McNamara and Vo Nguyen Giap meet at a 1997 conference on the Vietnam War. The two exchanged recollections of the war they helped wage nearly thirty years prior.
Reproduced by permission of AP/Wide World Photos.

war—condemned the book as dishonest and self-serving. They charged that McNamara's memoir never explained why he continued to send American soldiers to die in Vietnam in 1966 and 1967, after he had privately concluded that U.S. involvement in the war was doomed to fail. "Mr. McNamara must not escape the lasting moral condemnation of his countrymen," stated one *New York Times* editorial. "His regret cannot be huge enough to balance the books for our dead soldiers. The ghost of those unlived [the people who died in Vietnam] circle close around Mr. McNamara. Surely he must in every quiet and prosperous moment hear the ceaseless whispers of those poor boys in the infantry, dying in the tall grass, platoon by platoon, for no purpose. What he took from them cannot be repaid by prime-time apology and stale tears, three decades late."

In 1999 McNamara cowrote a second book on the Vietnam War with several scholars and historians. This book, called *Argument without End: In Search of Answers to the Vietnam Tragedy,* provided excerpts from a series of meetings between American and Vietnamese scholars, policy makers, and military officers who were involved in the Vietnam War. Participants in these meetings, which were held from 1995 to 1998, included McNamara, Vo Nguyen Giap (leader of North Vietnamese military forces during the war; see entry) and Nguyen Go Thach (a former foreign minister of Vietnam).

Sources

Halberstam, David. *The Best and the Brightest.* New York: Random House, 1972.

Hendrickson, Paul. *The Living and the Dead: Robert McNamara and Five Lives of a Lost War.* New York: Knopf, 1996.

Karnow, Stanley. *Vietnam: A History.* New York: Viking, 1983.

Kearns, Doris. *Lyndon Johnson and the American Dream.* New York: Signet Books, 1976.

McNamara, Robert S., et al. *Argument without End: In Search of Answers to the Vietnam Tragedy.* Public Affairs, 1999.

McNamara, Robert S., with Brian VanDeMark. *In Retrospect: The Tragedy and Lessons of Vietnam.* New York: Times Books, 1995.

"Mr. McNamara's War." *New York Times,* April 12, 1995.

Shapley, Deborah. *Promise and Power: The Life and Times of Robert McNamara.* Boston: Little, Brown, 1993.

Bobby Muller

Born 1946
Long Island, New York

U.S. Marine; founder of the Vietnam Veterans of America (VVA)
and the International Campaign to Ban Landmines (ICBL)

Vietnam veteran Bobby Muller is one of America's best-known advocates for the men and women who served in the Vietnam War, as well as for people all around the world who have been scarred by war. A former Marine lieutenant whose war injuries left him a paraplegic (unable to use his legs), Muller was a key figure in the creation of both the Vietnam Veterans of America (VVA) and the Vietnam Veterans of America Foundation (VVAF). In the 1990s he cofounded the International Campaign to Ban Landmines (ICBL), an organization dedicated to ending the use of landmines around the world.

"[The dedication of the Vietnam Veterans Memorial] rekindled that sense and gave the beginning of [a feeling that] it's okay to be a Vietnam vet—you don't have to be ashamed or embarrassed."

Muller enlists in the Marine Corps

Robert Muller was born in 1946 in Long Island, New York. The eldest of two sons of Robert and Edith Muller, Bobby grew up in a New York City suburb. After graduating from high school in 1964, he enrolled at nearby Hofstra University. In the meantime, the United States had dramatically increased its involvement in an armed conflict in Vietnam.

American involvement in Vietnam's affairs had begun in the 1950s, when the U.S. government sent generous mili-

tary and financial aid packages to the young country of South Vietnam to help it establish a strong economy and a democratic government. But by the early 1960s America had become gravely concerned that South Vietnam was on the verge of falling to the Communist nation of North Vietnam and its Viet Cong allies in the South. U.S. analysts claimed that if the South were overrun by the Communists, other nations would become more vulnerable to a Communist takeover. When North Vietnamese and Viet Cong attacks pushed South Vietnam to the brink of collapse in the mid-1960s, the United States escalated its involvement in the conflict. Before long, America had assumed primary responsibility for both the ground war in the South and the air war against the North.

As Muller pursued his studies at Hofstra, he watched events unfold in Vietnam with growing interest. "Back in late '66, early '67, everybody was very rah, rah, Vietnam," he recalled in *The Bad War: An Oral History of the Vietnam War.* "I was in business school at Hofstra, and in the last part of my junior year I was doing very well, Dean's list, management as a specialty." Around this time, however, several professors told him that military experience would help his future career. In addition, Muller began to feel that by not serving in Vietnam, he was missing out on a significant event in his nation's history. These factors convinced him to enlist in the U.S. Marine Corps and request an infantry assignment.

Muller graduated from Hofstra with a degree in business administration in the spring of 1968. He then reported to the Marines for officer training. Muller excelled in his training, and in the fall of 1968 he was sent to Vietnam as a Marine lieutenant.

Tour of duty ends with life-threatening bullet wound

Muller spent the next several months leading patrols and missions in some of the most dangerous countryside in Vietnam. During this time, he endured long, difficult marches through the jungle and fierce firefights with enemy forces. As the months passed, Muller became disillusioned with the whole war effort. He became convinced that American military policies in Vietnam were ineffective and that the South

Vietnamese military was incapable of defending itself without U.S. help. At the same time, he developed a grudging admiration for the enemy, which he described in *The Bad War* as "tough, hard, and dedicated."

Muller spent eight months in Vietnam before suffering a crippling injury in combat against North Vietnamese forces in April 1969. "I caught a bullet through the chest," he said in *The Bad War.* "It went through both lungs, severed the spinal cord. Your spinal cord has all those nerves, right? Boom, when something goes through that sucker, that rings a bell, and it was just stunning. I felt like I was in a kaleidoscope and everything was fragmented and multicolored and boom. I'll never forget the sequence of thoughts: ' . . . I've been hit. I got it right in the gut. My girl, she's going to kill me.' Then I said, 'I don't got to worry about that, I'm going to die.'"

Muller was quickly evacuated to a nearby military hospital, where doctors raced to save his life. "They put in the medical records that had I arrived one minute later, I'd have been dead, because both lungs had collapsed," Muller recalled. "All I know is that I woke up with tubes everywhere. But I was stunned, amazed, overwhelmed and ecstatic over the fact that I woke up at all."

Muller's spinal cord injury made him a paraplegic and forced him into a wheelchair. After returning to the United States, he was sent to the Kingsbridge VA (Veterans Administration) Hospital in the Bronx in New York City for rehabilitation. VA facilities such as the one in Kingsbridge are meant to help American military veterans who suffer from physical and emotional problems. But many facilities in the VA hospital system did not have adequate resources to provide good treatment in the 1970s, and the Bronx hospital to which Muller was sent was filthy, understaffed, and overcrowded. In fact, the facility neglected even the most basic needs of the veterans. These horrible conditions made a deep impression on Muller, who endured several months at the facility before being released.

Antiwar activist and veterans' advocate

In the early 1970s Muller became an active member of the antiwar movement. In addition, he gained a reputation during this time as a crusader on behalf of Vietnam veterans,

A "Bad War" Indeed

Bobby Muller began his tour of duty in Vietnam in the fall of 1968. Upon arriving in the war-torn country, he grabbed a ride with a helicopter so that he could join his platoon out in the jungle. But when the helicopter pilot located Muller's platoon, he saw that they were engaged in a fierce battle with enemy forces. The helicopter quickly landed, dropping Muller off as enemy mortars exploded all around the landing zone. As the helicopter flew off, Muller found his platoon, which had suffered several casualties in the battle. In the following passage from *The Bad War,* Muller recalls his initial impressions of the war after finding his platoon:

> My guys had, I think, three killed and eight wounded. We had to get medevac ships [medical evacuation helicopters] in to lift them out.
>
> Before the medevacs come in, we called in supporting arms [bombing strikes designed to wipe out enemy forces in the immediate area]. In training they give you the "Mad Minute," which is very impressive but doesn't hold a candle to the real thing, when you walk in [guide] your artillery and call in your jet strikes just beyond your perimeter. It was awesome. Awesome. And I got so pumped, I said, 'Ain't nobody going to [mess] with us. Not

who he believed were being terribly neglected by their own country. As an advocate for his fellow veterans, he worked tirelessly to improve their medical care and assist them in their efforts to establish postwar careers.

Muller also returned to Hofstra, where he earned a law degree in 1974. One year later he married Virginia Estevez, the sister of a Vietnam veteran who had committed suicide after returning to the United States. The couple soon settled in Huntington, New York.

In 1978 Muller cofounded the Vietnam Veterans of America (VVA), an organization dedicated to providing for the needs of the men and women who served their country in Vietnam. As president of the VVA, Muller played an important role in convincing the U.S. government to give additional medical help and financial compensation to veterans who had been exposed to Agent Orange during the war. This flammable chemical was used throughout the war by U.S. forces to *when we can do what we've just done to those poor [people].'*

So in come the medevacs, throw in the dead and the wounded, the chopper lifts off, maybe fifty meters off the deck. And all around us all of a sudden Prrow! Prrow! Prrow! . . . . Chopper starts to wobble. Boom! It goes down in the valley. Everybody on board is killed. . . . That was my first afternoon. I said, 'All right. A little reality therapy right off the bat' . . . .

Next day I take out a patrol. Guys leaving the perimeter cross themselves [a religious gesture that symbolizes devotion to God]. Each one looked at me and right off the bat, I understood that it wasn't a game. Lots of fear and very, very intense. And it was my introduction to the absurdity of it all because we were out in no-man's land, and they didn't have the helicopters to lift us out, so a couple of days later they had us walk out. We had to go down to the valley and walk along the river bed. There were supposed to be NVA [North Vietnamese Army] regiments in the area. For three or four days from sunrise to sunset we walked, sometimes along the bank, sometimes in water up to your waist, with the banks coming in vertical drops right to the river. I kept saying to myself if there was an NVA regiment in the area, forget it, we're dead. They could have set up an ambush any one of countless places. All I remember thinking from the get-go was the absolute stupidity of this entire . . . war. I waited three days from sunrise 'till sunset to get blown away.

destroy jungle areas used by Communist forces. After the war, however, many American veterans suffered serious health problems that were caused by exposure to Agent Orange and other toxic chemicals used by the U.S. military in Vietnam.

In 1980 Muller helped establish the Vietnam Veterans of America Foundation (VVAF), an organization dedicated to providing humanitarian assistance to victims of war around the world. The next year he led the first delegation of Vietnam veterans to visit Vietnam since the war's end in 1975. These activities, along with milestones such as the 1982 dedication of the Vietnam Veterans Memorial in Washington, D.C., helped give America's Vietnam veterans—who had long felt ignored or forgotten by their fellow citizens—a belated sense of pride in their military service. "Look, we shared something that was powerful, and it shouldn't be forgotten," Muller said in *The Bad War*. "What it means differs to different people, but [the dedication of the Vietnam Veterans Memorial] rekindled that sense and gave the beginning of [a feeling that] it's okay

Landmines Remain a Deadly Problem around the World

Statistics compiled by the United Nations and the U.S. government indicate that approximately 110 million landmines remain planted in the ground in nearly seventy different countries around the world. Analysts estimate that removing these mines, which injure and kill thousands of people every year, would cost an estimated $33 billion. In addition, various nations own an additional 100 million landmines that could be used at any time. This figure is expected to increase in the future, even though more than 120 countries signed a treaty in 1997 that banned them from making, using, or purchasing landmines. More than fifty nations—including the United States, China, and Russia—refused to sign the agreement, and they continue to manufacture landmines.

to be a Vietnam vet—you don't have to be ashamed or embarrassed."

Leads the fight to ban landmines

In 1987 Muller was named president of the VVAF. As president, he established several VVAF-sponsored clinics that manufacture and distribute wheelchairs and prosthetics (artificial limbs) to people—both soldiers and civilians—who have been maimed and crippled by war.

Muller's work on behalf of the VVAF soon led him to turn his attention to a problem that afflicted dozens of countries around the world: the presence of millions of landmines that had been planted during periods of war. Antipersonnel landmines are small explosive devices that are placed in the ground in order to injure enemy forces. These deadly devices, which are capable of blowing off entire arms and legs, remain active for years. In many cases, they remain in place long after a war has ended, killing and maiming farmers, children, and other people who step on them. Some analysts estimate that these landmines claim 26,000 lives a year around the world.

In 1992 Muller and Jody Williams founded the International Campaign to Ban Landmines (ICBL). The ICBL eventually brought together more than a thousand organizations—including children's welfare groups, religious organizations, and environmental groups—to call for a worldwide ban on the production and use of landmines around the world. "These weapons have become probably the most destabilizing factor in third world countries today that are recovering from conflict," Muller explained in the *New York Times*. "Three dollar antipersonnel landmines have killed more people than all the Cold War weapons of mass destruction combined."

In October 1997 the ICBL and its coordinator, Jody Williams, were awarded the Nobel Peace Prize for their efforts to end the use of landmines. Two months later, 121 countries signed an agreement called the Ottawa Treaty, which formally banned all members from using, producing, selling, or storing landmines.

The Ottawa Treaty was a great triumph for the ICBL. But the United States, China, Russia, and a number of other nations declined to sign the treaty, citing a variety of military and security concerns. Their refusal to agree to the ban deeply disappointed Muller and other activists who had worked on the landmine issue for so many years. But they recognized that the Ottawa Treaty represented an important first step in eliminating the threat of landmines around the world. With this in mind, Muller launched the Campaign for a Landmine Free World in 1998. This organization is dedicated to fulfilling the goals of the international landmine treaty (which went into effect in March 1999) and working for an eventual worldwide ban on landmine production and use.

Sources

"Ex-Marine Hates Mines and His Battle Pays Off." *New York Times,* December 3, 1997.

Figley, Charles R., and Seymour Leventman, eds. *Strangers at Home: Vietnam Veterans Since the War.* Brunner/Mazel, reprint 1990.

MacPherson, Myra. *Long Time Passing: Vietnam and the Haunted Generation.* Garden City, NY: Doubleday, 1984.

Willenson, Kim. *The Bad War: An Oral History of the Vietnam War.* New York: New American Library, 1987.

"Wounds That Will Not Heal." *Time,* July 13, 1981.

Ngo Dinh Diem

Born January 3, 1901
Quang Binh Province, Vietnam
Died November 1, 1963
Saigon, Vietnam

President of South Vietnam, 1954–1963

Ngo Dinh Diem.
Reproduced by permission of AP/Wide World Photos.

N go Dinh Diem served as the president of South Vietnam during the early years of the Vietnam War. He came to power in 1954, immediately after the Geneva Accords divided the newly independent Vietnam into two sections—Communist-led North Vietnam and U.S.-supported South Vietnam. Diem gained the support of the United States because of his strong opposition to communism. But his corrupt, ineffective, and sometimes brutal government became highly unpopular with the South Vietnamese people over the next few years. The U.S. government finally withdrew its support in 1963, after Diem crushed a Buddhist uprising. A few months later, Diem was killed during the overthrow of his government by a group of military generals.

Rises quickly in the government ranks

Ngo Dinh Diem was born January 3, 1901, in the village of Phu Cam in Quang Binh province in central Vietnam. He was the third of eight children in a devout Catholic family. His father, Ngo Dinh Kha, was an important official under the Vietnamese Emperor Thanh Thai. At the time of Diem's birth,

Vietnam was a colony of France. The French colonial government removed Thanh Thai from power in 1907. Diem's father then resigned from his position in protest and returned to Phu Cam to become a teacher and farmer.

Diem received his early education at his father's private school and at Catholic schools in Hue. He considered becoming a priest, like one of his brothers, but instead studied law and government at the College Hau Bo in Hanoi. An excellent student, Diem graduated at the top of his class. After completing his education, he entered public service and began moving up the ranks in government. French colonial officials often promoted his career because he was Catholic.

Diem became a provincial governor at age twenty-five. During this time, he increased his popularity by riding through villages on horseback and personally addressing the concerns of the peasants. In 1929 he learned that a group of Communists was encouraging people to rise up against the provincial government. From this time on, Diem was a strong opponent of communism.

Comes into conflict with the French

In 1932 the French colonial government made eighteen-year-old Bao Dai the new emperor of Vietnam. The following year, with the support of the French, Bao Dai appointed Diem as his interior minister. Diem immediately began pressuring the colonial authorities to give the Vietnamese people more control over their own government. When the French refused, he resigned after three months in office. At that point, the French authorities began to view Diem as a potential threat to their rule. They kept a close watch on his activities, threatened to arrest him, and removed his brother Ngo Dinh Khoi from his position as governor of Quang Nam province.

For the next ten years, Diem lived quietly in Hue. He emerged from seclusion during World War II (1939–1945), when international events began to loosen France's grip on its colonies in Indochina. In the early years of the war France suffered a series of military defeats in Europe and surrendered to Germany. Unable to protect its colonies, the French government allowed Japan to occupy Vietnam and set up military bases there in the 1940s. Various factions in Vietnam—including Vietnamese Communists under Ho Chi Minh (see entry), known as the Viet Minh—viewed the Japanese occupation as an opportunity to gain control of the country.

Diem wanted to prevent the Communists from taking over Vietnam. First, he approached the Japanese and asked them to help him establish his own government. When this effort failed, he tried to see Bao Dai in order to convince him not to join forces with the Communists. But on his way to visit the emperor, Diem was kidnapped by Viet Minh agents and taken to a remote area near the Chinese border. He was held captive for six months. During this time, he learned that his brother Khoi had been shot to death by the Viet Minh. Finally, Diem was granted a meeting with Communist leader Ho Chi Minh, who asked him to join the Viet Minh in their fight to gain Vietnam's independence from France. Despite the fact that he believed he would be killed if he did not cooperate, Diem refused Ho's offer. To his surprise, he was then released.

In 1945 the Allied forces (which mainly consisted of the United States, Great Britain, and the Soviet Union) defeated both Germany and Japan to win World War II. As soon as Japan was defeated, the Viet Minh launched a military campaign to take control of Vietnam. This so-called August Revolution was successful, as the Viet Minh captured large areas of the country. In September 1945 Ho Chi Minh formally declared Vietnam's independence from both the French and the Japanese. But it soon became clear that France was not willing to give up its former colony. In 1946 war erupted between the French and the Viet Minh.

Gathers political support as an alternative to Communist rule

For the next four years, Diem traveled around Vietnam trying to gather political support. He presented himself as a true nationalist who opposed both the French and the Communists. In 1950 Diem left Vietnam following an attempt on his life. Over the next few years, he lived quietly overseas while war raged between the Viet Minh and the French. During this time, Diem gradually gained the support of a number of important people. He met with Pope Pius XII at the Vatican. He also went to the United States and met with a number of prominent church and government officials, including Francis Cardinal Spellman, Hubert Humphrey, and Senator John F. Kennedy (see entry).

In 1953 Diem went to Europe. He began to gain political support from the large community of Vietnamese exiles in Paris. The following year, the French and Viet Minh signed the Geneva Peace Accords, ending the Indochina War. The peace agreement divided Vietnam into two sections. The northern section, which was led by a Communist government under Ho Chi Minh, was officially known as the Democratic Republic of Vietnam but was usually called North Vietnam. The southern section, which was led by a U.S.-supported government under Emperor Bao Dai, was known as the Republic of South Vietnam.

Concerned about his future, Bao Dai asked Diem to be prime minister in his government. The emperor knew that Diem had American connections and was popular among the Vietnamese living abroad. In July 1954 Diem returned to the South Vietnamese capital of Saigon and began establishing his government. He was one of the only non-Communist Vietnamese leaders known to American officials, so the U.S. government felt obligated to support him. It felt that Diem was the best hope for keeping South Vietnam out of Communist control. The U.S. government began supplying Diem with financial aid and sent Colonel Edward Lansdale (see entry) to advise him.

Refuses to hold national elections

Shortly after becoming prime minister, Diem began taking steps to increase his hold on power. In 1955 he called for an election to let the South Vietnamese people decide whether he or Bao Dai should control the government. Diem's brother Ngo Dinh Nhu (see page 300) then fixed the election results so that Diem received 98.2 percent of the vote. That October, he proclaimed himself president of the Republic of Vietnam. Lacking any other non-Communist alternatives, the U.S. government recognized Diem's government and tried to improve his image by exchanging diplomatic visits with South Vietnam.

Under the terms of the Geneva Accords, the two parts of Vietnam were supposed to hold nationwide free elections in 1956 in order to reunite the country under one govern-ment. But Diem, along with U.S. government officials, wor-ried that holding elections in Vietnam would bring power to the Communists who had led the nation's war for independ-ence from France. American leaders felt that a Communist government in Vietnam would increase the power of China and the Soviet Union and threaten the security of the United States. As a result, Diem and his American advisors refused to hold the elections.

"Our policy is one of peace. [Nothing] will divert us from our goal: the Unity of our land, but Unity in freedom, not in slavery," Diem explained in a speech. "We do not reject the principle of elections as a peaceful and democratic means of realizing this unity. Still, though elections may form one of the pillars of true democracy, they are senseless if they are not absolutely free. When we see the system of oppression prac-ticed by the Viet Minh, we cannot but be skeptical as to the pos-sibility of obtaining conditions for a free vote in the North."

Diem's government loses support

Over the next few years, the situation in Vietnam dete-riorated rapidly. Ho Chi Minh and other Communist leaders in North Vietnam grew angry when Diem refused to hold the elections as scheduled. They were determined to reunite the country under a Communist government, by force if neces-sary. In 1960 former Viet Minh supporters in South Vietnam united with other opponents of Diem to form the National Liberation Front (NLF), which later became known as the Viet Cong. The goals of this organization included overthrowing Diem and establishing a coalition government in South Viet-nam with Communist representation. Before long, Viet Cong guerrilla fighters had begun taking control of large areas of the South Vietnamese countryside.

As Diem struggled to maintain his hold on power, his government became more and more unpopular among the South Vietnamese people. Diem threw hundreds of his politi-cal rivals into prison camps, where many were tortured or killed. He also refused to institute land reforms to help the peasant farmers make a decent living from their labor. Instead, he returned land to the wealthy landlords who exploited the peasants. Diem also filled important positions in his government with his family and friends. Many of these people were corrupt and used their positions for personal gain.

One of Diem's closest advisors was his brother Ngo Dinh Nhu, known as Brother Nhu. Nhu controlled a secret police force that terrorized people he considered a threat to Diem's government. Nhu's wife, Madame Ngo Dinh Nhu (see entry), acted as an honorary first lady and official hostess in the Diem government. She used her influence to convince the president to outlaw divorce, dancing, gambling, fortune-telling, and a variety of other activities. Many people viewed these rules, and the harsh punishments for breaking them, as unfair restrictions on their personal freedom.

When John F. Kennedy became president of the United States in 1961, he tried to convince Diem to make changes in the way he was ruling South Vietnam. Kennedy wanted Diem to introduce policies that would help the nation's struggling peasant population and stamp out widespread corruption in the government. He also urged Diem, who was Catholic, to show respect for Buddhism, the religion practiced by most South Vietnamese families. The United States hoped that by making these changes, the Diem government could reverse its drop in popularity and strengthen its hold on power. During this time, however, Kennedy also continued sending financial aid and military advisors to South Vietnam to help Diem fight the Communists.

Crushes Buddhist uprising

In 1963 a series of incidents convinced the Kennedy administration to end its support for Diem's government. That May, Diem attended a Catholic holiday celebration in the city of Hue. During the celebration, Catholic religious banners lined the streets. A few days later, however, the president refused to allow a group of Buddhists to fly religious banners at a celebration honoring the birth of Buddha. This discriminatory treatment outraged the Buddhist majority in Hue, and thousands of demonstrators took to the streets in a major protest against Diem's government. Diem's troops responded with violence, attacking the protestors and killing several people.

In June a Buddhist monk set himself on fire in public as a form of protest against Diem's repression of the Buddhist religion. Shocking pictures of the monk's suicide quickly appeared in the United States and all around the world. The photographs stunned many Americans and convinced them to focus greater attention on their country's involvement in South Vietnam. The pictures also triggered a wave of intense international criticism against Diem's government and its treatment of Vietnamese Buddhists. But President Diem and his ruling family reacted defiantly to the criticism. In fact, Brother Nhu and Madame Nhu proclaimed that "if the Buddhists want to have another barbecue, I will be happy to supply the gasoline." These remarks horrified President Kennedy and other American officials.

Killed during the overthrow of his government

In August 1963 U.S. ambassador Henry Cabot Lodge (see entry) reported that an influential faction in the South Vietnamese military wanted to overthrow Diem. By this time, U.S. government officials recognized that Diem was so unpopular among his own people that they could no longer support him. "We are launched on a course from which there is no turning back: the overthrow of the Diem government," Lodge wrote in a cable to Washington. "There is no turning back because there is no possibility the war can be won under a Diem administration." At this point, U.S. officials made it clear that they would like to see someone else lead South Vietnam.

On November 1, 1963, a group of South Vietnamese generals led by Duong Van "Big" Minh launched a coup to overthrow Diem's government. Diem and Brother Nhu fled the presidential palace and hid in the Chinese section of Saigon. They agreed to surrender if they were allowed to leave the country safely, and Big Minh agreed. But before Diem and his brother could make their escape, they were discovered and shot to death by military troops. Madame Nhu was out of the country at the time.

After Diem's death, Big Minh became the new president of South Vietnam. But his rule lasted only a short time before it was ended by another coup. Control of the government changed several more times over the next few years. Lacking a strong non-Communist Vietnamese leader to support in place of Diem, the United States became more and more deeply involved in the war.

Sources

Hammer, Ellen J. *A Death in November: America in Vietnam.* 1987.

Prochnau, William. *Once Upon a Distant War.* New York: Vintage Books, 1995.

Young, Marilyn B. *The Vietnam Wars, 1945–1990.* New York: Harper-Collins, 1991.

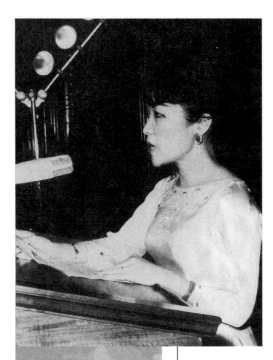

Madame Ngo Dinh Nhu (Tran Le Xuan)

Born in 1924
Hanoi, Vietnam

South Vietnamese political figure

Madame Ngo Dinh Nhu is one of the most controversial figures of the early Vietnam War. As the sister-in-law of Ngo Dinh Diem (see entry), who served as the president of South Vietnam from 1954 to 1963, Madame Nhu acted as the unofficial first lady and held a great deal of influence in the government. She was beautiful and charming but also proved to be devious and power-hungry. She often embarrassed the president with her outrageous behavior and insensitive remarks. Many historians claim that she contributed to the downfall of Diem's government.

A privileged childhood

Madame Nhu was born in 1924 in Hanoi, Vietnam. Her name at birth was Tran Le Xuan, which means "beautiful spring" in Vietnamese. She was the second of three children born into a wealthy and prominent family. Her father, Tran Van Chuong, was a Paris-educated attorney, and her mother, Madame Chuong, was descended from Vietnamese royalty. At the time of Madame Nhu's birth, Vietnam was a colony of France. Both sides of her family had earned great fortunes serving in the French

Madame Ngo Dinh Nhu.
Reproduced by permission of AP/Wide World Photos.

colonial government. Madame Nhu grew up in a luxurious home with twenty servants to take care of her every need.

During her teen years, Madame Nhu attended a prestigious French-speaking high school in Vietnam. Although she was highly intelligent, she was a poor student and dropped out before completing her education. In 1943 she married Ngo Dinh Nhu, a man nearly twice her age who was the younger brother of Ngo Dinh Diem. At that time, Diem was just beginning to attract attention as a political figure. He positioned himself as a true nationalist who opposed both the French and the Vietnamese Communists known as the Viet Minh. The French colonial government resented Diem's political activities and struck back at him by dismissing his brother Nhu from his job in the National Library.

For the next few years, Madame Nhu and her husband lived quietly in Da Lat, and she gave birth to four children. In the meantime, the Viet Minh and the French entered into a war for control of Vietnam. As this war continued into the 1950s, Diem traveled to the United States and Europe trying to gain political support. He hoped to form his own government as an alternative to the French and the Communists. In 1953 Ngo Dinh Nhu organized demonstrations in Saigon in support of his brother. The following year, the French and Viet Minh signed the Geneva Peace Accords ending the Indochina War.

The peace agreement divided Vietnam into two sections. The northern section, which was led by a Communist government under Ho Chi Minh (see entry), was officially known as the Democratic Republic of Vietnam but was usually called North Vietnam. The southern section, which was led by a U.S.-supported government under Emperor Bao Dai, was known as the Republic of South Vietnam. Knowing that Diem had American connections and was popular among the Vietnamese living abroad, the emperor asked Diem to become prime minister of South Vietnam. In July 1954 Diem returned to the South Vietnamese capital of Saigon and began establishing his government. The U.S. government felt obligated to support him because it felt that Diem was the best hope for keeping South Vietnam out of Communist control.

Acts as first lady of South Vietnam

Once Diem took office, Madame Nhu and her husband moved into the presidential palace in Saigon. Diem and his brother Nhu immediately began taking steps to increase their hold on power. In 1955 Diem called for an election to let the South Vietnamese people decide whether he or Bao Dai should control the government. Nhu then fixed the election results so that his brother received 98.2 percent of the vote. That October, Diem proclaimed himself president of the Republic of Vietnam. He hired family members to fill many of the important positions in his government. For example, his brother Nhu was the interior minister and head of the secret police force. Madame Nhu's father was named ambassador to the United States, her mother became a representative to the United Nations, and two of her uncles became cabinet ministers.

Madame Nhu claimed an influential position in the government as well. Since Diem never married, she acted as the unofficial first lady and hostess for the president. Beautiful and charming, Madame Nhu enjoyed entertaining important people by throwing fancy parties. But she also held strong opinions on political issues and never hesitated to express them to her husband and Diem. In fact, a *Time* magazine cover story described her influence by stating that she "rules the men who rule the nation."

Madame Nhu increased her personal power by creating an anti-Communist organization called the Vietnamese Women's Solidarity Movement. Many of the members were the wives of government officials. They used their influence to lobby the government on a variety of issues concerning women and families. For example, they convinced the government to pass the Family Code and the Law for the Protection of Morality. These measures outlawed divorce, contraceptives, dancing, fortune-telling, gambling, and other activities. In fact, one law said that a married person could not be seen in public with a person of the opposite sex without being charged with the crime of adultery. Madame Nhu viewed these laws as protecting the morality of Vietnamese women, but many people thought that the laws unfairly restricted their personal freedom.

Contributes to the fall of Diem's government

Over the next few years, the situation in Vietnam deteriorated significantly. Ho Chi Minh and other Communist leaders in North Vietnam were determined to reunite the two parts of the country under a Communist government. In 1960 former Viet Minh supporters in South Vietnam united with other opponents of Diem to form the National Liberation Front (NLF), which later became known as the Viet Cong. The goals of this organization included overthrowing Diem and establishing a coalition government in South Vietnam with Communist representation. Before long, Viet Cong guerrilla fighters had begun taking control of large areas of the South Vietnamese countryside.

As Diem struggled to maintain his hold on power, his government became more and more unpopular among the South Vietnamese people. Madame Nhu contributed to the problem by interfering with the president's decisions and attacking his political opponents. She often embarrassed Diem and created new enemies for his administration. At one point, U.S. Ambassador J. Lawton Collins told Diem that his sister-in-law was a troublemaker and asked him to send her away. But Diem refused to take this advice due to family loyalty.

In 1963 a series of incidents convinced the United States to end its support for Diem's government. Diem, who was Catholic, often discriminated against his country's Buddhist majority. In May thousands of demonstrators took to the streets of the ancient city of Hue in a major protest against Diem's government. Diem's troops responded with violence, attacking the protestors and killing several people.

In June a Buddhist monk set himself on fire in public as a form of protest against Diem's repression of the Buddhist religion. Shocking pictures of the monk's suicide quickly appeared in the United States and all around the world. The photographs stunned many Americans and convinced them to focus greater attention on their country's involvement in South Vietnam. The pictures also triggered a wave of intense international criticism against Diem's government and its treatment of Vietnamese Buddhists.

But Madame Nhu reacted to the criticism with defiance. She accused the U.S. government of using the Buddhists to aid in the overthrow of Diem's government. She

Ngo Dinh Nhu (1910–1963)

Ngo Dinh Nhu—the younger brother of South Vietnamese President Ngo Dinh Diem (see entry) and husband of the notorious Madame Nhu—was born on October 7, 1910, near the city of Hue in central Vietnam. Educated in Paris, he worked at the National Library in Hanoi until the French colonial government dismissed him due to his brother's political activities.

During the Indochina War between the French and the Communist-led Viet Minh, Nhu emerged as a capable, behind-the-scenes political organizer. In 1953 he led demonstrations in Saigon calling for a new government headed by his brother Diem. He also created a political movement, called the National Union for Independence and Peace, which opposed both the French and the Communists.

In 1954 the French and Viet Minh signed the Geneva Peace Accords ending the Indochina War. The peace agreement divided Vietnam into two sections— Communist North Vietnam under Ho Chi Minh, and U.S.-supported South Vietnam under Emperor Bao Dai. Nhu formed a coalition of South Vietnamese nationalist groups called the Front for National Salvation. These groups pressured Bao Dai to appoint Diem prime minister.

Once Diem became prime minister, Nhu came up with a plan to help his brother remove Bao Dai from power. They held national elections to decide whether Diem or Bao Dai should control the government. Then Nhu used his secret police force to fix the elections so that Diem won by a huge margin. Diem declared himself president of the Republic of Vietnam in October 1955. Then, with the support of Nhu's secret police, he used harsh measures to destroy his political opponents.

During Diem's nine-year rule in South Vietnam, Nhu was the president's closest advisor. He held a great deal of power as the head of the secret police and the founder of the Can Lao Party. This secret political organization consisted of 16,000 members, many of whom were high officials in the South Vietnamese

also created controversy by saying that she would "clap hands at seeing another monk barbeque show." Her insensitive remarks horrified U.S. officials, who had been pushing Diem to be more tolerant of the Buddhists. In fact, one high-ranking American told President John F. Kennedy (see entry) that "Madame Nhu is out of control." At this time, Kennedy decided that Diem and his family were so unpopular among

Ngo Dinh Nhu. *Reproduced by permission of AP/Wide World Photos.*

By the early 1960s Diem's government had become very unpopular among the South Vietnamese people. Part of the reason was that Nhu and other family members used corruption and brutality to maintain their hold on power. The problems with the Diem government came to international attention in 1963, when the South Vietnamese armed forces used violence to break up a Buddhist protest. In response, a Buddhist monk committed suicide by burning himself to death in public. Nhu reacted to this tragic situation with defiance. In fact, he outraged many people by declaring that "if the Buddhists want to have another barbecue, I will be happy to supply the gasoline."

Diem's handling of the Buddhist uprisings led U.S. officials to withdraw their support for his government. On November 1, 1963, a group of South Vietnamese military generals launched a coup to overthrow Diem. Both the president and his brother Nhu were assassinated by their political rivals during the coup.

government or army. In fact, membership in the party was often required for people to move up the ranks in the government. Nhu used the Can Lao party to spy on his political opponents and intimidate people into going along with his ideas. Can Lao members also became involved in criminal activities and used the proceeds to enrich themselves.

their own people that the United States could no longer support them.

On November 1, 1963, a group of South Vietnamese generals led by Duong Van "Big" Minh launched a coup to overthrow Diem's government. While there is no evidence that the U.S. government participated in the coup, it is clear that American leaders did not try to prevent it. Madame Nhu was out of the country on a speaking tour at the time. But Diem and his brother Nhu were captured and killed by their political rivals. Upon hearing about the death of her husband and brother-in-law, Madame Nhu told the *New York Times,* "If the news is true, if really my family has been treacherously killed with either official or unofficial blessing of the American Government, I can predict to you all that the story of Vietnam is only at its beginning." After her family fell from power in South Vietnam, Madame Nhu went into exile in Rome, Italy.

Sources

Boetcher, Thomas D. *Vietnam: The Valor and the Sorrow.* Boston: Little, Brown, 1985.

Karnow, Stanley. *Vietnam: A History.* New York: Penguin Books, 1984.

Prochnau, William. *Once Upon a Distant War.* New York: Vintage Books, 1995.

Young, Marilyn V. *The Vietnam Wars 1945–1990.* 1991.

Nguyen Cao Ky

Born September 8, 1930
Son Tay, Vietnam

South Vietnamese military officer and political leader; premier of South Vietnam, 1965–67

"Our only object is to restore peace and return prosperity to [South Vietnam] after defeating the Communists."

N guyen Cao Ky was a top pilot in the South Vietnamese air force during the early years of the Vietnam War. He quickly increased his military rank and political power as the government of South Vietnam changed several times in the early 1960s. In 1964 Ky became head of South Vietnam's air force. A year later, he helped overthrow the government and became the youngest premier in Vietnamese history. Although Ky made some positive changes as the leader of South Vietnam's government, he also launched a violent crackdown against Buddhists who disagreed with his policies.

A top South Vietnamese military pilot

Nguyen Cao Ky was born September 8, 1930, in Son Tay province. Ky's hometown was located twenty-five miles northwest of Hanoi, which eventually became the capital of North Vietnam. But at the time he was born, Vietnam was a colony of France known as French Indochina. Ky's father was a schoolteacher. His family also included two older sisters.

Ky attended high school in Hanoi. After graduating in 1948, he enrolled in a French military academy in northern

Nguyen Cao Ky.
Reproduced by permission of Corbis Corporation.

303

Vietnam. Once he had completed his military education, he volunteered for pilot training. In 1951 Ky left Vietnam to train with the French air force. He flew practice missions in France, Algeria, and Morocco over the next few years. In 1954 Ky returned to Vietnam as a fully trained military pilot. By this time, however, Communist-led Viet Minh forces had defeated the French to gain Vietnam's independence.

The Geneva Accords of 1954, which ended the war between the French and the Viet Minh, divided Vietnam into two sections. The northern section, which was led by a Communist government under Ho Chi Minh (see entry), was officially known as the Democratic Republic of Vietnam but was usually called North Vietnam. The southern section, which was led by a U.S.-supported government under Ngo Dinh Diem (see entry), was known as the Republic of South Vietnam. During this time, Ky moved to South Vietnam and quickly rose through the ranks in the nation's air force.

The Geneva peace agreement also provided for nationwide free elections to be held in 1956, with a goal of reuniting the two sections of Vietnam under one government. But U.S. government officials worried that holding free elections in Vietnam would bring power to the Communists who had led the nation's war for independence from France. They felt that a Communist government in Vietnam would increase the power of the Soviet Union and threaten the security of the United States. As a result, the U.S. government and South Vietnamese President Diem refused to hold the elections. Ky spent 1956 in the United States, where he received additional training as a fighter pilot.

North Vietnamese leaders grew angry when the South Vietnamese government failed to hold the required elections. The Communists remained determined to reunite the country, by force if necessary. Within a short time, a new war began between the two sections of Vietnam. North Vietnam's main weapon in this phase of the Vietnam War was a group of South Vietnamese guerrilla fighters known as the Viet Cong.

The U.S. government sent money, weapons, and military advisors to help South Vietnam defend itself against the Viet Cong. Some of the Americans in Vietnam were agents for the Central Intelligence Agency (CIA). In 1960 Ky began flying secret missions for the CIA. He and other pilots used South Vietnamese military planes to drop guerrilla fighters and sabotage experts by parachute into North Vietnam. The idea behind these missions was to isolate the Viet Cong guerrillas operating in South Vietnam from the Communist leadership in North Vietnam.

Head of South Vietnam's air force

Over the next few years, however, the Viet Cong took control of large areas of the South Vietnamese countryside. Part of the reason for the Communist success was that Diem's government was very unpopular with the people. In November 1963 a group of South Vietnamese military leaders overthrew the government and assassinated Diem. Duong Van Minh, known as "Big Minh," became the new leader of South Vietnam.

But this was only the first in a series of political changes in South Vietnam. In January 1964 General Nguyen Khanh took control of the government from Big Minh. Ky was one of several key military figures involved in the overthrow of Big Minh's government. In appreciation of his support, Khanh named Ky as the head of South Vietnam's air force.

At this time, Ky became the leader of a group of youthful South Vietnamese military officers known as the "Young Turks." They put pressure on the older military officers who had taken charge of the government. As a result, South Vietnam saw several more changes in leadership over the next year.

Meanwhile, Ky continued to build his own reputation as a top pilot and military leader. He implemented a number of changes that made the air force the most effective part of the South Vietnamese armed forces. Ky also became known as a playboy. He was often seen at popular nightclubs dressed in a stylish black flight suit. He also carried a gun in a holster in public, which led people to refer to him as "The Cowboy."

Premier of South Vietnam

Through the early 1960s the United States deepened its military involvement in Vietnam. In 1965 President Lyndon Johnson (see entry) sent American combat troops to South Vietnam. In June of that year Ky joined forces with two other South Vietnamese generals, Nguyen Van Thieu (see entry) and Nguyen Huu Co, to overthrow the government once again. The three military leaders then formed the National Leader-

Excerpt from Nguyen Cao Ky's Memoir
Twenty Years and Twenty Days

In 1976 Nguyen Cao Ky published a book about his experiences in the South Vietnamese government during the war, *Twenty Years and Twenty Days*. In the following excerpt, Ky admits that South Vietnam needed U.S. help to fight the Communists. But he claims that the Americans did not understand the basic needs and concerns of the Vietnamese people. Ky defends the good intentions of his government and says that the United States interfered with its ability to gain the trust and loyalty of the South Vietnamese people.

Alongside the military war, fought with bombs and bullets, we had to fight another war—one to convince our own people that South Vietnam offered a way of life superior to that of the Communists.

It was a war for the hearts and minds of the people.

It was not, as some thought, a matter of simple materialism, a philosophy that started with filling bellies. Ambassador Ellsworth Bunker [the man who served as U.S. ambassador to South Vietnam, 1967–73] was hopelessly wrong when he told me on one occasion, "People are drifting toward communism because they are poor. If you give the people everything they want—television sets, automobiles, and so on—none of them will go over to communism."

Poor Bunker! He was trying to impose American standards of life on people he did not understand, people who basically had no desire for the so-called good things of the American way of life . . . .

Yet we had one ace in our hand, if only we could play the hand properly, an ace

ship Committee to rule South Vietnam. This takeover marked the ninth change of political leadership in less than two years since Diem was assassinated.

The American military officials in South Vietnam supported Ky over the other two generals for the position of premier. The premier oversaw the day-to-day operations of the government. The U.S. officials thought that Ky would make the best premier because he was outspoken, held the respect of the country's armed forces, and was a Buddhist (the religion of the majority of citizens in South Vietnam). Thanks to the American support, Ky became the youngest premier in Vietnam's history.

Upon taking office, Ky surprised many people by admitting that the war against the Viet Cong was progressing slowly. He claimed that South Vietnam's political instability had that did not even exist in the Communist deck of cards. It was freedom, the world's most precious—yet most elusive—treasure. The freedoms that [U.S. President Franklin D.] Roosevelt had preached, not only the freedom from fear and want, but the freedom for us to choose our leaders, and the freedom to boot them out if they proved unworthy of the trust reposed in them . . . .

But if we held an ace, we also held a deuce [an undesirable card]. For while I was preaching the need for freedom, I was not always free myself. True, we were not puppets [controlled by the United States], yet we never achieved the standing or appearance of an independent, self-governing country. The Americans criticized us for not having a highly developed system of government, but how could we have that when every Vietnamese in Saigon referred to the American ambassador as "the Governor General"?

The Americans did not seek this; they were not colonists, but South Vietnam had been a colony until the defeat of the French, and in many ways it remained virtually a colony, though without the restrictions imposed by the French. We still lacked our own identity.

We never produced a leader to unite the country with its many religious and political factions. The North had one in Ho Chi Minh; rightly or wrongly, the Communists believed in him and fought and died for him. He had a charisma [attractive personality] that won many supporters even in the West and not all of them were Communists. Neither Diem [Ngo Dinh Diem, leader of South Vietnam, 1954–63], nor Thieu [Nguyen Van Thieu, leader of South Vietnam, 1967–75]—both backed by the Americans—won the hearts of even the South Vietnamese.

destroyed people's confidence in the government and undermined the war effort. He expressed his determination to restore order and establish a stable, democratic government in South Vietnam. "Our only object is to restore peace and return prosperity to the country after defeating the Communists," he stated.

But Ky also became the subject of controversy shortly after taking office. Several months earlier, he had said in an interview with British journalist Brian Moynahan that he admired Adolf Hitler, the brutal German dictator whose policies resulted in the murder of millions of people during World War II (1939–45). When Ky came to power, these comments created a stir in various parts of the world. But Ky claimed that his statements had been misunderstood. "I had in mind the idea that Vietnam needed above all leadership and a sense of discipline in order to face the criminal aggression of communism," he explained. "The idea is far from me praising Hitler or adopting his view."

Ky did make some positive changes in South Vietnam. He improved the armed forces, introduced land reform programs, built new schools and hospitals, and removed corrupt officials from power. But he also took some harsh steps to silence people who disagreed with his policies. For example, he launched military attacks against Buddhist protestors in the cities of Danang and Hue in the spring of 1966. In both cases U.S. troops helped the South Vietnamese military crush the Buddhist uprisings.

In June 1966 Ky improved his political position in South Vietnam by meeting with President Johnson in Hawaii. During a two-day conference, the two men agreed that South Vietnam needed to make further social and economic reforms and hold national elections. Three months later, Ky followed through on a promise to Johnson by organizing a convention to create a new constitution for South Vietnam. A large percentage of voters turned out to select representatives to attend the convention.

Ky claimed that the large voter turnout showed that his policies enjoyed strong public support. But some observers said that Ky and his government could not hold on to power without the help of American troops. "The military junta [government] in Saigon would not last a week without American bayonets to protect it," Neil Sheehan (see entry) wrote in the *New York Times*.

Loses power and leaves the country

In 1967 South Vietnam held a presidential election in order to make the government seem more legitimate and democratic. The two main candidates were Ky and one of the generals who had helped him overthrow the government, Nguyen Van Thieu. But the nation's top military leaders felt that Ky's comments about Hitler and handling of the Buddhist uprisings had damaged his reputation. They pressured Ky to give up his bid for the top office and instead run as Thieu's vice president. According to American observers, the military leaders also rigged the elections so that their preferred candidates would win. So when the results came in, Thieu was the new president of South Vietnam and Ky was the vice president.

Ky and Thieu never really got along. In his book *Twenty Years and Twenty Days,* Ky said that Thieu "wanted power and glory but he did not want to have to do the dirty work." Relations between the two men got even more tense after North Vietnam launched the Tet Offensive in 1968. During this time, six of Ky's main military supporters were killed in a bombing incident that was supposedly ordered by Thieu.

In 1971 Thieu took steps to reduce Ky's power by disqualifying him as a presidential candidate in the next election. Ky responded by announcing his retirement from politics. He went back to his position as head of the air force and became a vocal critic of Thieu's government. In 1973 the United States withdrew its troops from Vietnam. Then in 1975 North Vietnam launched a final attack in hopes of taking over South Vietnam.

As Communist forces won a series of battles in central Vietnam, Thieu decided to remove his forces from the region. This action resulted in the collapse of the South Vietnamese army, which triggered a wave of panic and chaos across much of the country. Ky criticized Thieu's decision as a "strategic error" that led to "the eventual disintegration of our entire armed forces."

Over a matter of weeks, North Vietnam's forces rolled across the South Vietnamese countryside, capturing city after city. In early April Ky led a demonstration in the capital city of Saigon. Along with 400 other military officers, he publicly declared that he would never leave Vietnam. Ky hoped that his words would help calm South Vietnamese citizens, who were afraid of what might happen if North Vietnam won the war. A few weeks later, the Communists captured Saigon to end the Vietnam War.

When Saigon fell, Ky went back on his promise and fled from Vietnam on an American military helicopter. He moved to the United States with his wife, Dang Tuyet Mai, and six children. Ky eventually opened a liquor store in Los Angeles, California. In 1985 he filed for bankruptcy when he was unable to repay his business loans and gambling debts.

Sources

Harrison, James Pincklney. *The Endless War: Vietnam's Struggle for Independence*. New York: McGraw-Hill, 1982.

Lacouture, Jean. *Vietnam: Between Two Truces*. New York: Random House, 1966.

Nguyen Cao Ky. *Twenty Years and Twenty Days*. New York: Stein and Day, 1976.

Nguyen Thi Dinh

Born in 1920
Ben Tre Province, Vietnam
Died in 1992

Viet Cong military leader

Nguyen Thi Dinh was the best-known female revolutionary of the Vietnam War. She began her career at the age of sixteen, when she began recruiting peasants to join the fight to gain Vietnam's independence from France. When the country was divided into Communist-led North Vietnam and U.S.-supported South Vietnam in 1954, Dinh remained in South Vietnam and led the resistance to the government of Ngo Dinh Diem (see entry). She was one of the founding members of the National Liberation Front opposition group, which later became known as the Viet Cong. During the Vietnam War, Dinh organized a number of antigovernment demonstrations by large groups of women. She became the highest-ranking female member of the Viet Cong.

Fights for Vietnam's independence from France

Nguyen Thi Dinh was born in 1920 in Ben Tre province in southern Vietnam. She grew up as one of ten children in a poor family of farmers. At the time of her birth, Vietnam was a colony of France. One of her older brothers was part of a group of Vietnamese revolutionaries who fought to gain their country's independence from French rule. Dinh admired

"There are two seasons in the South, the dry season and the rainy season. But under the regime of Ngo Dinh Diem . . . the people were battered by wind and rain all year round."

her brother and began participating in anti-French resistance activities when she was sixteen.

In 1938 Dinh married a fellow revolutionary who was a member of the Indochinese Communist Party, which had been founded by Ho Chi Minh (see entry) and other future North Vietnamese leaders in 1930. The following year, French authorities arrested her husband shortly before she gave birth to a son. In 1940 Dinh was arrested as well and sent to prison in Ba Ra, South Vietnam. She was released three years later due to poor health, but her husband died in prison in 1944.

Around that time, France suffered a series of military defeats during World War II (1939–45) and surrendered to Germany. Unable to protect its colonies in Indochina, the French government allowed Japan to occupy Vietnam and set up military bases there. A group of Communist-led revolutionaries known as the Viet Minh viewed the Japanese occupation as an opportunity to gain control of the country.

In 1945 the Allied forces (which mainly consisted of the United States, Great Britain, and the Soviet Union) defeated both Germany and Japan to win World War II. As soon as Japan was defeated, the Viet Minh launched a military campaign to take control of Vietnam. This so-called August Revolution was successful, as the Viet Minh captured large areas of the country. In September 1945 Ho Chi Minh formally declared Vietnam's independence from both the French and the Japanese.

But it soon became clear that France was not willing to give up its former colony. After a year of negotiations, war erupted between the French and the Viet Minh in late 1946. Dinh joined the Viet Minh and began fighting against French forces in Ben Tre province. She also remained active in the Communist Party and was elected to the executive committee of the Women's Union. As an important member of the Viet Minh resistance in the South, Dinh visited Ho Chi Minh in the northern city of Hanoi in 1946. She convinced the Communist leader to send money and a shipment of weapons to help the Viet Minh fight the French in the South.

Leads resistance to the Diem government

After nine years of war, the Viet Minh finally defeated the French in 1954. The Geneva Peace Accords, which formally ended the war, divided Vietnam into two sections—Communist North Vietnam under Ho Chi Minh, and U.S.-supported South Vietnam under Ngo Dinh Diem. According to the terms of the peace agreement, the two parts of Vietnam were supposed to hold nationwide free elections in 1956 in order to reunite the country under one government. But U.S. government officials worried that holding free elections in Vietnam would bring power to the Communists who had led the nation's war for independence from France. They felt that a Communist government in Vietnam would increase the power of China and the Soviet Union and threaten the security of the United States. As a result, the South Vietnamese government and its American advisors refused to hold the elections.

Many people in Vietnam were angry when the Diem government failed to hold the elections as scheduled. The Communist leadership of North Vietnam remained determined to reunite the country, by force if necessary. In addition, some citizens of South Vietnam grew resentful of Diem, who put many of his political opponents in prison and used other harsh measures to maintain his hold on power. "There are two seasons in the South," Dinh wrote in her memoir *No Other Road to Take,* "the dry season and the rainy season. But under the regime of Ngo Dinh Diem . . . the people were battered by wind and rain all year round."

Over the next few years, several groups of South Vietnamese citizens began organizing opposition to the Diem government. In 1960 Dinh became a founding member of the National Liberation Front (NLF). This Communist-led group consisted mostly of people who had supported the Viet Minh during the war against the French. Its main goals were to overthrow the Diem government and establish a new government in South Vietnam that included Communist representation. The NLF, which later became known as the Viet Cong, recruited peasants throughout the South Vietnamese countryside to fight Diem's army using tactics of guerrilla warfare. Dinh and other Viet Cong fighters believed that Diem and his American supporters were interfering with the independence and reunification of Vietnam.

Dinh played an active role in the South Vietnamese resistance to the Diem government. She was elected to the central committee of the Ben Tre Communist Party. She also trained and armed former Viet Minh supporters, recruited peasants to join the revolutionary movement, and led guerrilla attacks against government troops in the countryside. In addition, Dinh organized a number of large-scale demonstrations against the Diem government.

Organizes the Long-Haired Army

In March 1960 Dinh led a group of women in a mass protest in the village of Phuoc Hiep. As part of Diem's campaign to wipe out the Viet Cong presence in rural villages, a group of South Vietnamese army soldiers had occupied Phuoc Hiep. The soldiers had arrested and executed twenty young men, then buried the bodies around the army post as a warning to other villagers not to become involved with the Viet Cong. Dinh and other NLF leaders met to decide how to respond to this violence. "We discussed ways to put a stop to the enemy's killing while still maintaining the initiative," she recalled in her memoir. "Everyone unanimously agreed that we should organize immediately a large group of women who would push their way into Mo Cay district town to denounce the crimes of the soldiers in Phuoc Hiep."

Dinh recruited 5,000 South Vietnamese women from six different villages to participate in the demonstration. They marched to the district headquarters in Mo Cay and remained there for five days and nights. The women sang revolutionary songs, tried to convince the soldiers to join the Viet Cong, and refused to leave until their demands were met. Finally, the government agreed to withdraw its troops from Phuoc Hiep. Throughout the Vietnam War, Dinh and the NLF often used groups of women in large-scale protests. The women demonstrators became known as the Doi Quan Toc Dai or Long-Haired Army.

Dinh remained active in the Communist Party and in the NLF for the rest of the war. She served on the NLF central committee and acted as head of the NLF Women's Union. In 1965 she was named deputy commander of the NLF armed forces, which was the highest combat position held by a woman during the war. In 1975 the Communist forces from North Vietnam and the NLF captured the South Vietnamese capital of Saigon to win the Vietnam War. The country was finally reunited under a Communist government and renamed the Socialist Republic of Vietnam. After the war ended, Dinh served on the central committee of the Vietnamese Communist Party. In 1982 she was named head of the Women's Union of the Socialist Republic of Vietnam. She died in 1992.

Sources

Eisen, Arlene. *Women and Revolution in Vietnam*. London: Zed Books, 1984.

Nguyen Thi Dinh. *No Other Road to Take: Memoir of Mrs. Nguyen Thi Dinh*. Translated by Mai V. Elliott. New York: Cornell University Southeast Asian Studies Program, 1976.

Nguyen Van Thieu

Born April 5, 1923
Phan Rang, Vietnam

South Vietnamese military and political leader;
president of the Republic of Vietnam, 1967–75

Nguyen Van Thieu.
Courtesy of the Library of Congress.

Nguyen Van Thieu served as the president of South Vietnam from 1967 until Communist forces took over the country in 1975. When he first came to power, the South Vietnamese government was highly unstable. The country's leadership had changed nine times in less than two years. Thieu brought a degree of stability to South Vietnam during his eight years in office. But his hold on the country became steadily weaker as he lost the support of the United States. When U.S. troops withdrew from Vietnam in 1973, Thieu refused to honor the terms of the Paris peace agreements. His actions reduced support for his government among the South Vietnamese people and ultimately helped North Vietnam win the war.

Fights against the Communist Viet Minh

Nguyen Van Thieu, whose name means "one who ascends" in Vietnamese, was born on April 5, 1923, near Phan Rang in Ninh Thuan province in central Vietnam. At the time of his birth, Vietnam was a colony of France and was known as French Indochina. Thieu was the youngest of five children in a successful family of farmers and fishermen. Two of his brothers also became public officials in South Vietnam.

Thieu attended schools in Saigon and Hue. In 1945 he joined a revolutionary group known as the Viet Minh that was fighting to gain Vietnam's independence from France. Thieu joined the Viet Minh out of feelings of patriotism for his homeland. But he quit the group when he realized that many other members were fighting to establish a Communist government over Vietnam. "By August of 1946, I knew that Viet Minh were Communists," he said in a *Time* magazine interview. "They shot people. They overthrew the village committee. They seized the land."

At this time, Thieu switched his loyalties to the side of the French. He graduated from a French military academy in 1949, and he received further military training in France and in Hanoi in the early 1950s. Thieu soon proved himself to be a skilled but cautious military commander. In 1954 he led an attack that drove the Viet Minh out of his native village.

The Vietnam War begins

Despite Thieu's success, however, the Communist-led Viet Minh forces defeated the French later that year to gain Vietnam's independence. The Geneva Accords of 1954, which ended the war between the French and the Viet Minh, divided Vietnam into two sections. The northern section, which was led by a Communist government under Ho Chi Minh (see entry), was officially known as the Democratic Republic of Vietnam but was usually called North Vietnam. The southern section, which was led by a U.S.-supported government under Ngo Dinh Diem (see entry), was known as the Republic of South Vietnam.

The peace agreement also provided for nationwide free elections to be held in 1956, with a goal of reuniting the two sections of Vietnam under one government. But U.S. government officials worried that holding free elections in Vietnam would bring power to the Communists who had led the nation's war for independence from France. They felt that a Communist government in Vietnam would increase the power of the Soviet Union and threaten the security of the United States. As a result, the U.S. government and South Vietnamese President Diem refused to hold the elections.

North Vietnamese leaders grew angry when the South Vietnamese government failed to hold the required elections. The Communists were determined to overthrow Diem and reunite the country, by force if necessary. Within a short time, a new war began between the two sections of Vietnam. One of North Vietnam's main weapons in the Vietnam War was a group of South Vietnamese guerrilla fighters known as the Viet Cong. The U.S. government sent money, weapons, and military advisors to help South Vietnam defend itself against North Vietnam and the Viet Cong.

Rises through the ranks of South Vietnam's military

Over the next few years, Thieu continued to move up in the ranks of the South Vietnamese military. He became superintendent of the national military academy for several years, where he earned the respect of many young officers. He also went to the United States for further training in 1957 and 1960. The U.S. government sponsored these training programs in the hopes of building a strong South Vietnamese military.

By 1963, however, the Viet Cong controlled large areas of the South Vietnamese countryside. Part of the reason for the Communists' success was that Diem's government was very unpopular with the people. To protect himself, Diem stationed an armored division just outside of Saigon and put Thieu in charge of it. But this proved to be a mistake. In November 1963 a group of South Vietnamese military leaders overthrew the government and assassinated Diem. Thieu's division played an active role in the overthrow of Diem by firing artillery on the presidential palace.

General Duong Van Minh, known as "Big Minh," became the new leader of South Vietnam. He rewarded Thieu for his help by making him a member of the twelve-man Military Revolutionary Council that controlled the government. But Thieu and other young military officers—whom the U.S. military advisors in Vietnam called the "Young Turks"—were not impressed with Big Minh's leadership. In January 1964 they helped General Nguyen Khanh take control of the government from Big Minh.

South Vietnam saw several more changes in leadership over the next year. Throughout these changes, Thieu remained one of the most powerful figures in the government. When Tran Van Huong came to power in 1965, Thieu was named deputy prime minister in charge of defense. In this position, he argued that South Vietnam should resist calls for a negotiated settlement and expand its military operations against the North. He was pleased when the United States launched bombing campaigns against North Vietnam and began sending American combat troops to the country.

President of the Republic of Vietnam

In June 1965 Thieu joined forces with two other young military officers, Nguyen Cao Ky (see entry) and Nguyen Huu Co, to overthrow the government of South Vietnam for the ninth time since Diem was assassinated. The trio then formed the National Leadership Committee to rule South Vietnam, with Thieu as its chairman. Although this was technically the highest position in the government, Thieu found himself overshadowed by Ky, who handled day-to-day government operations as premier.

In 1966 Thieu and Ky traveled to Hawaii to meet with U.S. president Lyndon Johnson (see entry). During this conference, they agreed to establish a constitution for South Vietnam and to hold national elections. In 1967 South Vietnam held a presidential election in order to make the government seem more legitimate and democratic. The two main candidates were Thieu and Ky. But the nation's top military leaders pressured Ky to give up his bid for the top office and instead run as Thieu's vice president. According to American observers, the military leaders also rigged the elections so that their preferred candidates would win. For example, they stationed troops in several provinces to influence voters and prevent their opponents from holding protests.

Thieu was sworn in as the president of the Republic of Vietnam on October 31, 1967. In his speech at the ceremony, he declared that he would "open wide the door to peace [with North Vietnam] and leave it open." However, he also said that he was "determined not to accept a surrender."

Thieu did make some positive changes as president of South Vietnam. He launched a campaign to remove corrupt officials from the government. He also distributed land to 50,000 families and passed laws that protected tenants from unfair practices by landlords. But he also used harsh measures to silence his political enemies and maintain his hold on power.

In 1969 U.S. president Richard Nixon (see entry) announced a plan to withdraw American combat forces from Vietnam gradually and turn the main responsibility for fighting the war over to the South Vietnamese government and military. Thieu reacted bitterly to Nixon's announcement. He resented the suggestion that South Vietnamese forces had not participated in the war over the previous several years. He also recognized that when the United States departed, his government would be more vulnerable to the Communist forces of North Vietnam. Still, Thieu had no choice but to accept Nixon's plan.

As the American forces began leaving Vietnam, Thieu had to recruit and train new South Vietnamese military units to replace them. In order to do this, he set up programs to draft citizens into the military and increased taxes to pay for more weapons and training. These actions angered many people in South Vietnam. They felt they had already sacrificed enough, and they wanted peace. Realizing that his policies were unpopular, Thieu took steps to ensure that he would remain in power. He passed laws to disqualify Ky and some of his other major opponents from running in the next presidential election. As a result, Thieu was reelected president of South Vietnam in 1971.

Refuses to honor peace agreements

In 1973 negotiators for the United States and North Vietnam reached an agreement on a peace treaty in Paris. Under the terms of the agreement, North Vietnam agreed to drop its demands for a coalition government (one that included Communist representation) in South Vietnam. In exchange, the United States agreed to allow some North Vietnamese troops to remain in the South as long as they promised not to resume military aggression. The treaty also stated that all U.S. troops were required to leave South Vietnam.

The agreement left Thieu in charge of the South Vietnamese government. But it also created a Committee of

National Reconciliation that included political representatives from North Vietnam. This organization was charged with supervising elections for a new government in which all parties—including Communists—could take part.

Thieu was outraged by the terms of the peace agreement. He told U.S. officials that he would never agree to its conditions. But Nixon administration officials warned Thieu that America was going to go forward with the agreement whether Thieu approved of it or not. Fearful that the United States would cut off all aid to his government, Thieu reluctantly dropped his objections to the treaty.

A short time after the agreement took effect and U.S. troops withdrew from Vietnam, Thieu began violating the peace treaty. He refused to hold elections or form a new government and he took steps to silence his opponents. He also ordered bombing missions and military attacks on areas of the countryside that were controlled by the Communists. These operations disrupted farming and other business activities in South Vietnam. Before long, there were widespread shortages of food and other supplies. As the South Vietnamese people suffered from hunger and other hardships, Thieu's government became even more unpopular.

In 1975 North Vietnam launched a final offensive in hopes of taking control of South Vietnam. As Communist forces won a series of battles in central Vietnam, Thieu decided to remove his forces from the region. This action resulted in the collapse of the South Vietnamese army, which triggered a wave of panic and chaos across much of the country. Over a matter of weeks, North Vietnam's forces rolled across the South Vietnamese countryside, capturing city after city.

On April 20 U.S. ambassador Graham Martin (see entry) asked Thieu to resign for the good of the country. The next day, Thieu gave a tearful, three-hour speech that was broadcast on Vietnamese radio and television. He blamed the United States for the Communists' success. He claimed that the U.S. government had abandoned South Vietnam and forced him to sign the Paris agreements.

On April 26, 1975, Thieu fled from South Vietnam on an American transport plane. The plane also included Thieu's wife, Nguyen Thi Mai Anh, and their two children, as well as fifteen tons of their belongings. The family went to Taiwan and Great Britain before settling in the United States. Thieu has lived in the Boston area since the 1980s. Some reports claim that he is a billionaire. In 1992 he told an interviewer that he was ready to return to Vietnam and lead the country again.

Sources

Current Biography, June 1968.

Isaacs, Arnold R. *Without Honor: Defeat in Vietnam and Cambodia.* 1984.

Nguyen Tien Hung, and Jerrold L. Schecter. *The Palace File.* New York: Harper and Row, 1986.

Werner, Jayne, and Luu Doan Huynh, eds. *The Vietnam War: Vietnamese and American Perspectives.* 1993.

Richard M. Nixon

Born January 9, 1913
Yorba Linda, California
Died April 22, 1994
New York, New York

Thirty-seventh president of
the United States, 1969–1974

Richard M. Nixon became president of the United States at the peak of American involvement in the Vietnam War. During his election campaign, he promised to achieve "peace with honor" in Vietnam, meaning that he planned to end U.S. involvement without allowing South Vietnam to fall to Communist forces. Nixon's main strategy to end the war was "Vietnamization," which involved withdrawing American combat troops gradually over time while also taking steps to strengthen the South Vietnamese government and military for its own defense. While the Vietnamization program did result in the withdrawal of U.S. forces from Vietnam in early 1973, it failed to prevent the fall of South Vietnam. North Vietnamese forces captured the South Vietnamese capital of Saigon to win the war two years later. By this time, Nixon had resigned from office in disgrace over the Watergate scandal.

A rapid rise in politics

Richard Milhous Nixon was born January 9, 1913, in Yorba Linda, California. His parents, Francis Anthony and Hannah Milhous Nixon, were working-class people who strug-

Nixon claimed the 1968 Republican nomination by promising to bring the American people "peace with honor" in Vietnam.

Richard Nixon.
Courtesy of the Library
of Congress.

gled to support their family by running a lemon farm and grocery store. In 1922 the Nixons moved to Whittier, California. Richard was a good student at Whittier High School and Whittier College. He played football and worked hard to make the starting team, but he soon learned that his real talent was in debate. He earned a scholarship to Duke University Law School in North Carolina in 1934 and graduated three years later near the top of his class.

After earning his law degree, Nixon returned to Whittier and worked for a law firm there, becoming a partner in 1939. During this time he met Thelma Catherine Ryan, known by the nickname Pat. The couple were married in 1940 and eventually had two daughters, Patricia and Julie. During World War II, Nixon joined the U.S. Navy. He served in the South Pacific between 1942 and 1946 and resigned with the rank of lieutenant commander.

Upon completing his military service, Nixon began a rapid rise to prominence in politics. In 1946, at the age of thirty-three, he was elected to serve California in the U.S. House of Representatives. Running as a Republican, Nixon used aggressive campaign tactics to defeat his opponent, Jerry Voorhis, a liberal Democrat who had served five terms in office.

Once in Congress, Nixon became a member of the influential House Un-American Activities Committee (HUAC). At this time, the United States and the Soviet Union were involved in an intense rivalry, as both nations competed to spread their political philosophies and influence around the world. This period, which was known as the Cold War, created an atmosphere of suspicion and distrust in the United States. The HUAC was formed in order to uncover and expose Communists within the U.S. government.

As a member of this committee, Nixon led an investigation into the activities of an American diplomat named Alger Hiss, who was suspected of passing secret U.S. documents to the Soviet Union. Hiss was eventually convicted of perjury (lying while under oath to tell the truth) in a controversial case. The Hiss investigation first brought Nixon to national attention. He used it and the strong anticommunist sentiments of the period to promote his own career.

Becomes vice president of the United States

After serving two terms in the House of Representatives, Nixon was elected to represent California in the U.S. Senate. Once again, he defeated a liberal Democrat by running an aggressive, negative campaign. His opponent, Helen Gahagan Douglas, protested against Nixon's "dirty tricks" and gave him the nickname "Tricky Dick." In 1952 Republican presidential candidate Dwight Eisenhower asked the young senator to be his vice-presidential running mate. Eisenhower chose Nixon because he was young, enjoyed strong support in California, and was well-known for his anticommunist activities. Eisenhower easily defeated Democratic candidate Adlai Stevenson in the general election, and Nixon became vice president of the United States just six years after he started his political career.

During his two terms as vice president, Nixon mainly concentrated on foreign policy. He made frequent official visits to other countries on behalf of the U.S. government. In 1956 Nixon traveled to South Vietnam. Two years earlier, Communist-led Viet Minh forces had won the Indochina War to gain Vietnam's independence from France. The Geneva Peace Accords, which formally ended the war, had divided the country in two parts: North Vietnam, with a Communist government under Ho Chi Minh (see entry), and South Vietnam, with a U.S.-supported government under Ngo Dinh Diem (see entry).

The peace agreement had also provided for nationwide free elections to be held in 1956 to reunite the two parts of Vietnam under one government. But President Eisenhower and other U.S. leaders worried that national elections would bring power to the Communists. They felt that a Communist government in Vietnam would increase the strength of China and the Soviet Union and threaten the security of the United States. As a result, Diem and his American advisors refused to hold the elections as scheduled. Nixon's official visit to South Vietnam showed that Diem had the support of the U.S. government.

Eisenhower and Nixon were reelected in 1956. Toward the end of the decade, the president suffered a series of health problems. Nixon exercised greater power during this time and increased his public approval ratings. As the 1960 elections approached, Nixon received the Republican nomination for the presidency. His Democratic opponent was John F. Kennedy (see entry), a U.S. senator from Massachusetts. Kennedy ran a tough campaign that put Nixon on the defensive. Kennedy surged ahead in the polls after the first nationally televised presidential debate between the two candidates. Nixon appeared nervous and irritable compared to the calm and handsome Kennedy. Nixon ended up losing by only 113,000 popular votes in one of the closest presidential elections ever.

After being defeated in his bid for the presidency, Nixon returned to California. He ran for governor of the state in 1962 but lost again. Afterward, he announced his retirement from politics, telling reporters that "you won't have Nixon to kick around anymore." For the next few years, Nixon worked in a law firm in New York City. But he also kept his hand in politics, supporting various Republican candidates and making occasional visits to foreign leaders. Before long, he launched a remarkable political comeback.

Leads the United States out of Vietnam as president

During the time that Nixon was out of politics, the United States had become more and more deeply involved in Vietnam. The Communist leaders of North Vietnam grew angry when South Vietnamese President Diem refused to hold national elections to reunite the two parts of the country. Before long, tensions between the two sides erupted into war. President Kennedy sent U.S. military planes and advisors to help South Vietnam defend itself. His successor, Lyndon Johnson (see entry), sent American combat troops to fight on the side of South Vietnam in 1965. But increasing U.S. involvement failed to defeat the Communists. Instead, the war turned into a bloody stalemate, and the American public became bitterly divided over the government's policies toward Vietnam.

The debate over Vietnam had a strong effect on the 1968 presidential election. Tired of being criticized for leading the United States into the war, Johnson decided not to run for reelection. As the Democratic Party tried to select a new candidate for the presidency, their nominating convention in Chicago was interrupted by violent antiwar protests. Nixon claimed the Republican nomination by promising to bring the American people "peace with honor" in Vietnam. He ended up winning the election over Democrat Hubert Humphrey and

independent candidate George Wallace to become the thirty-seventh president of the United States.

During his election campaign, Nixon had indicated that he had a "secret plan" for ending U.S. involvement in the Vietnam War. After taking office in January 1969, he began outlining his plan to the American people. Nixon promised to withdraw American combat forces gradually over time, while

Richard Nixon meets with American troops in Vietnam.
Reproduced by permission of AP/Wide World Photos.

also taking steps to strengthen the South Vietnamese government and military. He noted that this plan—which became known as "Vietnamization"—would enable the United States to end its involvement in the war without allowing South Vietnam to fall to communism. He began implementing this plan in June 1969, when he withdrew the first 25,000 American troops from Vietnam. Nixon also opened peace talks in Paris with North Vietnamese officials.

At the same time, however, Nixon expanded the war into the neighboring countries of Cambodia and Laos. In 1969 he authorized U.S. bombing raids to wipe out Communist base camps in the border regions. Then in the spring of 1970 Nixon sent U.S. ground troops into Cambodia. He explained that this "incursion" would destroy enemy supply lines, force the North Vietnamese into serious negotiations, and reduce the pressure on South Vietnam so that the Vietnamization program would have time to work. But many Americans viewed the invasion of neutral Cambodia as an escalation of the war. They felt that Nixon had broken his promise to bring American troops home and reach a peaceful settlement. The antiwar movement reacted to the invasion of Cambodia by launching protests across the country. During one of these protests, on the campus of Kent State University in Ohio, four students were shot to death during a confrontation with National Guard troops.

Over the next two years, Nixon managed to quiet the antiwar movement by continuing to move forward with his Vietnamization program. The last American combat troops withdrew from Vietnam in 1972, and the United States reached a peace agreement with North Vietnam in January 1973. When the Paris Peace Accords were signed, many Americans praised Nixon and his administration for their direction of the war effort. The president's supporters argued that his strong leadership enabled the United States to negotiate a cease-fire that allowed it to leave South Vietnam "with honor." Opponents of the war, however, were more critical of Nixon's record in Vietnam. They charged that Nixon's heavy use of bombing resulted in thousands of civilian deaths and injuries, and that U.S. air strikes virtually destroyed large sections of the country. Finally, Nixon's critics argued that he spent four years smashing Vietnam and neighboring countries, only to settle for a peace agreement that was similar in most respects to ones that he had turned down in the late 1960s.

In the months following the signing of the treaty, both South Vietnam and North Vietnam kept fighting in violation of the cease-fire agreement. But the continuing hostilities did not prevent American lawmakers from taking a series of steps designed to ensure that the United States would never again become entangled in Vietnam. For example, Congress overwhelmingly passed the Case-Church Amendment, which explicitly prohibited future U.S. military involvement in Indochina. In November 1973 Congress passed the so-called War Powers Act. This legislation put new limits on the president's powers to commit U.S. troops to military operations without congressional approval. Nixon resented these limits on his military authority, but by this time he lacked the political power to fight Congress.

Resigns in disgrace over the Watergate scandal

During the presidential election of 1972, Nixon was reelected by a huge margin of almost 18 million popular votes over Democratic candidate George McGovern (see entry). But a short time later, his political career was threatened by the Watergate scandal. In the spring of 1972 a group of people associated with Nixon's reelection campaign had broken into the Democratic National Committee offices at the Watergate hotel in Washington, D.C., and stolen secret campaign information. As the investigation into the burglary unfolded in early 1973, it became clear that members of the Nixon administration—and possibly the president himself—had tried to cover up the burglary. The investigation also showed that Republican agents had engaged in a wide range of illegal activities against Democrats and other political opponents over the past few years.

Nixon's vice president, Spiro Agnew (see entry), resigned from office in October 1973 over charges that he had accepted bribes while he was governor of Maryland. Gerald R. Ford, a Republican senator from Michigan, became Nixon's new vice president a short time later. By 1974 Congress had gathered enough evidence to begin impeachment hearings against Nixon. (The U.S. Constitution says that elected officials can be impeached, or brought up on legal charges, and removed from office if they are convicted of crimes.) Rather than face impeachment, Nixon became the first president in American history to resign from office in disgrace on August 9, 1974. Ford took over as president and granted Nixon an official pardon, meaning that he would never stand trial for any crimes he had committed while in office. By the time the Watergate investigation ended, thirty members of the Nixon administration had been sent to prison.

Nixon's legacy as president was forever tarnished by his involvement in the Watergate scandal. Historians have since claimed that Nixon's behavior in office permanently reduced the level of trust that the American people placed in their leaders. Among the most promising developments during Nixon's presidency was the improvement of relations between the United States and China. Nixon made a historic visit to the Communist-led nation in 1972 to formally open diplomatic relations and trade between the two countries. He also held summit meetings with Leonid Brezhnev, leader of the Soviet Union, that began to ease Cold War tensions. Many people found it interesting that Nixon helped improve relations between the United States and these Communist countries, given his earlier reputation as a tough opponent of communism.

After leaving office, Nixon lived quietly in New Jersey for many years. He eventually reemerged on the political scene as an elder statesman. He often traveled overseas to visit foreign leaders, and he acted as an advisor to Republican presidents Ronald Reagan and George Bush. Nixon also published his memoirs and several other best-selling books over the years. He died of a stroke on April 22, 1994, in New York City. All four living former presidents attended his funeral.

Sources

Ambrose, Stephen E. *Nixon.* 3 vols. New York: Simon and Schuster, 1987, 1989, 1991.

Kimball, Jeffrey. *Nixon's Vietnam War.* Lawrence, KS: University Press of Kansas, 1998.

Morris, Roger. *Richard Milhous Nixon: The Rise of an American Politician.* New York: Holt, 1990.

Nixon, Richard M. *The Memoirs of Richard Nixon.* New York: Grosset and Dunlap, 1978.

Nixon, Richard M. *No More Vietnams*. New York: Arbor House, 1985.

Randolph, Sallie G. *Richard M. Nixon, President*. New York: Walker, 1989.

Ripley, Peter C. *Richard Nixon*. New York: Chelsea House, 1987.

Wicker, Tom. *One of Us: Richard Nixon and the American Dream*. New York: Random House, 1991.

Tim O'Brien

Born October 1, 1946
Austin, Minnesota

American writer and Vietnam War veteran

"It was the most terrible summer of my life. My conscience kept telling me not to go [to Vietnam], but my whole upbringing told me I had to."

A ward-winning author Tim O'Brien is one of America's best-known writers about the Vietnam War. A Vietnam veteran, O'Brien has drawn upon his wartime experiences to write several classic literary works about the conflict, including *Going after Cacciato* (1978), *The Things They Carried* (1990), and *In the Lake of the Woods* (1994).

Growing up in Minnesota

Tim O'Brien was born in the small town of Austin, Minnesota, on October 1, 1946. His parents were William T. O'Brien, an insurance salesman, and Ava (Schulz) O'Brien, a schoolteacher. Looking back on his childhood, O'Brien described himself as a shy and lonely youngster who had difficulty making friends. As he grew older, he used magic tricks as a way to gain approval and applause from his peers. "There's a real appeal in that for a lonely little kid in a lonely little town, to get that kind of love and applause and to feel you have some control," O'Brien recalled in *Booklist*.

After graduating from high school, O'Brien enrolled at Macalester College in St. Paul, Minnesota. He eventually became one of Macalester's leading student activists. In fact, he campaigned for a wide range of social and political causes around campus, ranging from efforts to reform the college's grading system and its policies toward women students to participation in demonstrations against the Vietnam War.

The Vietnam War was a conflict that pitted the U.S.-supported nation of South Vietnam against the Communist nation of North Vietnam and its Viet Cong allies in the South. The Viet Cong were guerrilla fighters who wanted to overthrow the South Vietnamese government and unite the two countries under one Communist government. In the late 1950s and early 1960s the United States sent money, weapons, and military advisors to South Vietnam to help it fend off the Viet Cong. In 1965 President Lyndon Johnson (see entry) sent American combat troops to fight on the side of South Vietnam. But deepening U.S. involvement in the war failed to defeat the Communists. Instead, the war settled into a bloody stalemate, and the American public became bitterly divided about how to proceed in Vietnam.

O'Brien receives his draft notice

In 1968 O'Brien graduated from Macalester with a bachelor's degree in political science. An honor student, he was offered a full scholarship to continue his education at Harvard University. But then he received his draft notice to report for duty in the U.S. Army. O'Brien spent the next several months agonizing about whether to obey the draft. He thought about going to jail or fleeing the country in order to avoid being sent to fight a war in which he did not believe. But he knew that many of his family and friends would be angry and ashamed of him if he did not answer his country's call. "It was the most terrible summer of my life," he told the *New York Times*. "My conscience kept telling me not to go, but my whole upbringing told me I had to."

O'Brien finally decided to obey his draft notice. But he later confessed in the *New York Times Magazine* that he did so only because "I could not bear the prospect of rejection . . . by my family, my country, my friends, my hometown. I would risk conscience and rectitude [moral righteousness] before risking the loss of love. . . . I was a coward. I went to Vietnam."

O'Brien in Vietnam

O'Brien arrived in Vietnam in February 1969. He was assigned to an infantry unit in Quang Ngai Province, a region of central South Vietnam along the South China Sea. O'Brien soon learned that he had been sent to one of the country's deadliest places. Viet Cong guerrilla fighters roamed throughout the forests and villages of the region, despite the best efforts of American infantry squads and airpower.

O'Brien spent the next several months taking part in patrols deep into the Quang Ngai countryside. His unit regularly passed through My Lai, a village where hundreds of unarmed peasants had been brutally massacred by U.S. troops only a few months earlier. The My Lai atrocity was concealed from the American public and U.S. soldiers for more than a year, but O'Brien recalled that the atmosphere surrounding the village was tense and hateful. "The My Lai area . . . scared . . . me, to be honest with you," he told *Booklist*. "It was a spooky, evil place on the earth. . . . It scared everybody, and that was before we knew what had gone on."

As the weeks passed by, O'Brien became accustomed to the death and destruction that surrounded him. "Back in 1969, the wreckage was all around us, so common it seemed part of the geography, as natural as any mountain or river," he wrote in the *New York Times Magazine*. "Wreckage was the rule. Brutality was S.O.P. [standard operating procedure]. Scalded children, pistol-whipped women, burning hooches [huts], free-fire zones [regions in which U.S. soldiers had approval to shoot anyone they saw], body counts, indiscriminate bombing and harassment fire, villages in ash, M-60 machine guns hosing down dark green tree lines and any human life behind them."

Returning home

In March 1970 O'Brien was discharged from the U.S. Army with the rank of sergeant. He returned home with a Purple Heart medal he received after suffering a minor shrapnel wound while out on patrol. Years later, O'Brien marveled at the swift change in environment that he and other soldiers experienced when they left the jungles of Vietnam to return to their hometowns. "It was fast and effortless, just like gliding out of a nightmare," he recalled in *Publishers Weekly*.

Upon returning to America, O'Brien enrolled at Harvard University to pursue a degree in government. But the year he spent in Vietnam continued to haunt him, and he began to compose a journal in which he described his wartime experiences. As O'Brien worked on the book, he spent hours thinking about the grim and horrible events that he witnessed during the war. But he also spent a lot of time reflecting about the ways in which Vietnam gave him a greater appreciation for love, friendship, and the simplest pleasures of life.

O'Brien's first book, *If I Die in a Combat Zone, Box Me Up and Ship Me Home,* was published in 1973. This nonfiction work described all stages of O'Brien's Vietnam experience—from military training through combat to homecoming—in a series of story-like essays that were praised for their realism and honesty. "In a style which is lucid [easily understood], relaxed, razor-sharp, and consciously dispassionate, the wasteland of Vietnam unreels before us [in O'Brien's memoir]," wrote one reviewer in *The New Statesman.*

Writing about the war

O'Brien followed up *If I Die in a Combat Zone* with *Northern Lights* (1975), his first novel. The story follows two brothers whose lives become endangered during a stormy cross-country ski trip. One of the brothers is a Vietnam War veteran who is loved by his patriotic father, while the other is the family "failure" who did not fight for his country. As the ski trip turns into a perilous struggle, however, it is the "failure" who takes the lead in ensuring their survival.

Northern Lights received mixed reviews from critics, but the experience of writing a novel convinced O'Brien to dedicate himself to a literary career. "There came a point when I had to decide where I was going to devote my time," he told *Publishers Weekly,* "and I decided that I wanted to be a writer and not a scholar." He dropped out of Harvard in 1976 and began writing full-time.

Going after Cacciato

In 1978 O'Brien published *Going after Cacciato,* a novel that wove two storylines together into one powerful work. Part of the novel describes the experiences of one battered, war-weary platoon of U.S. infantrymen as they struggle to survive in Vietnam.

The other section of the book follows the war-ravaged fantasies of one member of the unit. Assigned to night guard duty, the soldier imagines chasing an actual deserter from the platoon—Cacciato—all across Vietnam to the streets of Paris, France.

Going after Cacciato was widely hailed as one of the finest books ever written about the Vietnam War. It won the prestigious National Book Award and established O'Brien as one of the country's leading voices on the war. It also led many Vietnam veterans to contact him by telephone or letter to share their own wartime experiences. O'Brien confessed, however, that their letters and phone calls left him with mixed feelings. "It has been a bittersweet experience," he told the *Christian Science Monitor.* "The letters mean a lot because I had wanted to touch on something that was common to us all. But I found myself involved in so many hour-long phone calls from shattered guys that it was like reliving the war all over again."

The Things They Carried

In the mid-1980s O'Brien concentrated on writing projects that explored a variety of non-Vietnam topics. But in 1990 he returned to the Vietnam War again with a short story collection called *The Things They Carried.* Many of the events described in *The Things They Carried* closely mirrored O'Brien's own experiences. In addition, many of the interrelated stories are set in O'Brien's home state of Minnesota or in Quang Ngai Province, where he was stationed during the war. Moreover, the collection features several characters who are closely based on soldiers that O'Brien met in Vietnam. Finally, the volume is narrated by a character named "Tim O'Brien." Still, O'Brien has described the book as a work of fiction.

When *The Things They Carried* was published, it immediately attracted a great deal of popular and critical attention. *Booklist* hailed it as a "compassionate, complex, magnificent novel of self-acceptance and renewal." The *New York Times Book Review* offered a similar assessment, calling the collection "one of the finest books, fact or fiction, written about the Vietnam War. . . . By moving beyond the horror of the fighting to examine with sensitivity and insight the nature of courage and fear, by questioning the role that imagination plays in helping to form our memories and our own versions of truth, [O'Brien] placed *The Things They Carried* high up on the list of best fiction about *any* war." And *Publishers Weekly* commented that "O'Brien's meditations—on war and memory, on darkness and light—suffuses [spreads through] the entire work with a kind of poetic form, making for a highly original, fully realized novel. . . . The book is persuasive in its desperate hope that stories can save us."

The Things They Carried received several literary awards in the months following its publication, and it was nominated for a number of other prestigious honors. Since then, O'Brien's collection has retained a prominent place in discussions about enduring Vietnam War literature. In fact, *The Things They Carried* is now generally regarded as the single greatest work of literature ever written about the American experience in Vietnam.

Returning to Vietnam

O'Brien wrote about Vietnam once again in 1994's *In the Lake of the Woods*. This novel explores the disappearance of a woman after her husband's political career is destroyed by revelations that he was present at the My Lai massacre in Vietnam. *In the Lake of the Woods* received several honors, including recognition from the *New York Times Book Review* as the best book of fiction of 1994. But it did not enjoy the same level of critical or popular success as *The Things They Carried.*

O'Brien also made a special journey to Vietnam in 1994. He returned to Quang Ngai Province, the region where he had served during the war. During his trip, he met many men and women who had been caught up in the war, including former Viet Cong officers and survivors of the My Lai massacre. Upon returning to the United States, O'Brien said that the trip helped heal some of the lingering emotional wounds from his first Vietnam experience. "There was a new Vietnam in my thoughts," he told *Booklist*. "It's a nice feeling to find the geography, to walk in the backyard again and not really remember what happened so much as feel blown away by the utter peace that's replaced what was horror."

O'Brien continues to explore a variety of subjects in his writing. His 1998 novel *Tomcat in Love,* for example, centered on the relationships between men and women. But he remains best known for his works on the Vietnam War. Indeed, it is the power of O'Brien's Vietnam-related works that led the *San Francisco Examiner* to call him the "best American writer of his generation" in 1998.

Sources

Beidler, Philip D. *Re-Writing America: Vietnam Authors in Their Generation.* Athens: University of Georgia Press, 1991.

Kaplan, Steven. *Understanding Tim O'Brien.* Columbia, SC: University of South Carolina Press, 1994.

Mort, John. "The Booklist Interview: Tim O'Brien." *Booklist,* August 1994.

O'Brien, Tim. *If I Die in a Combat Zone, Box Me Up and Ship Me Home.* New York: Delacorte, 1973.

O'Brien, Tim. *In the Lake of the Woods.* Boston: Seymour Lawrence/Houghton Mifflin, 1994.

O'Brien, Tim. *The Things They Carried.* Boston: Seymour Lawrence/Houghton Mifflin, 1990.

O'Brien, Tim. "The Vietnam in Me." *New York Times Magazine,* October 2, 1994.

Schroeder, Eric James. *Vietnam, We've All Been There: Interviews with American Writers.* Westport, CT: Praeger, 1992.

"Tim O'Brien." *Dictionary of Literary Biography Documentary Series,* Vol. 9: *American Writers of the Vietnam War,* Detroit: Gale Research, 1991.

Tim Page

Born in 1944
London, England

English photojournalist

Tim Page was a talented combat photographer who courted death on numerous occasions while covering the Vietnam War. He documented the war from 1965 to 1969, when a serious shrapnel wound nearly took his life. Page then disappeared from public view until the late 1970s, when Michael Herr (see entry) wrote about his Vietnam exploits in the best-selling book *Dispatches*. Herr's book sparked renewed interest in Page's life and enabled the photographer to revive his career. Today, Page ranks as the most famous of the photojournalists who covered the war in Vietnam.

Early life of adventure and danger

Tim Page was born in England in 1944. The son of a British sailor who was killed in World War II, Page was put up for adoption as an infant. He recalled his childhood in the London suburbs as a happy one, but at age seventeen he ran away from home in search of adventure.

Page spent the next few years traveling around Asia. He supported himself by a variety of means during this time,

"Page was known as a photographer who would go anywhere, fly in anything, snap the [camera] shutter under any conditions, and when hit [wounded] . . . go at it again in bandages."

Sanford Wexler in The Vietnam War: An Eyewitness History

Tim Page.
Reproduced by permission of AP/Wide World Photos.

including jobs as a cook and a light-bulb salesman. But he spent most of his time seeking out new adventures, experiences, and parties (he became a frequent user of marijuana and other illegal drugs during this time). Before long, Page was very familiar with both the criminal underworlds and the traditional cultures of nations all across Southeast Asia.

Page's travels eventually took him to Laos, where a civil war was raging between Communist guerrillas and the U.S.-supported government. Shortly after entering the war-torn country in 1964, he became a freelance photographer for United Press International (UPI). It was in Laos that Page first developed his reputation as a fearless photojournalist, for he often roamed deep into the countryside in order to cover the violent clashes between the Laotian military and the guerrillas.

Travels to Vietnam

In February 1965 Page left Laos for Vietnam, where U.S. involvement in another civil war was deepening. The Vietnam War was a conflict that pitted the U.S.-supported nation of South Vietnam against the Communist nation of North Vietnam and its Communist guerrilla fighters (known as Viet Cong) in the South. At first, the United States sent money, weapons, and military advisors to South Vietnam to help it fend off the Viet Cong and their North Vietnamese allies. But this assistance failed to put down the Communist threat, and in March 1965—one month after Page's arrival in the country—President Lyndon Johnson (see entry) sent American combat troops to fight on the side of South Vietnam. Over the next few years, the United States sent hundreds of thousands of troops to fight in the war. But deepening U.S. involvement failed to defeat the Communists. Instead, the war settled into a bloody stalemate, and the American public became bitterly divided over the conflict.

Page quickly became known as one of the most fearless of the photojournalists who were covering the war. Indeed, Page spent a good part of the late 1960s grabbing rides on helicopters or motorcycles to go deep into combat areas, where he captured a wide range of images on film. As Sanford Wexler noted in *The Vietnam War: An Eyewitness History,* "Page was known as a photographer who would go anywhere, fly in anything, snap the [camera] shutter under any conditions, and when hit [wounded] . . . go at it again in bandages." Many fellow journalists and U.S. soldiers thought that Page's behavior was crazy or at least foolhardy, but everyone recognized that his risky actions often produced stunning pictures that most other photographers could never obtain.

Some of Page's photos showed fierce firefights or army helicopters swooping over rice fields, while others preserved the emotions of captured Viet Cong suspects or Vietnamese children weeping over the bodies of family members. Page also took many photographs of the American soldiers who served during the late 1960s, a period when drug use, rock and roll music, antiwar protests, and general war-weariness were all influencing troop attitudes and military performance. "Perhaps Page's most striking pictures are of the GIs," wrote William Shawcross in his introduction to *Tim Page's Nam*. "Poor whites and blacks plucked from the ignorant and often innocent island of America's heart and cast without understanding or preparation into an utterly alien and terrifying world. In his pictures and . . . in his commentary Page records the 'sixties-psychedelic side of the GI culture, the inanity [absurdity] of their predicament and the refuge they took in dope and rock [music]."

For his part, Page recognized that the war took a terrible toll on both the Vietnamese people and U.S. troops. He became a strong opponent of American military involvement in the region. But he also confessed that he found his years of photojournalism in Vietnam to be intensely exciting and strangely glamorous. "Page fed on every wretched, insane, heroic, perilous, convulsive, inhuman, controversial, grotesque, paradoxical, beautiful hour of his Vietnam years," commented Paul Dean in the *Los Angeles Times Book Review*. "When not flying on drugs he was high on the buccaneering thrill of it all."

Repeatedly wounded in the field

Page was wounded on four different occasions during his four years in Vietnam. In 1965 he was hit by shrapnel in the legs and stomach during an attack on the coastal city of Chu Lai. A year later, Buddhist groups led antigovernment riots in the South Vietnamese city of Danang. The South Vietnam government responded with a violent crackdown, during which Page suffered shrapnel wounds in the head, back, and arms.

Page recovered from his wounds and resumed working. One day, he hopped a ride with a Coast Guard boat out into the South China Sea. He had gone out with the boat to relax for the day, but American jet fighters in the area mistakenly identified the boat as a Viet Cong vessel. The U.S. planes immediately launched a fierce attack on the defenseless boat. "I had never seen anything like it in my life," recalled Page. "Here's two Phantoms and a B-57 strafing us with twin Vulcans [machine guns] blazing, giving us a stem-to-stern strafing. They hit some gas drums, which started cooking off, and I watched a guy get his hand blown off. The skipper went up to the bridge to try and signal to the jets that we were friendlies and they blew him away. They made nine passes, and blasted the living hell out of the ship. Everybody on board was killed or wounded, I had pieces of commo wire coming out of my head like porcupine quills, a bone sticking out of my arm and countless shrapnel punctures." In fact, Page suffered more than 200 individual wounds, and he floated in the South China Sea for several hours before he was finally rescued.

This attack convinced Page to leave Vietnam for awhile. Many of his friends had been warning him that he seemed destined to die in the war, and he began to think that they might be right. But the 1968 Tet Offensive—a major North Vietnamese invasion of the South that was barely turned back by U.S. and South Vietnamese forces—lured Page back to the region. He soon resumed his daring ways, roaming deep into the jungle in search of memorable photographs and stories.

On the verge of death

One day in 1969, Page secured a ride on an army helicopter that was heading out into the countryside. During the trip, the helicopter was diverted to pick up two wounded American soldiers. When the helicopter landed, Page and a sergeant leaped out to retrieve the soldiers. The sergeant promptly stepped on a land mine that blew off both of his legs. The explosion also drove a big piece of shrapnel into the base of Page's brain. The photographer collapsed onto the floor of the helicopter. As he lay there he heard someone estimate that he had only twenty minutes to live. But Page remained alive through the helicopter ride back to the U.S. base, and doctors revived him two or three different times after his heart stopped. He was later transferred to a hospital in Tokyo, where doctors told him he would suffer permanent paralysis of his left side.

After being transferred to medical facilities in the United States, Page started a comprehensive rehabilitation program. The program eventually helped him regain the use of his left side, but the photographer remained hospitalized for nearly eighteen months before he was released.

Page struggled both emotionally and financially during the mid-1970s. Suffering from depression and lingering memories of the war, he sank into alcohol and drug abuse. This behavior made it difficult for him to hold down a steady job. Finally, a brief marriage ended in divorce during this period.

In the late 1970s Page filed a lawsuit against Time-Life Corporation, for whom he worked during most of his time in Vietnam. The photographer claimed that the company never adequately compensated him for the injuries that he suffered while covering the war. He eventually received an out-of-court settlement of $125,000.

Revival of interest in Page's career

In the late 1970s the public spotlight abruptly turned to Page again. In 1977 Vietnam journalist Michael Herr (see entry) published *Dispatches,* a critically acclaimed war memoir that included extensive comments about Page. Herr's remarks about Page's remarkable years in Vietnam sparked a major surge of interest in the photojournalist's work. This interest intensified two years later, when the Vietnam War film *Apocalypse Now* was released. At that time, it was revealed that one of the movie's main characters—an eccentric photographer played by actor Dennis Hopper—was partly based on Page. In 1980 the British Broadcasting Corporation (BBC) made a documentary film about Page's life. During this same period, an exhibition of the photojournalist's Vietnam pictures was held at the Institute of Contemporary Arts in London. And in 1983 a collection of some of his finest work was published in *Tim Page's Nam.*

Excerpt from *Tim Page's Nam*

Writing in *Tim Page's Nam*, photojournalist Tim Page offered his own perspective on the basic character of the war in Vietnam:

> When you got down to it, it was less of a battle of the technical toys, more about the stamina of the people out there on the ground; between the folks who lived there and the white devils who had come to try and push them out of their own backyards at flashpoint. Not to say that millions of them did not get napalmed, strafed, shot and blitzed trying to stay in their yards.
>
> Most of the time we spent slogging about in vicious circles looking for him, trying to discern [figure out] who was who. The average GI had no more idea who was a VC [Viet Cong] than who was a "friendly farmer"; a lot of friendly farmers got blown away. The maxim [rule] was shoot first, ask questions later. Few Vietnamese tried living in their so-called "Free Fire Zones," where anything was target practice.
>
> Vietnam would normally have ranked as one of the most beautiful spots on this planet. Instead, it was a daunting place to operate a coordinated antiguerrilla campaign. Vietnam was very hot and very wet during the monsoon, but during the dry season there wasn't a drop to drink even in the jungle. The hill country was ravenous: it could eat a whole brigade and its supporting aviation and artillery units alive for breakfast; the swamps and paddies could eat the reserves for lunch. Gear dropped apart in a million mysterious mildewed ways, the body seemed to grow things that existed only in horror movies. The day-to-day stuff, a shower, a hot meal, a clean rack, were a matter of supreme skill coupled with the problem of just staying alive.

In 1980 Page accepted a magazine assignment and returned to Vietnam for the first time since the war's end in 1975. In 1985 he visited the country again on his own. He collected the photographs from that visit into a book called *Ten Years After: Vietnam Today* (1987). Since then, he has returned to Vietnam on a number of occasions for book projects such as 1995's *Derailed in Uncle Ho's Victory Garden*.

In 1988 Page published an autobiographical account of his experiences during the war. *Kirkus Reviews* described *Page after Page: Memoirs of a War-Torn Photographer* as a "woozy memoir . . . of [an] eccentric and adventurous life on the edges of society and in the midst of jungle warfare." *Publishers Weekly,* meanwhile, called Page's memoir "a story that is alternately hilarious and heartrending."

Produces *Requiem* tribute

In the mid-1990s Page started work on a new project that he intended as a tribute to two close friends who had been lost in Vietnam. The two men, photojournalists Dana Stone and Sean Flynn (son of movie legend Errol Flynn), had both disappeared in the jungles of Cambodia during the spring of 1969, and they had never been heard from again. Page intended to collect the war photos of Flynn and Stone and publish them together in a special book. As he worked on the project, though, he eventually decided to expand it to include the camera work of other photojournalists who had died or disappeared during the war. The final result, which Page produced in collaboration with fellow Vietnam photojournalist Horst Faas, was the 1997 book *Requiem: By the Photographers Who Died in Vietnam and Indochina*. This powerful collection of images won several important awards and earned widespread critical praise.

In 1999 Page and Faas presented an exhibition of selected works from the *Requiem* book in the United States. The exhibition included pictures from 135 photojournalists—including seventy-two North Vietnamese—who died or were lost in the wars in Vietnam, Laos, and Cambodia during the 1960s and 1970s. The *Requiem* exhibition also appeared in Japan and Great Britain. In 2000 the exhibition was moved to Vietnam. It was shown in Hanoi in early 2000 and was scheduled to be permanently housed in Ho Chi Minh City (formerly Saigon) later that year, when the nation celebrated the twenty-fifth anniversary of the end of the war.

Sources

Andrews, Owen, et al. *Vietnam: Images from Combat Photographers*. Washington: Starwood, 1991.

Herr, Michael. *Dispatches*. New York: Knopf, 1977.

Page, Tim. *Derailed in Uncle Ho's Victory Garden: Return to Vietnam and Cambodia*. New York: Touchstone, 1995.

Page, Tim. *Page after Page: Memoirs of a War-Torn Photographer*. New York: Atheneum, 1989.

Page, Tim. *Ten Years After: Vietnam Today*. New York: Knopf, 1987.

Page, Tim. *Tim Page's Nam*. New York: Knopf, 1983.

Pham Van Dong

**Born March 1, 1906
Quang Ngai province, Vietnam**

**Premier of North Vietnam, 1955–75, and of the
reunited Socialist Republic of Vietnam, 1975–86**

"A national liberation
war is by its very nature
a people's war. . . .
Our people are fighting
for their liberty, their
life, their honor."

Pham Van Dong.
*Courtesy of the Library
of Congress.*

P ham Van Dong served as the premier of North Vietnam
both before and during the Vietnam War. He was recognized as one of three most powerful leaders of North Vietnam
during these years, along with Ho Chi Minh (see entry) and
General Vo Nguyen Giap (see entry). In fact, these three men
were sometimes referred to as the "iron triangle." When Ho
died in 1969, Pham Van Dong emerged as the main spokesman
for the Communist government of North Vietnam. After
North Vietnam defeated South Vietnam and reunited the two
halves of the country in 1975, Pham Van Dong served another
decade as premier of the Socialist Republic of Vietnam.

Joins the resistance at an early age

Pham Van Dong was born March 1, 1906, in Quang
Ngai province in central Vietnam. At the time of his birth,
Vietnam was a colony of France known as French Indochina.
His father was a wealthy and educated man who served in the
cabinet of Emperor Duy Tan. Pham Van Dong attended French
schools in Saigon and Hue. One of his classmates was Ngo
Dinh Diem (see entry), who went on to become president of

South Vietnam. Outside of the classroom, Pham Van Dong was known as a top soccer player.

In 1925 Pham Van Dong entered the University of Hanoi. During his college years, he became an active member of the Thanh Nien youth league and led a student strike against the French colonial government. Under pressure from the French, he fled to China in 1930. There he joined a group of other young revolutionaries, including eventual North Vietnamese leader Ho Chi Minh, in forming the Indochinese Communist Party.

Upon returning to Vietnam, Pham Van Dong was arrested for his anti-French activities and served six years in Con Son prison. After being released in 1939, he returned to China. Two years later, he helped Ho Chi Minh create the Viet Minh, a Communist-led Vietnamese nationalist group. The Viet Minh were determined to fight to gain Vietnam's independence from French colonial rule.

"Uncle Ho's best nephew"

During World War II (1939–45), France was forced to give up some of its control over Vietnam. When the war ended in 1945, the Viet Minh launched a successful revolution to regain control of the country. That September, Ho Chi Minh formally declared Vietnam's independence and named himself president of the country. Pham Van Dong became foreign minister in the new Communist government. In this position, he represented Vietnam in formal negotiations with the French. People began calling him "Uncle Ho's best nephew" because of his close ties to the Vietnamese president.

But the negotiations fell apart when it became clear that France was not willing to give up its former colony. War erupted between the French and the Viet Minh in late 1946. During this conflict, which became known as the Indochina War, Pham Van Dong commanded the Viet Minh forces in Quang Ngai province. After nine years of fighting, the Viet Minh defeated the French in 1954. Once again, Pham Van Dong represented the Communists in negotiations with the French. These talks, held in Geneva, Switzerland, produced an agreement known as the Geneva Accords.

The Geneva Accords, which ended the Indochina War, divided Vietnam into two sections. The northern section, which was led by a Communist government under Ho Chi Minh, was officially known as the Democratic Republic of Vietnam but was usually called North Vietnam. The southern section, which was led by a U.S.-supported government under Ngo Dinh Diem, was known as the Republic of South Vietnam.

The peace agreement also provided for nationwide free elections to be held in 1956, with a goal of reuniting the two sections of Vietnam under one government. But U.S. government officials worried that holding free elections in Vietnam would bring power to the Communists who had led the nation's war for independence from France. They felt that a Communist government in Vietnam would increase the power of China and the Soviet Union and threaten the security of the United States. As a result, South Vietnamese President Diem and his American advisors refused to hold the elections.

Premier of North Vietnam

Shortly after negotiating the Geneva Accords, Pham Van Dong became premier of the North Vietnamese government. In this position, he introduced a series of changes designed to transform North Vietnam into a Communist nation. For example, he established land reform programs to take land away from wealthy landlords and give it to poor farmers.

Pham Van Dong also tried to negotiate an agreement with his old classmate Diem. He proposed that the two sections of Vietnam reduce their levels of troops and begin trading with one another. He also continued to press for free national elections to reunite the country. But Diem and his American advisors refused to compromise with Pham Van Dong. As a result, North Vietnamese leaders became determined to overthrow Diem and reunite the country by force. Within a short time, a new war began between the two sections of Vietnam.

In the late 1950s and early 1960s the U.S. government sent money, weapons, and military advisors to help South Vietnam. Pham Van Dong responded by accusing the United States of violating the Geneva Accords and trying to establish South Vietnam as a separate nation. Still, American involvement in the Vietnam War continued to increase. In 1965 President Lyndon Johnson (see entry) authorized U.S. bombing missions over North Vietnam and sent American combat troops to South Vietnam.

Issues warnings about Communist determination

But deepening U.S. involvement failed to defeat the Communists. Instead, the Vietnam War turned into a bloody stalemate. As the conflict dragged on, Ho Chi Minh became ill and faded from public view. At the same time, Pham Van Dong's power gradually increased. When Ho died in 1969, Pham Van Dong took charge of the North Vietnamese war effort. He consistently refused to consider any negotiated settlement that did not include a complete withdrawal of American forces and Communist participation in a coalition government in South Vietnam.

Pham Van Dong often gave interviews to Western journalists during this time. Knowing that the American people were growing tired of the war, he frequently spoke about the Communists' determination to fight as long as necessary to achieve a complete victory. "A national liberation war is by its very nature a people's war, a long war, one that can last for tens of years," he told reporter Wilfred Burchett in 1966. "Our people are fighting for their liberty, their life, their honor."

The following year, a reporter for the *New York Times* asked the North Vietnamese premier how long he expected the war to last. Pham Van Dong replied, "What I used to tell our friends was that the younger generation will fight better than we—even kids just so high. They are preparing themselves. That's the situation. How many years the war goes on depends on you [the Americans] and not on us."

Government struggles after the war

In 1973 North Vietnam and the United States finally reached an agreement to end American involvement in Vietnam. Under the terms of the Paris Peace Accord, the United States withdrew its troops from Vietnam later that year. But the peace agreement did not end the Vietnam War. Both North

Vietnam and South Vietnam began violating the terms of the treaty within a short time.

Once the American troops left, Pham Van Dong worked to reconstruct North Vietnam and strengthen its economy. Then in 1975 he approved a new military offensive designed to overthrow the government of South Vietnam and reunite the two parts of the country once and for all. This coordinated attack swept across the South Vietnamese countryside in the spring of 1975. In April the Communists captured the South Vietnamese capital of Saigon to win the Vietnam War.

After winning the war, the Communist leaders of North Vietnam reunited the two halves of the country to form the Socialist Republic of Vietnam. In 1976 Pham Van Dong became premier of the new country. He then introduced a series of changes designed to transform Vietnam into a socialist society. For example, the government took control of all farmland and business activities and placed restrictions on the lives of the Vietnamese people. These changes created terrible hardships for the Vietnamese. Before long, hundreds of thousands of Vietnamese people decided that they could not live under the new government and began fleeing the country as refugees.

Over the next few years, the economic situation in Vietnam continued to deteriorate. Hunger and poverty became widespread problems. Pham Van Dong admitted that his government was struggling to achieve its goal of bringing peace and prosperity to the Vietnamese people. "Yes, we defeated the United States. But now we are plagued by problems," he stated. "Waging a war is simple, but running a country is very difficult."

By the 1980s the situation had become so desperate that the Communist government was forced to make a series of economic reforms. These reforms restored some private property and free-market business incentives in Vietnam. As Vietnamese leaders recognized the need for reform, they began pressuring some of the early Communist leaders to step down. Pham Van Dong resigned from his position as premier in 1986, after more than thirty years in office.

Sources

Current Biography, 1975.

"An Interview with Pham Van Dong." *Time,* November 11, 1985.

Pham Van Dong. *Selected Writings.* 1977.

Pham Van Dong. *Twenty-Five Years of National Struggle.* 1970.

Phan Thi Kim Phuc

Born c.1963
Trang Bang, South Vietnam

Vietnamese woman who appeared in a famous photograph that showed young victims of a U.S.-ordered napalm attack; became a symbol of forgiveness and healing after she laid a wreath at the Vietnam Veterans Memorial in 1996

"Behind that picture of me, thousands and thousands of people, they suffered—more than me. . . . Their whole lives were destroyed, and nobody took that picture."

I n 1972 a nine-year-old Vietnamese child named Phan Thi Kim Phuc was photographed running naked down a country road after suffering terrible burns from a U.S.-ordered napalm attack on her village. The photograph received a Pulitzer Prize and became one of the most enduring images of the Vietnam War's violence and cruelty. Twenty-four years later, however, Kim Phuc also became a symbol of reconciliation when she laid a wreath at the Vietnam Veterans Memorial in memory of the U.S. soldiers who died in the war.

Growing up in wartime

Phan Thi Kim Phuc was born in the early 1960s near the village of Trang Bang in South Vietnam's Central Highlands region. Kim Phuc's family and other members of the Trang Bang community were farmers who led a simple existence. But during Kim Phuc's early childhood, war engulfed the Central Highlands and all of South Vietnam.

The Vietnam War was a grim conflict between the U.S.-supported nation of South Vietnam and the Communist nation of North Vietnam and its guerrilla allies—known as the Viet

Cong—who operated in the South. The war began in the mid-1950s, when Communists first initiated efforts to take over South Vietnam and unite it with the North under one Communist government. But the United States strongly opposed the Communist maneuvers because of fears that a takeover might trigger Communist aggression in other parts of the world. As a result, the United States provided military and financial aid to South Vietnam in the late 1950s and early 1960s.

In 1965 the United States escalated its involvement in the Vietnam War. It sent thousands of American combat troops into the South and executed hundreds of air raids against Communist targets. But deepening U.S. involvement in the war failed to defeat the joint Viet Cong-North Vietnamese forces. Instead, the war settled into a bloody stalemate that eventually claimed the lives of more than 58,000 U.S. soldiers and caused bitter internal divisions across America. The United States finally withdrew from Vietnam in 1973. Two years later, Communist forces captured the South Vietnamese capital of Saigon to bring the war to a close.

Suffers terrible wounds in napalm attack

Kim Phuc received her wounds in June 1972, when a battle between North Vietnamese and South Vietnamese troops erupted on the outskirts of Trang Bang. As the fight continued, U.S. military officers who were leading the South Vietnamese forces received reports that the village had been abandoned by civilians. With this information in hand, an American commander ordered South Vietnamese planes to attack the village. He ordered this assault because he thought that enemy forces might be hiding in the abandoned village.

In reality, however, some Vietnamese civilians remained in Trang Bang. As the fighter planes approached, young Kim Phuc and the other villagers took refuge in a small religious temple called a pagoda. When a bomb hit the building, the frightened villagers fled out into the open. But as they looked around for other shelter, another plane flew over the village and dumped a load of napalm on them. Napalm was often used by American forces to destroy areas held by enemy forces during the Vietnam War. It is a gasoline-like chemical that sticks to surfaces—including skin—and burns nearly anything it touches.

When the South Vietnamese fighter plane dumped its cargo of napalm on Trang Bang, Kim Phuc and several other villagers were struck. The attack killed some of the villagers and maimed others. Kim Phuc was one of those who were mutilated by the napalm. The substance fell on her back, chest, and arms and quickly burned her flesh away. "I saw my hand, my arm burning," Kim Phuc recalled in *Maclean's*. "I thought, 'Oh, my goodness, I become ugly girl, not normal like before.'" Frightened and in tremendous pain, she tore off her burning clothing and ran blindly down a nearby road, where she was joined by several other terrified children.

The air attack was witnessed by several journalists, who rushed to the roadway to meet the frightened children. One of the journalists—a twenty-one-year-old South Vietnamese photographer with the Associated Press named Huynh Cong "Nick" Ut—took a picture of Kim Phuc just before she reached the reporters. In the photo, she is naked and screaming in pain, her arms held away from her horribly burned body.

Kim Phuc collapsed a few minutes later. Ut and other journalists poured water over her wounds. Ut then carried her to a car and rushed her to a hospital fifteen miles away. Afterward, he sent his photograph to the Associated Press, which published it in newspapers and magazines around the world.

The photograph immediately triggered a storm of angry reaction from the American people, most of whom had come to see the Vietnam War as a terrible and tragic event. The picture also won the Pulitzer Prize. In the years since its first appearance, it has remained one of the most frequently reproduced images of the entire Vietnam conflict. As the *Christian Century* noted, "the instantly famous photograph was used again and again to symbolize the horror of war."

A long and painful recovery

After she was hospitalized, Kim Phuc was near death for several days. She then regained some of her strength, and it became clear that she would survive her wounds. But the napalm attack still left her horribly disfigured. Her chin had been fused to her chest by scar tissue, and burns covered much of her small body. The pain she suffered was so great that she lost consciousness whenever nurses washed and bandaged her wounds. "That is a terrible time for me," she remembered in *Maclean's*.

Kim Phuc was not forgotten, however. Ut organized a fund-raising drive to help pay for her care, and American surgeons working in Vietnam repaired her damaged body the best they could. In August 1973, fourteen months after she was first admitted to the hospital, Kim Phuc was finally released.

Life was difficult for Kim Phuc in the late 1970s and early 1980s. She remained in constant pain because of her injuries, and like many other Vietnamese, she had difficulty adjusting to life under Communist rule. But her circumstances improved in the early 1980s. At that time, the Vietnamese government began using her injuries to criticize the United States, which remained a bitter political foe. At first, Kim Phuc liked the renewed attention, for it reassured her that she had not been forgotten. But interviews and other government-sponsored activities interfered with her studies, and after a while she began resisting her role as a propaganda tool. ("Propaganda" refers to methods used by a government or group to spread a political message or point of view.)

In 1986 Kim Phuc received permission to go to Cuba—another Communist nation—to study pharmacology (the science of drug composition and use). During her time there, she fell in love with Huy Toan, another Vietnamese student who had relocated to Cuba to pursue his studies. When the couple married in 1992, they were given a trip to Moscow for their honeymoon. On their return flight, however, their plane stopped in Canada to refuel. At that time, Kim Phuc and her husband quietly left the plane and requested political "asylum" (protection from one's native government).

The couple's decision to make a new life for themselves in Canada was a very brave one. Kim Phuc recalled in the *New York Times* that they had "no clothes, no money, no family, no friends, no knowledge—nothing at all [in Canada]." But they received housing and legal assistance from Nick Ut and Nancy Pocock, a member of Canada's Quaker Committee for Refugees. A short time later, their request for refugee status was approved by the Canadian government. This ruling allowed them to begin building a new life for themselves in Canada. Kim Phuc and Huy Toan eventually settled in Toronto, where they had a son, Thomas.

Kim Phuc visits the Wall

When Kim Phuc first arrived in Canada, she was reluctant to talk about her wartime experiences. But she also hated the fact that wars continued to rage in many parts of the world. After a while, she became convinced that her story might help people understand the horrible nature of war and convince them to work harder for the cause of peace. As a result, she began making herself available for interviews once again. "I wanted to share my experience with people so that they feel better," she explained in the *New York Times*. "Behind that picture of me, thousands and thousands of people, they suffered—more than me. They died. They lost parts of their bodies. Their whole lives were destroyed, and nobody took that picture."

In 1996 the leadership of the Vietnam Veterans Memorial Fund invited Kim Phuc to attend Veterans' Day ceremonies at the Vietnam Veterans Memorial in Washington, D.C. The memorial, commonly known as "the Wall," pays tribute to the 58,000 American men and women who died during the Vietnam War. Kim Phuc accepted the invitation. On November 11, 1996, she joined Norm McDaniel, a former Vietnam POW (prisoner of war), in laying a wreath at the Wall in memory of America's fallen soldiers. She then delivered a brief speech to the assembled crowd, which gave her two standing ovations. "I have suffered a lot from both physical and emotional pain," she told the gathered audience. "Sometimes I could not breathe. But God saved my life and gave me faith and hope. Even if I could talk face to face with the pilot who dropped the bombs, I would tell him, 'We cannot change history, but we should try to do good things for the present and for the future to promote peace.'"

American Vietnam veterans who attended the ceremony expressed deep appreciation and admiration for Kim Phuc's presence. "It important to us that she's here, part of the healing process," said one veteran. They also agreed that her appearance had a tremendous emotional impact on them. "When we realized who she was, we all started bawling," one veteran told the *New York Times*.

Meets the American who ordered the bombing

The most emotional moment of Kim Phuc's appearance at the Vietnam Veterans Memorial, however, was her meeting with John Plummer, the U.S. commander who ordered the 1972 attack on her village. After leaving the U.S. military in 1982, Plummer had become the pastor of a Methodist Church in Virginia. But the memory of the bombing attack on Trang Bang and the death and pain it caused remained with him, even though he had ordered the attack in the mistaken belief that the village had been abandoned. "[Kim Phuc's] photograph was indelibly burned into my heart and soul and was to haunt me for many, many years," Plummer told the *Christian Century.*

Shortly before the 1996 Veterans Day events, Plummer learned that Kim Phuc was scheduled to take part in the ceremonies at the Wall. He decided to attend the ceremony in the hope that he might have a chance to apologize to her for his role in the bombing. But as the ceremony progressed, he learned that Kim Phuc's one- and three-year-old cousins had been killed by the napalm attack. "Being in a pretty precarious emotional state already, this just pushed me over the edge," he recalled in *Christian Century.* "I began to shake all over as wracking sobs were torn from my body."

After the ceremony, Plummer's friends and family members told Kim Phuc that he was in the crowd. She quickly agreed to meet him, and in a matter of moments they had an emotional meeting. "She saw my grief, my pain, my sorrow," Plummer recalled in *Christian Century.* "She held out her arms to me and embraced me. All I could say was 'I'm sorry; I'm so sorry; I'm sorry' over and over again. At the same time she was saying 'It's all right; It's all right; I forgive; I forgive.'" Plummer later said that Kim Phuc's comforting words finally gave him a sense of peace about his experiences in the Vietnam War.

Since the 1996 Veterans' Day services at the Wall, Kim Phuc has remained very busy caring for her family and speaking about her wartime experiences. In 1997 she was named goodwill ambassador for the United Nations Educational, Scientific, and Cultural Organization (UNESCO). She continues to correspond with both Nick Ut and John Plummer, and she regularly sends money to her parents, who still live in Vietnam.

Sources

Chisholm, Patricia. "An Extraordinary Capacity to Forgive." *Maclean's,* February 10, 1997.

Chong, Denise. *The Girl in the Picture: The Story of Kim Phuc, the Photograph, and the Vietnam War.* New York: Viking, 2000.

"A Picture of Forgiveness." *The Christian Century,* February 19, 1997.

Sciolino, Elaine. "A Painful Road from Vietnam to Forgiveness." *New York Times,* November 12, 1996.

Pol Pot

**Born May 19, 1928
Kompong Thom Province, Cambodia
Died April 1998
Preah Vihear, Cambodia**

**Cambodian political leader; head of the
Cambodian Communist rebel group
known as the Khmer Rouge**

P ol Pot is widely considered to be one of the most evil political leaders in modern history. During the Vietnam War, he
led a group of Communist rebels known as the Khmer Rouge
who were fighting for control of the neighboring country of
Cambodia. When the Khmer Rouge took over the Cambodian
government in April 1975, Pol Pot and his followers went on a
murderous rampage that led to the deaths of an estimated two
million Cambodian citizens. Their reign of terror ended only
after Vietnamese forces successfully invaded Cambodia in 1979.

Develops radical communist ideas

The man who became known as Pol Pot was born on
May 19, 1928, in Kompong Thom province, Cambodia. His
name at birth was Saloth Sar. He changed his name to Pol Pot,
which means "the original Cambodian," years later when he
became leader of the Khmer Rouge. Pol Pot's parents were
landowners who traced their ancestors back to Cambodian
royalty. He had a very strict and sheltered childhood in the
capital city of Phnom Penh, where he attended an elite
Catholic school.

Pol Pot is considered to
be one of the most evil
political leaders in
modern history.

Pol Pot.
*Reproduced by permission of
AP/Wide World Photos.*

At the age of twenty, Pol Pot received a scholarship to study radio electronics in France. During his time there, he became active in the Communist Party. He also met his future wife, Khieu Ponnary, who was the first Cambodian woman to earn a college degree. Some sources say that Pol Pot left France without earning a degree because he failed to pass his final examinations three times in a row. These sources claim that Pol Pot later formed a deep hatred for intellectuals because of his own academic failures. But in one of his rare interviews, Pol Pot claimed that he did not complete his education because he concentrated on political activities instead. "As I spent most of my time in radical activities, I did not attend many classes," he admitted. "The state cut short my scholarship, and I was forced to return home."

Pol Pot returned to Cambodia in the early 1950s. At that time, Cambodia—like its neighbor Vietnam—was a colony of France. In 1954 a group of Communist-led Vietnamese nationalists known as the Viet Minh defeated the French after nine years of war. The agreement that ended this war divided Vietnam into two sections, Communist-led North Vietnam and U.S.-supported South Vietnam. At the same time, France granted independence to its other colonies in Indochina, including Cambodia. Prince Norodom Sihanouk (see entry)—who had been named king of Cambodia by the French in 1941, but later had fought for Cambodian independence—gave up his throne in order to become president of Cambodia in 1955.

During this time, Pol Pot remained active in the Cambodian Communist movement. This movement had grown out of the resistance to French colonial rule and had links to the Vietnamese Communists. It was generally critical of Sihanouk's government. But Sihanouk did not permit opposition to his rule. He called the Communists the Khmer Rouge, or "Red Cambodians," and forced them into hiding in the countryside. Pol Pot rose through the Communist ranks over the next few years. In 1962 he became the party's leader after the former leader was assassinated.

By the time Pol Pot took over leadership of the Cambodian Communist movement, his political views had become very radical. He and a few key supporters believed that the Cambodian people were superior to the rest of Indochina. They wanted to cleanse Cambodian society of what they considered impure elements, such as ethnic minorities and signs of other cultures. To achieve their goals, they planned to lead the people in a revolution that would restore the ancient glory of the country. Pol Pot kept the true nature of his plans secret from all but his closest advisors. Instead, he based his call for revolution on the need to overthrow the ineffective government of Sihanouk.

Leads the Khmer Rouge

During the 1960s Cambodia was increasingly threatened by a new war that had broken out in Vietnam. This war pitted North Vietnam and its secret allies, the South Vietnamese Communists known as the Viet Cong, against South Vietnam. North Vietnam wanted to overthrow the South Vietnamese government and reunite the two countries under one Communist government. But U.S. government officials worried that a Communist government in Vietnam would encourage other countries in Indochina to adopt communism. They felt that this would increase the power of China and the Soviet Union and threaten the security of the United States.

At first, the U.S. government sent money, weapons, and military advisors to help South Vietnam defend itself against North Vietnam and the Viet Cong. In 1965 President Lyndon Johnson (see entry) sent American combat troops to join the fight on the side of South Vietnam. The intense fighting with American troops encouraged the Viet Cong and North Vietnamese forces to move their base of operations across the border into eastern Cambodia. Like many other Cambodians, Pol Pot did not like the idea of Vietnamese forces operating in the country. After all, Vietnam and Cambodia had been involved in many violent border disputes over the years. These clashes had created very tense relations between the two countries. But Pol Pot also knew that the situation might provide him with an ideal opportunity to topple Sihanouk's government.

Pol Pot began organizing the Khmer Rouge as a revolutionary group in 1966. During this time, he remained behind the scenes as much as possible for his own protection. The Khmer Rouge slowly gained support from the Cambodian people over the next few years, as Cambodia became increasingly involved in the Vietnam War. In 1969 Sihanouk approved American bombing runs over Cambodian territory.

The Killing Fields

The Khmer Rouge, which ruled Cambodia from 1975 to 1979, was one of the most violent and destructive governments in modern history. The peaceful rice fields of the Cambodian countryside turned into "killing fields," or mass graves for the estimated two million people who died under the brutal Khmer Rouge rule. In fact, some historians have compared Cambodia under the Khmer Rouge to Germany under Adolf Hitler, when the Nazis murdered six million Jews during the Holocaust.

In 1984 British movie director Roland Joffe released *The Killing Fields,* a film about the horrors of life in Cambodia under the Khmer Rouge. It was based on an article by American reporter Sydney Schanberg that appeared in the *New York Times Magazine* in 1980. Both the article and the film follow the experiences of Schanberg and his Cambodian interpreter and guide, Dith Pran, during the Khmer Rouge takeover of Cambodia.

In the movie, Schanberg first arrives in Cambodia in 1972, when the Communist rebels known as the Khmer Rouge are involved in a civil war against Cambodian government forces. Schanberg reports on events in Cambodia with the help of Dith Pran, who helps him uncover stories and communicate with the local people. Over time, the two men develop a close friendship.

When the Cambodian capital of Phnom Penh is captured by the Khmer Rouge in 1975, Schanberg remains in the country to cover the story. He convinces Dith Pran to stay with him, at great risk to both of their safety. Schanberg manages to escape the city at the last minute, but he is unable to get a passport for Dith Pran. Although the reporter later wins a Pulitzer Prize for his coverage of the fall of Phnom Penh, he is consumed by guilt over leaving his friend behind.

For the next four years, Dith Pran struggles to survive the violence that

The bombing was intended to destroy the Vietnamese Communist bases along the border. But it mainly forced the North Vietnamese and Viet Cong forces to move deeper into Cambodia. It also disrupted the lives of the Cambodian people and caused them great hardship. As a result, many people threw their support behind the Khmer Rouge.

In 1970 a group of Cambodian officials led by Lon Nol (see entry) took control of the government while

Haing S. Ngor. *Reproduced by permission of AP/Wide World Photos.*

In *The Killing Fields,* the role of Dith Pran was played by Haing S. Ngor, a Cambodian doctor who had also endured several years of terror under the Khmer Rouge. After escaping to the United States, Ngor became an outspoken opponent of the Khmer Rouge and organized humanitarian aid missions to help Cambodian refugees. Sadly, the actor was murdered outside his home in Los Angeles in 1996. Some reports claim that he was killed by Khmer Rouge agents.

The Killing Fields became one of the most respected films of the Vietnam War era. It was popular with audiences, and it won three Academy Awards—including a best supporting actor Oscar for Ngor. Critics praised it for bringing the world's attention to the Cambodian tragedy through powerful images of war. As David Ansen wrote in a Newsweek review, "*The Killing Fields* paints a canvas of ravaged Cambodia so compelling and convincing you can't tear your eyes from the screen."

dominates his homeland under the Khmer Rouge. He pretends to be a simple taxi driver so the Communists will not kill him for being an "intellectual." Still, he suffers torture and terrible hunger at the hands of the Khmer Rouge. Finally, Dith Pran makes a dangerous journey to Thailand in 1979, where he is reunited with Schanberg.

Sihanouk was out of the country. Angry about the overthrow of his rule, Sihanouk joined forces with his former enemies, the Khmer Rouge, against Lon Nol's government. A short time later, U.S. and South Vietnamese combat forces mounted an invasion of Cambodia. Once again, the military operation pushed the Vietnamese Communists further into Cambodian territory and caused suffering for the Cambodian people.

Dith Pran (1942–)

One of the best-known survivors of the Khmer Rouge is Dith Pran, the Cambodian interpreter and guide whose life story became the basis for the award-winning movie *The Killing Fields*. Dith Pran was born on September 27, 1942, in the town of Siem Reap in northwestern Cambodia. He learned French and English during his school years and then became an interpreter for American military forces operating in Cambodia in 1960. When the Cambodian government broke off relations with the United States in 1965, Dith Pran found work in a hotel.

Five years later, a civil war erupted between Cambodian government forces and the Cambodian Communist rebels known as the Khmer Rouge. Dozens of reporters from around the world came to Cambodia to report on the situation, including Sydney Schanberg of the *New York Times*. Dith Pran worked as an interpreter for the foreign journalists. As the reporters learned of his energy, courage, and political connections, Dith Pran's services were in great demand.

In 1973 Dith Pran helped Schanberg break a big story. An American plane accidentally dropped twenty tons of bombs on the heavily populated Cambodian town of Neak Luong. About 150 people were killed, and another 250 were wounded. When rumors of the tragic mistake surfaced, the U.S. Embassy played down the destruction and tried to prevent reporters from reaching the town. Dith Pran helped Schanberg become the first journalist on the scene by arranging passage on a Cambodian military patrol boat.

Over time, Dith Pran and Schanberg became close friends. Dith Pran eventually received a salary from the *New York Times* and worked only with Schanberg. In 1975 Khmer Rouge forces surrounded the Cambodian capital of Phnom Penh. The U.S. Embassy was evacuated, and many foreign journalists left the country. But Schanberg decided to remain in Cambodia as long as possible to cover the Communist takeover. Dith Pran agreed to stay with him, despite the fact that both of their lives would be in great danger.

After Phnom Penh fell to the Khmer Rouge, Schanberg was allowed to leave the country. He desperately tried to find a way to take Dith Pran with him to the United States, including forging a passport. But Dith Pran was forced to remain in Cambodia under the Khmer Rouge. Dith Pran knew that the Communists would kill him for being an intellectual and helping the foreign

Dith Pran. *Reproduced by permission of Corbis Corporation.*

"killing fields," or mass graves containing thousands of bodies. "In the water wells, the bodies were like soup bones in broth," he said in Schanberg's book *The Death and Life of Dith Pran.* "And you could always tell the killing grounds because the grass grew taller and greener where the bodies were buried."

In the meantime, Schanberg won a Pulitzer Prize for his coverage of the fall of Phnom Penh to the Khmer Rouge. He also made numerous attempts to locate or get a message to Dith Pran. Finally, after the Vietnamese Army invaded Cambodia in 1979, Dith Pran escaped over the mountains into Thailand. Two of his companions were killed by a land mine during the dangerous journey. But Dith Pran made it to a refugee camp, where a joyful Schanberg met him and arranged for his passage to the United States.

journalists, so he destroyed all of his belongings and anything that would show his true identity. He spent the next four years working in labor camps and pretending to be a poor taxi driver.

Like many other Cambodians, Dith Pran suffered from disease and malnutrition during this time. At one point, he was nearly beaten to death by the Khmer Rouge for stealing a handful of rice to keep from starving. His father, three brothers, and one sister were all murdered by the Khmer Rouge. He recalled how the countryside of Cambodia turned into

Later that year, Schanberg wrote a major article for the *New York Times Magazine* about his search for Dith Pran. In 1984, director Roland Joffe used the story as the basis for his critically acclaimed film about the Cambodian tragedy, *The Killing Fields.* Since then, Dith Pran has found a home in New York City with his wife and children. He works as a staff photographer for the *New York Times.*

The Khmer Rouge continued to gather support from people who were upset over the country's involvement in the Vietnam War. With Sihanouk as its symbolic leader (although the former Cambodian president held no real power), the rebel group emerged as a legitimate political alternative to Lon Nol. The Khmer Rouge increased in size from 4,000 members to 80,000 members over the next few years. With help from the Vietnamese Communists, they defeated the Cambodian military in a series of battles. By 1973 the Khmer Rouge controlled 75 percent of the countryside of Cambodia and held the loyalty of nearly half of the population.

The Khmer Rouge takes control of Cambodia

After two more years of civil war, the Khmer Rouge captured the capital city of Phnom Penh and took control of the Cambodian government on April 17, 1975. Lon Nol escaped to the United States, but many members of his administration were murdered by the Khmer Rouge. Two weeks later, North Vietnamese forces captured the South Vietnamese capital of Saigon to win the Vietnam War.

Immediately after taking power, the Cambodian Communists began putting Pol Pot's radical ideas into place. They launched a brutal program designed to transform Cambodia into a simple farming society. As part of this destructive program, the Khmer Rouge renamed the nation Democratic Kampuchea and called the beginning of their rule Year Zero. They drove people out of cities and towns and forced them to work on communal farms in the countryside. They burned books, tore down buildings and temples, and destroyed cars, medical equipment, and other examples of "foreign technology." They also abolished money, prohibited religious practice, eliminated private property, ended all formal education, and forbade the publication of newspapers.

Worst of all, the Khmer Rouge murdered hundreds of thousands of Cambodian citizens in an effort to rid the country of ethnic minorities and "intellectuals" who opposed their rule. Some people were killed simply because they wore eyeglasses or spoke a foreign language. Many others were herded into forced labor camps, where they died of starvation, exhaustion, or disease. Most Cambodian doctors were killed, and those who survived were not allowed to use modern medicine.

As a result, epidemics of treatable diseases spread quickly through Cambodian society. People who managed to escape the country as refugees told of mass graves in the once-peaceful rice fields. Overall, historians estimate that as many as two million Cambodians—or one-fourth of the population—died under the Khmer Rouge.

Vietnamese invaders end the violence

During the four-year reign of terror of the Khmer Rouge, Cambodia was still involved in disputes with Vietnam over national borders and leadership of Indochina. Pol Pot disliked the Vietnamese and believed that the Cambodians were a superior race. As a result, he refused to acknowledge Vietnam as the most powerful nation in Indochina. Pol Pot also launched a series of military raids to reclaim Vietnamese territory that had once been part of Cambodia.

In December 1978 the Vietnamese government responded by sending troops into Cambodia to overthrow the Khmer Rouge. By January 1979 Vietnam's invasion forces had captured Phnom Penh. They immediately put an end to the brutal policies of the Khmer Rouge. They also established a new, pro-Vietnamese government under Prime Minister Hun Sen. The Vietnamese occupation forces sentenced Pol Pot to death, but they were not able to find him. The Khmer Rouge leader and 10,000 of his troops retreated to the jungles of Thailand, along the western border of Cambodia. From these hidden bases, the Khmer Rouge continued fighting for control of Cambodia using tactics of guerrilla warfare.

Even though the Vietnamese invasion of Cambodia had removed the violent Khmer Rouge from power, many countries around the world criticized Vietnam's actions. For example, the United States and other countries formed an economic embargo to punish Vietnam for its actions. The U.S. government also provided support to the Khmer Rouge and other Cambodian rebels fighting against the Hun Sen government.

Despite the international disapproval, Vietnam maintained its occupation of Cambodia for ten years before withdrawing its troops in 1989. Boosted by recognition from the United States and other countries, the Khmer Rouge remained a force in Cambodian politics during this time. In the 1990s, however, the Khmer Rouge gradually became a fringe movement and split into competing factions. In 1997 Pol Pot was taken prisoner by some of his rivals within the Khmer Rouge. He was held in a secret jungle hideout along the Thai border. He died under mysterious circumstances in April 1998. Khmer Rouge officials claimed that he died of a heart attack, but his body was cremated before the cause of death could be confirmed.

Sources

Chandler, David P. *Brother Number One: A Political Biography of Pol Pot.* Boulder, CO: Westview Press, 1992.

Chandler, David P. *The Tragedy of Cambodian History: Politics, War, and Revolution since 1945.* New Haven, CT: Yale University Press, 1991.

Kamm, Henry. *Cambodia: Report from a Stricken Land.* New York: Arcade Publishing, 1998.

Kirk, Donald. *Wider War: The Struggle for Cambodia, Thailand, and Laos.* New York: Praeger, 1971.

Ponchaud, Francois. *Cambodia: Year Zero.* New York: Holt, Rinehart, and Winston, 1977.

Schanberg, Sydney H. *The Death and Life of Dith Pran.* New York: Viking Penguin, 1980.

Dean Rusk

Born February 9, 1909
Cherokee County, Georgia
Died December 20, 1994
Athens, Georgia

U.S. secretary of state, 1961–69

As U.S. secretary of state from 1961 to 1969, Dean Rusk was one of America's major Vietnam War policy makers. Rusk supported U.S. military involvement in Vietnam because he viewed the conflict as an important test of America's determination to contain communism around the world. As the war's popularity diminished, though, Rusk's steady defense of U.S. actions in Vietnam made him a controversial figure. After leaving public life in 1969, he continued to consider the American effort in Vietnam to have been honorable and right.

> "I have not apologized from my role in Vietnam for the simple reason that I believe in the principles that underlay our commitment to South Vietnam and why we fought that war."

Escapes poverty through education

David Dean Rusk was born in February 1909 in Cherokee County, Georgia. His parents were Frances (Clotfelter) Rusk, a schoolteacher, and Robert Rusk, who worked as a farmer and postal worker after throat problems forced him to retire from the ministry. Rusk's parents struggled to provide their five children with clothing and shelter, but they taught their children to value education as a tool that could lift them out of poverty.

Dean Rusk.
Courtesy of United Nations.

Rusk took this message to heart. After completing high school in Atlanta in 1926, he used saved earnings and scholarship assistance to enroll at North Carolina's Davidson College. Rusk excelled in his course work at Davidson, where he also joined the country's Reserve Officer's Training Corps (ROTC) program. He graduated from Davidson with honors in 1931. He then received a prestigious Rhodes Scholarship, which enabled him to earn a master's degree in international relations from Oxford University in England in 1934.

In 1934 Rusk returned to the United States and accepted a faculty position with Mills College in California. Three years later, he joined the faculty of the University of California. That same year, he married Virginia Foisie, with whom he eventually had three children.

Military service brings new opportunities

In December 1940 Rusk was drafted into military service by the U.S. Army. An eight-year member of the ROTC, he was initially made an infantry captain. As World War II (1939–45) progressed, though, Rusk was transferred to posts that took greater advantage of his abilities as an administrator and analyst. From 1941 to 1943, he worked in Army Intelligence in Washington, D.C. He was then transferred to India, where he became an important member of General Joseph Stilwell's staff.

By the time Rusk was discharged from military service in 1946, he had gained a considerable reputation as a dedicated and talented administrator. He spent the next several years moving up through the diplomatic ranks in both the State Department and the War Department (now known as the Department of Defense). During this period, he emerged as an important voice on such issues as the Korean War, United Nations policies, and other international affairs. In addition, he became a recognized expert on European-Asian relations. Rusk was sympathetic to Asian peoples who wanted to be free of European colonialism, and he played an important part in President Harry Truman's decision to support Indonesian independence in 1949. Finally, Rusk became known during this period as a firm anti-Communist who believed that the United States should take the lead in defending the world from Communist aggression.

In 1952 Rusk left the State Department to accept the presidency of the Rockefeller Foundation, a charitable trust. He led the foundation for the next eight years, overseeing a variety of health, education, and economic programs within underdeveloped and impoverished countries. During this time, his reputation as one of the United States' leading foreign policy experts continued to grow.

Joins President Kennedy's cabinet

In 1960 John F. Kennedy (see entry) won election to succeed Dwight Eisenhower as president of the United States. As Kennedy prepared to take office in January 1961, he asked Rusk to join his administration as secretary of state. Rusk gladly accepted the invitation, which made him one of the nation's most powerful foreign policy makers.

After joining the Kennedy White House, Rusk once again proved his skills as a manager and administrator. In addition, he advised Kennedy on a host of major foreign policy issues, including the Cuban Missile Crisis of 1962. (This was a dangerous episode in which the United States and the Soviet Union moved to the brink of war after the U.S. discovered that Soviet missiles capable of showering nuclear warheads on many American cities had been installed in Cuba. The crisis passed only after the Soviets agreed to remove the missile threat in exchange for an American pledge not to invade Communist Cuba). But Kennedy became frustrated with Rusk's cautious style, and as time passed it became clear that the president placed greater value on the counsel of some other cabinet members, including Attorney General Robert Kennedy (see entry), Secretary of Defense Robert McNamara (see entry), and National Security Advisor McGeorge Bundy (see entry).

Rusk's visibility and influence increased during the presidency of Lyndon Johnson (see entry), who succeeded Kennedy after he was assassinated in November 1963. Rusk's steadiness, loyalty, and Southern background appealed to Johnson, a Texan. As a result, the secretary of state soon emerged as one of the Johnson administration's primary architects of U.S. policy toward the troubled nation of South Vietnam.

South Vietnam had been formed in 1954, after Vietnamese fighters known as Viet Minh had forced France to give up its colonial claims on the nation. But the Geneva Accords that ended the French-Vietnamese conflict created two countries within Vietnam. North Vietnam was headed by a Communist government under the revolutionary leader Ho Chi Minh (see entry). South Vietnam, meanwhile, was led by a U.S.-supported government under President Ngo Dinh Diem (see entry).

The Geneva Accords provided for nationwide free elections to be held in 1956 so that the two sections of Vietnam could be united under one government. But U.S. and South Vietnamese officials refused to hold the elections because they feared that the results would give the Communists control over the entire country. This decision greatly angered North Vietnam's leadership, which responded by launching a guerrilla war against the South with the help of Communist allies in the South known as the Viet Cong. The Communists started this campaign with the aim of eventually reuniting the country by force. The United States, however, fiercely opposed the Communist political philosophy. It sent military and financial aid to South Vietnam to help the country defend itself from the Viet Cong and their partners in the North.

Rusk and Vietnam

Rusk viewed the Vietnam War as an important test of America's determination to contain communism and maintain its position as the world's leading democracy. In fact, he warned that if the United States broke its commitment to defend South Vietnam from its Communist neighbors, China or Russia might invade other countries in the belief that America would not intervene. He thought that such an invasion might then trigger a nuclear war between the United States and either China or Russia.

This belief led Rusk to support more aggressive U.S. military policies toward Vietnam in the mid-1960s, when it appeared that the South was in danger of falling to the Communists. He abandoned his previous opposition to using American troops in the conflict and joined McNamara in advocating a military strategy of gradual escalation toward North Vietnam and the Viet Cong. Persuaded by this advice, Johnson committed large numbers of American troops to the South's defense. He also launched bombing campaigns and other new operations against the North. Before long, the

United States had assumed primary responsibility for defeating the Communists in Vietnam.

From 1965 to 1969, Rusk carried out Johnson's instructions regarding the Vietnam War. But deepening U.S. military commitments failed to defeat the Communists. Instead, the war dragged on with no end in sight, and the American public became bitterly divided about continued U.S. involvement in the conflict. As one of the Johnson administration's major architects of Vietnam policy, Rusk became a frequent target of the American antiwar movement and political leaders who opposed U.S. involvement. But Rusk never wavered in his defense of the U.S. military presence in Vietnam. "We believe that the South Vietnamese are entitled to a chance to make their own decisions about their own affairs and their own future course of policy . . . without having them imposed on them by force from North Vietnam or from the outside," he declared in one 1965 appearance before a Senate foreign relations committee.

In fact, Rusk eventually became one of the administration's leading spokesmen on the war effort. He even offered strong public defenses of policies he privately disagreed with, such as Johnson's decision to bomb cities in North Vietnam. "In innumerable congressional hearings and press conferences, Rusk expressed his certainty that an unconditional American withdrawal would be a fatal sign that the United States had lost its resolve to combat communism," pointed out the editors of *The Cold War, 1945–1991*. "He frequently acknowledged that there may have been flaws in this or that aspect of American policy, but he never waved in his support of the overall strategy the Johnson administration pursued."

Rusk Defends American Policies in Vietnam

As American involvement in the Vietnam War deepened in the mid-1960s, Secretary of State Dean Rusk became a leading defender of the Johnson administration's war policies. In February 1966 he testified before the U.S. Senate that America's position toward North Vietnam was actually quite reasonable:

"We are not asking anything from Hanoi except to stop shooting their neighbors in Laos and South Vietnam," he declared. "We are not asking them to give up an acre of territory. We are not asking them to surrender a single individual, nor to change the form of government. All we are asking them to do is to stop sending armed men and arms, contrary to specific agreements and contrary to international law, into South Vietnam for the purpose of shooting somebody. . . . We are not asking them to surrender a thing except their appetite to take over South Vietnam by force."

By the late 1960s Rusk's pro-war statements had transformed him into a favorite target of the antiwar movement. In fact, large antiwar demonstrations and protests became commonplace whenever the secretary made a public appearance. Around this same time, Rusk's son Richard publicly condemned him for his role in continuing an "immoral" war. These developments led Rusk to curtail his public appearances dramatically in the last year or so of his tenure.

Rusk retired from public life in 1969, when Richard Nixon (see entry) became president and established a new Republican administration to run the country. By the time he departed, Rusk had served as secretary of state for eight years, the second-longest stint in that office in American history. But despite his years of service and his widely acknowledged skills in managing the affairs of the State Department, he left the U.S. government as a deeply controversial figure whose name triggered strong negative reactions in many Americans. "Inevitably, he will be remembered as the man who defended the long and unpopular war in Vietnam," wrote Warren Cohen in *Dean Rusk*.

In 1970 Rusk joined the faculty of the University of Georgia at Athens, where he taught international law for more than two decades. He also reconciled with his son Richard, and the two worked together to produce Rusk's memoir *As I Saw It* (1990). In this memoir and in other remarks, Rusk remained steadfast in his belief that American military intervention in Vietnam was just and necessary. "I have not apologized from my role in Vietnam," he wrote in *As I Saw It*, "for the simple reason that I believe in the principles that underlay our commitment to South Vietnam and why we fought that war."

Sources

Cohen, Warren I. *Dean Rusk*. Totowa, NJ: Cooper Square, 1980.

Halberstam, David. *The Best and the Brightest*. New York: Random House, 1972.

Johnson, Lyndon B. *The Vantage Point: Perspectives of the Presidency, 1963–1969*. New York: Holt, Rinehart and Winston, 1971.

Rusk, Dean, as told to Richard Rusk. *As I Saw It*. New York: W. W. Norton, 1990.

Schoenbaum, Thomas J. *Waging Peace and War: Dean Rusk in the Truman, Kennedy, and Johnson Years*. New York: Simon and Schuster, 1988.

Jan Scruggs

Born in 1950
Bowie, Maryland

American Vietnam War veteran; cofounder of Vietnam Veterans Memorial Fund

Vietnam veteran Jan C. Scruggs is the person most responsible for the creation of the Vietnam Veterans Memorial, a Washington, D.C., monument that pays tribute to the 58,000 American men and women who died in the Vietnam War. Scruggs's efforts to build the memorial began in 1979, when he established the Vietnam Veterans Memorial Fund. Over the next three years, he and other dedicated volunteers worked tirelessly to see their vision become a reality. During this time they encountered several major obstacles, ranging from financial difficulties to controversy over the proposed memorial design. But Scruggs and his allies persevered, and in 1982 the Vietnam Veterans Memorial was formally dedicated.

Goes to Vietnam

Jan Scruggs was born in 1950 in the small town of Bowie, Maryland. He was the youngest of four children. His father, James, was a milkman, while his mother, Louise, worked as a waitress. He graduated from high school in 1968, at the height of American involvement in the Vietnam War.

"The Vietnam Veterans Memorial is conceived as a means to promote the healing and reconciliation of the country after the divisions caused by the war."

Bob Doubek, VVMF cofounder.

Jan Scruggs.
Reproduced by permission of Corbis Corporation.

This war pitted the United States and South Vietnam against the Communist nation of North Vietnam and Communist guerrillas—known as the Viet Cong—who lived in the South. The Communists wanted to overthrow South Vietnam's leaders and unite the two countries under one Communist government. But the United States strongly opposed these efforts, and during the mid-1950s the United States began sending money, weapons, and advisors to South Vietnam to help the country defend itself. In 1965 the United States escalated its involvement in the Vietnam War, sending thousands of American combat troops into the South and executing hundreds of air raids against Communist targets. But deepening U.S. involvement in the war failed to defeat the joint Viet Cong-North Vietnamese forces. Instead, the war settled into a bloody stalemate that eventually claimed the lives of more than 58,000 U.S. soldiers and caused bitter divisions across America. The United States finally withdrew from the Vietnam War in 1973. Two years later, Communist forces captured the South Vietnamese capital of Saigon to bring the war to a close.

When Scruggs earned his high school diploma, he decided to enlist in the U.S. Army. He believed that it was his patriotic duty to serve his country when it was at war. He completed basic training and was transferred to Vietnam, where he joined a combat infantry unit. Scruggs was one of only a handful of soldiers in his unit who had voluntarily joined the military. In fact, he estimates that 90 percent of his company was made up of draftees (men who were selected by the government for required military service).

Scruggs spent the next year in the jungles and mountains of Vietnam. The experience was a frightening and miserable one for him. "The massive protests against the war by then did little to help sagging morale," Scruggs recalled in the *Washington Post*. "Yet if the war was unpopular at home, it was probably liked even less by those whose fate it was to serve in Vietnam. It was a year-long nightmare. Half the men in my company were killed or wounded." Scruggs himself was wounded in action in 1969 by shrapnel from a rocket-propelled grenade attack.

As the months passed, though, Scruggs developed a deep respect and appreciation for his fellow soldiers. He also witnessed many acts of bravery, including one example of

heroic sacrifice that he would never forget. "Several months before leaving Vietnam I spent four hours of my life fifty feet from a North Vietnamese machine gun emplacement," he said in the *Washington Post*. "A dozen American youths were pinned down; several were wounded. We were able to retreat as one fellow exposed himself to the enemy gunners and drew their fire. He held his own for the few crucial minutes needed [so that we could] retreat with our wounded. Then came his screams. . . . We knew we were watching the man who had given his life for us die a horrible, excruciating death. We also knew he had a wife in Pennsylvania."

When Scruggs returned home in March 1970, his wartime experiences had made him an angry and disillusioned man. "The bitterness I feel when I remember carrying the lifeless bodies of close friends through the mire [deep, muddy ground] of Vietnam will probably never subside," he later wrote. This bitterness became even stronger when he realized that America did not seem to care about the men who served in Vietnam. Instead, the entire country seemed to regard the returning veterans as unpleasant reminders of a troubled period in American history. This attitude made Scruggs and thousands of other veterans feel forgotten and ignored.

At first, Scruggs had difficulty putting the war behind him and adjusting to life back in the United States. He spent the better part of a year drinking heavily and wandering aimlessly around the country. As time passed, however, he stopped his self-destructive behavior. In 1974 he married a young woman named Becky Fishman. He also returned to school, eventually earning a master's degree in education from American University in Washington, D.C. By the late 1970s, he was working in the U.S. Labor Department as a specialist in race and gender hiring issues.

Vietnam film sparks interest in building memorial

In March 1979 Scruggs saw *The Deer Hunter,* a film about the Vietnam War and the young American soldiers who fought in it. As Scruggs watched the movie, its storyline and imagery rekindled a flood of memories about the war and the men with whom he served. It also reminded him that the

United States had never expressed any meaningful thanks to the men and women who served their country during the Vietnam War. Scruggs decided that he wanted to try to correct that injustice. The next morning, he turned to his wife and announced, "I'm going to build a memorial to all the guys who served in Vietnam. It'll have the names of everyone who was killed."

A short time later, Scruggs began publicizing his concept of a monument that would honor the 58,000 Americans who were killed in Vietnam. His activities quickly attracted the attention of fellow Vietnam veterans Jack Wheeler and Bob Doubek, who shared his dream of creating a memorial to the nation's forgotten Vietnam soldiers. Together, the three men established a Vietnam Veterans Memorial Fund (VVMF) to raise the millions of dollars that would be needed to pay for the monument.

At first the organization had trouble getting started. Early fund-raising efforts were disappointing, and a comedian on national television made fun of Scruggs' vision of a memorial. Some critics even charged that the VVMF leaders were self-centered people who wanted to build a monument to themselves. But when Scruggs heard this complaint, he always replied that if America's Vietnam veterans waited around for someone else to honor their service, a monument would never be built.

Finally, some Americans who had actively opposed the war in the 1960s and early 1970s criticized the memorial idea. They claimed that the monument would honor U.S. involvement in an immoral war. But Scruggs and other VVMF officials emphasized that the monument would not make any political statements about American involvement in the war; it would simply pay tribute to Americans who were killed. "The Vietnam Veterans Memorial is conceived as a means to promote the healing and reconciliation of the country after the divisions caused by the war," explained Doubek.

Momentum builds for memorial

As the months passed, the efforts of hundreds of VVMF volunteers finally began to pay off. Boosted by the public support of such figures as First Lady Rosalynn Carter, former President Gerald Ford, antiwar Senator George McGovern (see entry), Vietnam General William Westmoreland (see entry), and entertainer Bob Hope, VVMF fund-raising appeals garnered responses from around the country. The VVMF gathered more than $8 million from more than 650,000 private donors in the early 1980s. The federal government did not contribute any money to the memorial fund. But it did set aside a two-acre section of land for the memorial in Washington, D.C.'s Constitutional Gardens, between the Washington Monument and the Lincoln Memorial.

In May 1981 the VVMF unveiled its proposed design for the monument. Created by a twenty-one-year-old Chinese-American art student named Maya Lin (see entry), the design featured a long, V-shaped wall of polished black granite that would be engraved with the names of American soldiers killed or missing-in-action in Vietnam. Much of the reaction to the design was positive. Several veterans' organizations—including the powerful Veterans of Foreign Wars (VFW) and the American Gold Star Mothers, half of whose membership had lost sons in Vietnam—declared their support for the design. Press reaction also was favorable. The *New York Times* stated that "[the design] honors these veterans with more poignancy, surely, than . . . more conventional monuments. . . . This design seems able to capture all of the feelings of ambiguity and anguish that the Vietnam War evoked in this nation."

But Lin's design attracted harsh criticism from other people. In *To Heal a Nation,* Scruggs and Joel Swerdlow admitted that some Vietnam veterans and other observers viewed the design as "unheroic, unpatriotic, below ground, and death-oriented." A bitter debate soon flared within America's veteran community over the proposed memorial, and before long the entire project seemed to be in jeopardy. This controversy angered and saddened Scruggs and the other VVMF volunteers, who had devoted countless hours to making the memorial a reality. The VVMF tried to address the concerns of the design's critics, but they failed to ease doubts about the project. "VVMF reassurances that the memorial would be exposed to sunlight all day, and that the names as displayed in Maya Lin's design would speak eloquently of sacrifice, commitment, and patriotism, never attracted as much attention as the attacks," wrote Scruggs and Swerdlow.

Support for "the Wall"

In 1981 the proposed design for the Vietnam Veterans Memorial was attacked by critics who felt that it failed to honor the American men and women who died in Vietnam. But many other observers, including veterans' groups and newspaper editors, defended Maya Lin's design. Following is an excerpt from a *New York Times* editorial that expressed support for the proposed monument:

> It used to be much simpler to build a monument. The roll of honor on bronze tablets, or the statue of the fallen warrior holding a flag appeared predictably on the village green. Anonymous generals and unknown soldiers furnish innumerable traffic islands. Forgotten heroes dot the nation's parks. The uniform changes, the heroes sit or stand or occasionally ride a horse, but the message remains the same: a noble cause well served.
>
> Nowadays, though, patriotism is a complicated matter. Ideas about heroism, or art, for that matter, are no longer what they were before Vietnam. And there is certainly no consensus yet about what cause might have been served by the Vietnam War.
>
> But perhaps that is why the V-shaped, black granite lines merging gently with the sloping earth make the winning design seem a lasting and appropriate image of dignity and sadness. It conveys the only point about the war on which people may agree: that those who died should be remembered.

Finally, after months of debate, the two sides agreed on a compromise that permitted construction of the memorial to go forward. Under the terms of this agreement, a statue of three young American soldiers and an American flag would be added to the two-acre plot near Lin's memorial. Construction of the memorial finally began in March 1982. Seven months later, it was ready to be presented to the American public.

The Vietnam Veterans Memorial

The Vietnam Veterans Memorial was formally dedicated on Veterans' Day weekend in November 1982 in front of a crowd that numbered in the thousands. The memorial features two tall walls set in the ground, each nearly 250 feet long, that meet at a V-shaped angle. Constructed of polished black granite, the walls have mirror-like surfaces that reflect the sky, the trees, and the faces of the men, women, and children who stand before them. On these walls, the names of more than 58,000 American soldiers who were lost in Vietnam are engraved.

Public reaction to the memorial—which soon became known simply as "the Wall"— was overwhelmingly positive. During the dedication weekend, Vietnam veterans, their families, and relatives of the men and women who were honored on the Wall all praised it as a touching and powerful tribute to their lost friends and loved ones. As more and more people went to see the memorial for themselves, the controversy over Lin's design quickly faded. Within months, the Wall became one of the most treasured sites in all of the United States.

Today, the Vietnam Veterans Memorial continues to be regarded as one of America's most beautiful and emotionally powerful monuments. It is also the most visited site in Washington, D.C., with an estimated 2.5 million visitors each year. And the memorial continues to be updated as U.S. casualty lists from the war are corrected (the Wall contained the names of 58,209 Americans who served in Vietnam as of Memorial Day 1997). Scruggs, meanwhile, continues to serve as president of the VVMF. The organization helps provide care for the Wall and coordinates activities and ceremonies on the monument grounds.

Sources

Hass, Kristin Ann. *Carried to the Wall: American Memory and the Vietnam Veterans Memorial.* Berkeley: University of California Press, 1998.

Isaacs, Arnold R. *Vietnam Shadows: The War, Its Ghosts, and Its Legacy.* Baltimore: Johns Hopkins University Press, 1997.

Katakis, Michael. *The Vietnam Veterans Memorial.* New York: Crown, 1988.

Scruggs, Jan C., ed. *Why Vietnam Still Matters: The War and the Wall.* Vietnam Veterans Memorial Fund, 1996.

Scruggs, Jan C., and Joel L. Swerdlow. *To Heal a Nation: The Vietnam Veterans Memorial.* New York: Harper and Row, 1985.

Vespa, Mary. "His Dream was to Heal a Nation with the Vietnam Memorial, but Healing Isn't over Yet." *People Weekly,* May 30, 1988.

Neil Sheehan

Born October 27, 1936
Holyoke, Massachusetts

American journalist

N eil Sheehan's career in journalism has been closely linked with the Vietnam War for nearly four decades. In the early and mid-1960s he provided acclaimed coverage of the conflict in Vietnam for United Press International and the *New York Times*. In 1971 he helped publish the so-called *Pentagon Papers,* a secret government history of the war. And in 1988 he published *A Bright Shining Lie: John Paul Vann and America in Vietnam*. This book, which took Sheehan sixteen years to complete, is regarded as one of the finest nonfiction works ever written about the Vietnam War.

A promising young journalist

Cornelius Mahoney "Neil" Sheehan was born in Holyoke, Massachusetts, on October 27, 1936. His parents were Cornelius Joseph and Mary (O'Shea) Sheehan, Irish immigrants who established a farm after resettling in America.

Sheehan was a bright youth who distinguished himself in academics. He earned a scholarship to attend Harvard University, graduating from the school with a degree in Mid-

Neil Sheehan.
Reproduced by permission of Corbis Corporation.

dle Eastern history in 1958. After school he entered the U.S. Army, working as a military reporter from 1959 to 1962 in Korea and Japan. He proved himself as a reporter during this period of military service, and when he left the army in 1962, the United Press International (UPI) news service promptly offered him a job.

UPI assigned Sheehan to Saigon in order to cover events in Vietnam, where America had become involved in a growing war. This war pitted the U.S.-supported nation of South Vietnam against the Communist nation of North Vietnam and its guerrilla allies (known as Viet Cong) in the South. The Viet Cong and North Vietnamese wanted to overthrow the South Vietnamese government and unite the two countries under one Communist government. But the United States stepped in to defend the South. U.S. leaders worried that if South Vietnam fell, other Southeast Asian nations might also turn to Communism. They knew that such a development would strengthen the Communist empire of the Soviet Union, America's great political and military rival of the era.

At first, Sheehan struggled with his new responsibilities and Vietnam's unfamiliar culture. As the months passed, however, Sheehan settled down and developed into an excellent reporter. "He arrived [in Vietnam] as the rawest of rookies and made all the raw-rookie mistakes," wrote William Prochnau in *Once Upon a Distant War*. "He also became one of the best correspondents ever to set foot in Vietnam, becoming a legendary figure himself."

When Sheehan arrived in South Vietnam in April 1962, the United States had already committed great amounts of money, weaponry, and military assistance to South Vietnam. He and the handful of other American reporters stationed in Saigon during this time supported the U.S. decision to defend the South. As Sheehan recalled in *A Bright Shining Lie*, "we shared the [American military] advisors' sense of commitment to this war. We regarded the conflict as our war too."

Covering the war

But as time passed, Sheehan and other reporters covering the war expressed growing concern about the situation in South Vietnam. Their observations convinced them that South

Vietnam's political and military leadership was very poor. In addition, the journalists discovered that American officials often tried to deceive them about the outcomes of battles and other aspects of the war.

As a result, Sheehan and other journalists made special efforts to learn about the true nature of things in Vietnam. They often risked their lives in pursuing news stories. Sheehan and other reporters often made helicopter trips into enemy territory or accompanied troops into battle. After a while, Sheehan became convinced that he was going to die in Vietnam, but he did not change his reporting methods.

The reporters also developed a network of American and Vietnamese information sources who were willing to provide honest assessments of the war. The most valuable of these secret sources was John Paul Vann, an American colonel who later became one of the most powerful U.S. officials in Vietnam. "Vann taught us the most, and one can truly say that without him our reporting would not have been the same," Sheehan wrote in *A Bright Shining Lie.* "He gave us an expertise we lacked. . . . He enabled us to attack the official optimism with gradual but steadily increasing detail and thoroughness."

When Sheehan and other correspondents realized that South Vietnam and its U.S. allies were actually making little progress in the war, their reports became more critical. Their coverage angered and embarrassed American military and political leaders. Some officials responded by accusing Sheehan and other journalists of exaggerating problems. A number of officials even suggested that the American reporters were betraying their country. But Sheehan dismissed such charges. In fact, he considered himself to be a patriot for telling the truth about the war to the American people.

Sheehan and the *Pentagon Papers*

In 1964 Sheehan left UPI to join the *New York Times.* He spent another year covering the war in Vietnam, then returned to the United States. In the late 1960s he served as the newspaper's chief White House and Pentagon correspondent. At the same time, he and wife Susan Sheehan, a writer, began to raise a family (they eventually had two daughters).

By 1971 Sheehan had become a strong critic of the war in Vietnam. In fact, he expressed great anger at America's military and political leadership, claiming that wartime policies were wasting tens of thousands of American and Vietnamese lives. Sheehan's changing perspective on Vietnam caught the attention of Daniel Ellsberg (see entry), a former top-level military analyst who had turned against the war. In February 1971 Ellsberg secretly delivered a copy of the *Pentagon Papers* to Sheehan. This massive collection of confidential government reports and documents showed that U.S. political leaders had repeatedly deceived both the American public and themselves about the war in Vietnam over the previous two decades.

Sheehan and other *New York Times* reporters spent months reviewing the documents to verify their accuracy and importance. On June 13, 1971, the *New York Times* published the first excerpts from the *Papers*. The publication of the documents caused a tremendous uproar across the United States. Members of the antiwar movement claimed that the *Pentagon Papers* proved that the U.S. government could not be trusted to tell the truth about the war in Vietnam. President Richard Nixon (see entry) and his administration, meanwhile, tried to prevent the *Times* from publishing any more excerpts. Nixon worried that their publication would make it harder for him to carry out his own Vietnam policies. But on June 30, 1971, the U.S. Supreme Court ruled that the *Times* and other papers had the constitutional right to publish the documents. A year later, all forty-seven volumes of the *Pentagon Papers* were published and made available to the American people.

The fight over the *Pentagon Papers* took a heavy toll on Sheehan. His honesty and patriotism were questioned, his family and friends were interviewed by federal investigators, and he was threatened with a variety of criminal charges, including theft of government property and violations of the federal Espionage Act. But the threat of criminal prosecution faded after the Supreme Court issued its June 30 ruling. In the meantime, the controversy increased his reputation as one of the country's best journalists. In 1971 he received the Drew Pearson Prize for excellence in investigative reporting. One year later, the *New York Times* received the prestigious Pulitzer Prize for publishing the *Pentagon Papers*.

Writing about John Paul Vann and Vietnam

In June 1972 John Paul Vann died in a helicopter crash in Vietnam. After Sheehan attended Vann's funeral, he decided

John Paul Vann (1924–1972)

John Paul Vann first served in Vietnam in 1962 as a military advisor to the South Vietnamese Army (ARVN). Vann was bright, brave, and devoted to the cause of defending the South from Communist forces. As time passed, however, he became very frustrated with South Vietnam's political and military leadership, which he viewed as incompetent and corrupt. Vann also emerged as an early critic of U.S. military policy in the war. But Sheehan noted in *A Bright Shining Lie* that "Vann . . . never ceased to believe that the war could be won if it was fought with sound tactics and strategy." By 1963 Vann was frequently offering his blunt opinions about the conflict to American journalists assigned to Vietnam.

Vann retired from the U.S. Army as a lieutenant colonel in 1963. Many observers believed that he resigned because of clashes with superior officers over his independent ways. But another factor was a statutory rape charge (a charge of having sex with a minor) that ruined his chances for career advancement in the military. In 1965, though, Vann returned to Vietnam as a high-ranking civilian (non-military person) with the Agency for International Development (AID).

Over the next five years, Vann's energy, grit, and dedication made him "one of the legendary Americans in Vietnam," observed the *Washington Post*. In May 1971 he was given authority over all U.S. military forces in central Vietnam, even though he was still a civilian. Some people who knew Vann claimed that he became much more ruthless and callous in his military tactics and attitudes during this time. In June 1972 Vann died in a helicopter crash in a remote valley in Vietnam.

to write a biography of the man. Sheehan believed that by examining Vann's life, he might also be able to shed some light on the entire war and America's role in it.

Sheehan began writing the biography of Vann in 1972. At first, he anticipated that the book would take three or four years to write. But the project ended up taking sixteen years, as the author struggled with physical ailments, financial problems, and his own disturbing memories of Vietnam. Sheehan's determination to tell Vann's story became an obsession, and as the years passed, friends and family members expressed concern about the author's physical and emotional well-being. Eventually, "the ordeal of [writing the book] became a legend that surpassed the legend of John Paul Vann," observed Prochnau.

In 1988 Sheehan's biography of Vann was finally published. The book, *A Bright Shining Lie: John Paul Vann and America in Vietnam,* received a tremendous critical and popular response. It became a national bestseller, and critics praised it as one of the finest books ever written about the Vietnam War. *New Republic* reviewer Richard Holbrooke—who served in the U.S. embassy in Vietnam and eventually became U.S. ambassador to the United Nations—wrote that "Sheehan has produced a book of vast ambition and scope that tells the entire story of the American tragedy in Vietnam through Vann's life and death." *Washington Monthly* critic Taylor Branch offered similar praise. He wrote that "by capturing within the life of one small obsessive daredevil the essence of something so vast and benumbing as Vietnam, Sheehan has written by far the best single account of the war." Sheehan's book eventually received numerous prestigious awards, including the 1988 Pulitzer Prize for nonfiction, the 1988 National Book Award for nonfiction, and the Robert F. Kennedy Award.

Looking back on Vietnam

The completion of *A Bright Shining Lie* enabled Sheehan to put some emotional distance between himself and his memories of the Vietnam War. But he continued to express bitterness about American involvement in the conflict. "In Vietnam, our political and military leaders simply could not conceive the possibility that we could lose," Sheehan stated in a 1988 *Publishers Weekly* interview. "Successive administrations deluded themselves into the fantasy that we could somehow perpetuate an American presence in the country. The American soldier became a victim of his own leadership, which is a bitter lesson to face."

Since the publication of *A Bright Shining Lie,* Sheehan has continued to devote his energies to writing. In 1992 he published another book about Vietnam, called *After the War Was Over: Hanoi and Saigon.* In 1995 he began researching and writing a history of the Cold War, the decades-long political and military rivalry between the United States and the Soviet Union. He also made a number of visits to Vietnam during the 1990s, including one with his two daughters.

Sources

Galles, Walter. "Publishers Weekly Interview." *Publishers Weekly,* September 2, 1988.

Holbrooke, Richard. "Front Man." *New Republic,* October 24, 1988.

Prochnau, William. *Once Upon a Distant War: David Halberstam, Neil Sheehan, Peter Arnett—Young War Correspondents and Their Early Vietnam Battles.* New York: Times Books, 1995.

Sheehan, Neil. *A Bright Shining Lie: John Paul Vann and America in Vietnam.* New York: Random House, 1988.

Sheehan, Neil. "Vietnam, and the Battle for Reality." *U.S. News & World Report,* October 24, 1988.

Wyatt, Clarence. *Paper Soldiers: The American Press and the Vietnam War.* New York: W. W. Norton, 1993.

Norodom Sihanouk

Born October 31, 1922
Phnom Penh, Cambodia

Cambodian monarch and political leader

N orodom Sihanouk has been an important figure in Cambodia through six decades of war and political instability. He first became the king of Cambodia in 1941, when his country was a colony of France. After participating in the movement to gain Cambodia's independence from French rule, he stepped down from the throne to become president in 1955. Over the next fifteen years, Sihanouk struggled to maintain his country's neutrality as war raged in neighboring Vietnam. During this time, a group of Communist revolutionaries known as the Khmer Rouge emerged to oppose his rule.

In 1970 Sihanouk was removed from power by his prime minister, Lon Nol (see entry). He then went into exile in China and joined forces with his former enemies, the Khmer Rouge. He became the symbolic head of state when the brutal Khmer Rouge took control of Cambodia in 1975, but returned to exile when Cambodia was conquered by Vietnam four years later. In 1993 the still-popular Sihanouk returned to the Cambodian government following United Nations-sponsored elections.

After many years in exile, Sihanouk remained popular among the Cambodian people. Many citizens considered him the "father of the nation."

Norodom Sihanouk.
Courtesy of the Library of Congress.

A member of Cambodia's royal family

Norodom Sihanouk was born on October 31, 1922, in Phnom Penh, the capital city of Cambodia. As the oldest of four children born to Prince Norodom Suramarit and Princess Monivong Kossamak, he came from a royal family that had ruled Cambodia for a more than a century. Sihanouk was educated in French schools in Saigon, Vietnam. He was also trained in music by his parents and eventually became quite skilled at playing the saxophone.

Throughout Sihanouk's early life, Cambodia—like its neighbor Vietnam—was a colony of France. In 1941 the French colonial government asked Sihanouk to become king of Cambodia. At this time, Sihanouk was eighteen years old and in his last year of school. French officials selected him to lead the colony because they thought he would be easy to control. A short time later, however, France suffered a series of defeats during World War II and surrendered to Germany. Unable to protect its colonies in Indochina, the French allowed Japan to occupy Cambodia and set up military bases there.

In 1945 the Allied forces (led by the United States, Great Britain, and the Soviet Union) defeated both Germany and Japan to win World War II (1939–45). As the Japanese pulled out of Indochina, Sihanouk took advantage of the situation to declare Cambodia's independence. But it soon became clear that France was not willing to give up its former colonies. In Vietnam, a group of Communist-led Vietnamese nationalists known as the Viet Minh began fighting the French to gain their country's independence. In the meantime, Sihanouk reached an uneasy agreement with French officials that prevented war in his country. But he eventually realized that achieving Cambodia's true independence was a key factor in his own power and popularity. In 1953 the king traveled to France to demand self-government for his country. When the French refused, Sihanouk went into exile in Thailand as a form of protest.

In 1954 the Viet Minh defeated the French after nine years of war. The agreement that ended this war divided Vietnam into two sections, Communist-led North Vietnam and U.S.-supported South Vietnam. At the same time, France granted independence to all of its colonies in Indochina, including Cambodia. Sihanouk immediately returned home.

Determined to play an active role in leading his newly independent country, he gave up his throne in order to run for elected office. Sihanouk was elected president of Cambodia in 1955, while members of his political party won all the seats in the National Assembly. This meant that Sihanouk effectively controlled the Cambodian government, even though he was no longer king. He was particularly popular among peasants, who viewed him as a beloved symbol of the country, but he was less well-liked among educated citizens and Communists.

Remains neutral during the Vietnam War

During his early years in office, Sihanouk accepted military and economic aid from the United States. He also took steps to modernize Cambodia's agricultural economy. But as time passed, Cambodia became threatened by a new war that had broken out in Vietnam. This war pitted North Vietnam and its secret allies, the South Vietnamese Communists known as the Viet Cong, against South Vietnam. North Vietnam wanted to overthrow the South Vietnamese government and reunite the two countries under one Communist government. But U.S. government officials worried that a Communist government in Vietnam would encourage other countries in Indochina to adopt communism. They felt that this would increase the power of Communist China and the Soviet Union and threaten the security of the United States.

In the late 1950s and early 1960s the U.S. government sent money, weapons, and military advisors to help South Vietnam defend itself against North Vietnam and the Viet Cong. Sihanouk declared that Cambodia would remain neutral, or refuse to take sides, in the conflict. In 1965 President Lyndon Johnson (see entry) sent American combat troops to join the fight on the side of South Vietnam. At this point, Sihanouk began to worry that increased U.S. involvement would expand the war into Cambodia. He decided to cut off diplomatic ties with the United States. Before long, Sihanouk's fears came true. The intense fighting with American troops encouraged the Viet Cong and North Vietnamese forces to move their base of operations across the border into eastern Cambodia.

Still determined to stay out of the war, Sihanouk reluctantly allowed the Communist forces to enter his country. As the Vietnam War progressed, the jungles of Cambodia became an important base for Vietnamese Communist activity. Many of North Vietnam's main supply routes and military roads—including the famous Ho Chi Minh Trail—ran through eastern Cambodia. In addition, many Viet Cong and North Vietnamese Army (NVA) units used the thick forests of Cambodia for secret bases in their war against the South.

By the late 1960s the war in Vietnam had caused severe economic hardship and growing political unrest in Cambodia. A group of Cambodian Communists known as the Khmer Rouge, under the command of a mysterious man named Pol Pot (see entry), began plotting an armed revolution against Sihanouk's government. North Vietnam provided significant assistance to the Khmer Rouge rebels. To increase his hold on power, Sihanouk reorganized the government and made his trusted advisor Lon Nol the prime minister. Together, they began working to remove the Vietnamese Communists from Cambodia.

In 1969 Sihanouk reestablished ties with the United States and allowed American forces to begin bombing Viet Cong and North Vietnamese bases along the border. But the bombing only pushed the Vietnamese Communists deeper into Cambodian territory. In addition, it caused suffering among the Cambodian people and convinced thousands of peasants that the government could not protect them. Many of these people turned their support to the Khmer Rouge. Lon Nol urged Sihanouk to increase the size of the Cambodian army in order to fight the North Vietnamese and crush the Khmer Rouge rebellion, but Sihanouk refused. He believed that such actions would only draw Cambodia deeper into the Vietnam War.

Sihanouk is removed from power

In March 1970 Sihanouk visited France. During his absence, a group of Cambodian leaders who were unhappy with his government made plans to overthrow him. Prime Minister Lon Nol and Deputy Prime Minister Sisowath Sirik Matak were among those involved in the plan. The Cambodian National Assembly voted to remove Sihanouk from power and make Lon Nol the new head of the government. Knowing that Lon Nol wanted to force the Vietnamese Communists out of Cambodia, U.S. officials backed him as the country's new leader. Sihanouk viewed the American support for Lon Nol as a betrayal. In fact, he claimed that the U.S. Central Intelligence Agency (CIA) had helped his enemies remove him from power.

After losing control of the government, Sihanouk moved to China, where he met with Vietnamese and Cambodian Communist leaders. He proclaimed himself the leader of Cambodia's "government in exile." He also agreed to join forces with his former enemies, the Khmer Rouge, in their efforts to overthrow Lon Nol's government. Over the next few years, the Khmer Rouge continued to gather support from people who were upset over the country's involvement in the Vietnam War. With Sihanouk's support, the rebel group emerged as a legitimate political alternative to Lon Nol. The Khmer Rouge increased its size and strength and managed to defeat the Cambodian military in a series of battles. Lon Nol's hold on power only grew weaker when the U.S. government withdrew its troops from Indochina in 1973.

Finally, on April 17, 1975, the Khmer Rouge captured Phnom Penh and took control of Cambodia. The Communists named Sihanouk as the symbolic leader of the country, although he held no real power. Two weeks later, North Vietnamese forces captured the South Vietnamese capital of Saigon to win the Vietnam War.

Immediately after taking power, the Khmer Rouge launched a brutal program designed to transform Cambodia into a simple farming society. As part of this transformation, the Khmer Rouge murdered hundreds of thousands of Cambodian citizens in an effort to rid the country of "intellectuals" who opposed their rule. Historians estimate that as many as two million Cambodians—or one-fourth of the overall population—died under the Khmer Rouge.

During this time, Cambodia was still involved in disputes with Vietnam over national borders and leadership of Indochina. In December 1978 the Vietnamese government sent troops into Cambodia to overthrow the Khmer Rouge. By January 1979 Vietnam's invasion forces had captured Phnom Penh. They immediately put an end to the brutal policies of the Khmer Rouge. At this time, Sihanouk appealed to the Vietnamese to allow him to form a coalition government in Cambodia. Instead, the occupation forces established a new pro-Vietnamese government under Prime Minister Hun Sen. When his efforts failed, Sihanouk returned to China and formed another government in exile that included Khmer Rouge representatives.

Even though the Vietnamese invasion of Cambodia had removed the violent Khmer Rouge from power, many countries around the world criticized Vietnam's actions. The United States and other countries formed an economic embargo to punish Vietnam. The U.S. government also provided support to Cambodian rebels fighting against the Hun Sen government, including the Khmer Rouge. Finally, both the United States and the United Nations formally recognized Sihanouk's coalition government as the legitimate rulers of Cambodia.

Returns to lead Cambodia

Despite the international reaction, Vietnam continued its occupation of Cambodia for ten years before withdrawing its forces in 1989. At this time, the United Nations stepped in to negotiate a settlement between the Khmer Rouge rebels and various other political parties. The UN arranged for national elections to choose a democratic government for Cambodia. Realizing that he would never win an election, Hun Sen agreed to turn over power to Sihanouk in 1991. After many years in exile, Sihanouk remained popular among the Cambodian people. In fact, many citizens considered him the "father of the nation."

After being named president once again in 1991, Sihanouk turned against the Khmer Rouge. He criticized the rebel group's leaders and said that they should be put on trial for war crimes. The Khmer Rouge gradually became a fringe movement and split into competing factions. In the UN-sponsored elections of 1993 Sihanouk's political party formally took control of the government. In September of that year Sihanouk was once again crowned king of Cambodia. He turned the everyday duties of running the country over to his two prime ministers, his son Norodom Ranariddh and former president Hun Sen. In 1997, however, fighting broke out between rival political factions that were loyal to the two prime ministers. Hun Sen managed to remove Norodom

Ranariddh from power that July. Since then, Sihanouk has held little formal political power in Cambodia. In 1999 he announced that he would soon step down from the throne due to failing health.

Throughout his leadership of Cambodia, Sihanouk became known for his unusual behavior. For example, as an amateur film-maker and songwriter, he sometimes handed out cassettes of his songs at United Nations meetings or made international advisors watch his feature films. He has also been known to consult astrologers before making important decisions and to suddenly become ill in times of crisis. Still, he remains popular among the Cambodian people.

Sources

Armstrong, John P. *Sihanouk Speaks*. New York: Walker, 1965.

Encyclopedia of World Biography. Detroit: Gale, 1998.

Kamm, Henry. *Cambodia: Report from a Stricken Land*. New York: Arcade Publishing, 1998.

Osborne, Milton E. *Sihanouk: Prince of Light, Prince of Darkness*. University of Hawaii Press, 1994.

Sihanouk, Norodom, with Wilfred Burchett. *My War with the CIA: The Memoirs of Prince Norodom Sihanouk*. New York: Pantheon, 1973.

Souvanna Phouma

Born October 7, 1901
Luang Prabang, Laos
Died January 1984
Laos

Prime Minister of Laos, 1951–1975

Souvanna Phouma.
Courtesy of the Library of Congress.

P rime Minister Souvanna Phouma led the nation of Laos for a total of twenty years, including the period from 1962 to 1975. During that time, the war in neighboring Vietnam repeatedly threatened to spill over into Laos. Souvanna tried to maintain a neutral position on the war, even as Communist rebels threatened his own nation. But Souvanna's efforts to remain neutral faltered in the early 1970s, when he approved massive U.S. bombing and reconnaissance missions against Communist forces in eastern Laos. In 1975 Communist forces seized control of Laos, and Souvanna's rule came to an end.

Member of the Laotian royal family

Souvanna Phouma was born October 7, 1901, into a family whose ancestors had ruled Laos for hundreds of years. During the late nineteenth century, however, France had taken control of Laos and the neighboring countries of Vietnam and Cambodia and combined them into one vast colonial holding known as French Indochina.

As a member of the Laotian royal family, Souvanna received a fine education in Vietnam and France. After earning an engineering degree, he returned home and secured a job in the Laotian government. During World War II (1939–45), Japanese forces rolled into French Indochina and seized control of the region. When Japan was defeated in 1945, it was forced to withdraw from the region. Nonetheless, France's longtime hold over the region was loosened.

In 1947 France gave Laos limited independence. Souvanna was given important responsibilities at this time. He served as minister of public transport, minister of planning, and minister of postal service and telegraphs over the next few years. In 1951 he was named prime minister of Laos. Two years later France granted the country full independence from colonial rule in a treaty that Souvanna helped negotiate.

As soon as France relinquished its claim on Laos, however, several Laotian political organizations clashed in a fierce struggle for power. The most prominent of these groups were the Pathet Lao (Lao Nation), a Communist movement that received support from Communist forces in Vietnam, and the Royal Lao, a non-Communist government supported by France. This battle for power temporarily knocked Souvanna out of power. But in 1956 he allied himself with the Pathet Lao rebels and regained his place as prime minister.

Turmoil in Laos

Upon returning to power, Souvanna tried to end the unrest that had rocked Laos over the previous years. But his uneasy relationship with the Pathet Lao crumbled again in 1958. At that time, both Laotian groups and influential outside forces like the United States objected to the presence of Communists in the government. When they pressured Souvanna to take a stronger anti-Communist stand, the Pathet Lao quit the coalition government and resumed their rebellion with the help of North Vietnam. Without the support of the Pathet Lao—whose leadership included Souvanna's younger half-brother, Prince Souphanouvong—Souvanna fell from power once again.

Laos continued to be rocked by political turmoil over the next few years, as various groups jockeyed for power. In 1962 Souvanna managed to put together another political coalition that restored him to his spot at the top of the nation's government and ended the fighting. This coalition included the Pathet Lao, but within a year the rebels quit the government and took up arms again in hopes of installing a Communist regime. As before, they were aided in their efforts by the Communist leaderships of North Vietnam and the Soviet Union.

Adopts neutral policy toward Vietnam War

When the Pathet Lao resumed hostilities in 1963, Souvanna Phouma turned to the United States for help. U.S. leaders responded by sending military and financial aid to the Laotian government. This aid was made secretly, however, because America leaders had previously promised to stay out of Laos's affairs. The United States' efforts to aid anti-Communist forces in Laos without being detected eventually became known as the "Secret War in Laos."

As Souvanna worked to beat the Communists and bring peace to his country, he also adopted a policy of neutrality toward the growing war in neighboring Vietnam. This conflict began in the mid-1950s, when South Vietnam refused to hold elections that would have united it and North Vietnam under one government. South Vietnam's stand angered the Communist leadership of North Vietnam, which responded by launching a war against the South with the help of Southern Vietnamese Communists known as the Viet Cong. America became involved in the war when it became concerned that the Communist aggression might succeed. In fact, the United States assumed primary responsibility for much of the war effort during the mid- and late 1960s. But U.S. military intervention ultimately failed, and South Vietnam fell to the Communists in 1975.

Souvanna tried to steer Laos away from involvement in Vietnam. But this became a very difficult task in the late 1960s. The North Vietnamese Army (NVA) used eastern Laos as a base for military activity in South Vietnam. In addition, a large section of the Ho Chi Minh Trail—the North's main supply and communications route into South Vietnam—ran through Laos. These factors, combined with the continued threat of the Pathet Lao, led the United States to conduct several bombing raids over the region.

In February 1971 South Vietnamese forces supported by U.S. artillery and air power made a major incursion (raid) into Laos in order to destroy Communist bases and smash the Ho Chi Minh Trail. But as the raid progressed, the South Vietnamese forces encountered heavy resistance from tens of thousands of NVA troops. After six weeks of heavy fighting, the South Vietnamese military was forced to call a ragged retreat out of Laos.

In 1973 the United States completed its military withdrawal from the region. The loss of America's military firepower greatly weakened Souvanna's government, which still faced the threat of the Pathet Lao. With the U.S. gone, Souvanna managed to negotiate a cease fire with the Pathet Lao and establish a new coalition government. But this new regime lasted only two years.

Souvanna's government is overthrown

In 1975 the Pathet Lao Communists finally seized control of the Laotian government. They removed Souvanna from office and replaced him with a Communist regime headed by Prince Souphanouvong. The Pathet Lao then initiated a brutal campaign to eliminate potential threats to its rule. They killed thousands of Laotians who were viewed as unfriendly to communism, including many government officials, teachers, and other professionals. This murderous campaign convinced hundreds of thousands of Laotians to flee the country. Souvanna, meanwhile, was allowed to serve as an advisor to the new government. He remained in that position until his death in 1984.

Sources

Castle, Timothy N. *At War in the Shadow of Vietnam: United States Military Aid to the Royal Lao Government, 1955–1975*. New York: Columbia University Press, 1993.

Fall, Bernard B. *Anatomy of a Crisis: The Laotian Crisis of 1960–1961*. Garden City, NY: Doubleday, 1969.

Stieglitz, Perry. *In a Little Kingdom: The Tragedy of Laos, 1960–1980*. Armonk, NY: M. E. Sharpe, 1990.

Toye, Hugh. *Laos: Buffer State or Battleground*. New York: Oxford University Press, 1968.

Oliver Stone

Born September 15, 1946
New York, New York

American Vietnam War veteran; film director

Oliver Stone.
Reproduced by permission of AP/Wide World Photos.

Vietnam veteran Oliver Stone is one of America's best-known film directors. Over the course of his career, he has written and directed films on many different subjects, from the world of high finance (1987's *Wall Street*) to the assassination of President John F. Kennedy (1991's *JFK*). But he first became famous for two Vietnam War films that received tremendous critical acclaim. These movies—*Platoon* (1986) and *Born on the Fourth of July* (1989)—provided movie audiences with powerful portraits of American soldiers' experiences in Vietnam.

Raised in a world of comfort and wealth

Oliver Stone was born September 15, 1946, in New York, New York. His parents were Louis Stone, a prominent stockbroker, and Jacqueline (Goddet) Stone. As a youngster, Stone attended elite schools in New York City and Connecticut and spent his summers living in France with his maternal grandparents. When he was sixteen, however, he was shocked to learn that his parents were divorcing and that his seemingly wealthy father was actually deeply in debt. "I thought they were very contented and that I was rich and that we had it made," Stone recalled in *Rolling Stone.* The break-up of Stone's family left the teenager feeling deeply disillusioned and rebellious.

In 1964 Stone graduated from high school and enrolled at Yale University, where he began to consider a writing career. But he dropped out of school after one year to join a teaching program. After undergoing training, he was assigned to teach English at a school in the South Vietnamese capital of Saigon. He arrived in the city in late 1965, just as the United States was beginning to commit American troops to the Vietnam War.

This conflict, which pitted the U.S.-supported nation of South Vietnam against the Communist nation of North Vietnam and its Viet Cong guerrilla allies, had actually begun in the mid-1950s. At that time, Communist forces began working to take over South Vietnam and unite it with the North under one Communist government. But the United States strongly opposed their activities because of fears that a takeover might trigger Communist aggression in other parts of the world.

As a result, the United States provided military and financial aid to South Vietnam in the late 1950s and early 1960s. When the South continued to struggle, American political and military leaders decided to introduce U.S. troops in hopes of wiping out the Communist threat. But deepening U.S. involvement in the war failed to defeat the joint Viet Cong-North Vietnamese forces. Instead, the war settled into a bloody stalemate that eventually claimed the lives of more than 58,000 U.S. soldiers and caused bitter internal divisions across America.

Stone in Vietnam

Stone spent six months in Saigon before returning to the United States. After returning home, however, he developed a deep desire to participate directly in the war as a soldier. This desire was due in part to his belief that wartime experiences might help him mature as a writer. But he also attributed his feelings to romantic visions of war, manhood, and adventure.

Stone volunteered for infantry duty in Vietnam, and in September 1967 he joined a platoon that was charged with patrolling a dangerous region near the Cambodian border. As soon as he arrived, Stone recalled in *Time* magazine, "I realized . . . that I'd made a terrible mistake. It was on-the-job training: Here's your machete, kid; you cut point [lead the platoon through the jungle]. You learn if you can, and if not you're dead. Nobody was motivated, except to get out. Survival was the key. It wasn't very romantic."

During Stone's year-long tour of duty in Vietnam, he fought in several deadly battles, was wounded twice, and witnessed the war's cruelty and violence on countless occasions. By the time he returned home in late 1968, Stone was convinced that American involvement in Vietnam was a terrible and tragic mistake.

Begins career in films

After returning to the United States, Stone studied film making at New York University with director Martin Scorsese and other instructors. He graduated in 1971 and spent the next few years trying to establish himself as a director and screenwriter. In the meantime, however, Stone's memories of Vietnam continued to haunt him, and he began abusing drugs and alcohol.

In 1976 Stone managed to gain control over his destructive drinking and drug use. Around this same time, he drew on the memories of his tour in Vietnam to write the script for *Platoon.* But film studios rejected the script because they did not believe that the American public would be interested in seeing a movie treatment of the controversial and unpopular war.

Stone's inability to gain financing for *Platoon* frustrated him, but he continued to build his reputation in the film industry. In 1977 he earned an Academy Award for his screenplay for *Midnight Express,* a dark and controversial film about a young American's imprisonment in Turkey for drug smuggling. He also wrote the screenplay for *Scarface,* a violent but popular film that was released in 1983. And in 1986 he wrote and directed *Salvador,* a critically acclaimed movie that the story of a photojournalist who reports on the civil war that engulfed the Central American country of El Salvador during the early 1980s.

Platoon and *Born on the Fourth of July*

In the mid-1980s Stone finally was able to gather enough money to begin filming *Platoon.* The story concerns a young American college dropout who volunteers to serve in Vietnam. Once he arrives, however, he is stunned by the violence, brutality, and confusing nature of the war. As the weeks go by, the young soldier works to maintain his morality and decency within a platoon that struggles to survive enemy attacks and internal disagreements.

Stone shot the film in the Philippines in less than two months and released it in 1986. *Platoon* was immediately popular across America when it appeared. A great commercial success, the movie also drew widespread praise. Reviewers and Vietnam veterans alike hailed the film for its realism and its powerful emotional impact. "For a long time after I saw *Platoon* the first time and then again after I saw it a second time, I wondered why I found the movie so powerful, so genuinely authentic," wrote the famous Vietnam War correspondent David Halberstam (see entry) in the *New York Times.* "Part of it is the acting and directing. One scene after another seems stunningly real. But the movie transcends all the individual scenes, no matter how good they are. Then finally I realized what it was. What Mr. Stone has captured and put together is the special reality of Vietnam, the loneliness of these men, how isolated they are and how on this terrain they are always foreigners." Stone's film ultimately won numerous prestigious awards, including Academy Awards for best picture and best director.

Stone followed up *Platoon* with *Wall Street,* a 1987 film that harshly attacked the greed and corruption of America's business world. He then turned his attention to another Vietnam film called *Born on the Fourth of July.* This movie is based on the autobiography of Ron Kovic (see entry), a young man who was crippled in combat in Vietnam. Stone's film begins by showing how Kovic's deep sense of patriotism convinced him to volunteer for military duty in Vietnam. It then details his horrifying experiences during the war and the firefight that left him a paraplegic (paralyzed from the chest down). The movie then tracks Kovic's experiences after he returns to the United States as he struggles to cope with his injuries and a deep sense that he has been betrayed by his country. But he eventually emerges from a haze of alcohol and self-pity to became a respected writer and antiwar activist.

Born on the Fourth of July proved to be another critical and commercial success for Stone. Reviewers praised actor Tom Cruise for his performance as Kovic. They also applauded the director for creating another gripping examination of the Vietnam War and its effect on the American men who fought in it. In 1990 Stone received his second best director Academy Award for his work on the film.

Becomes known for making controversial movies

Since *Born on the Fourth of July* appeared in 1989, Stone has become one of America's most controversial movie directors. In 1991 he released *JFK,* a film about the 1963 assassination of President John F. Kennedy (see entry). Stone was condemned by many reviewers and scholars who saw the film who charged that he altered basic historical facts surrounding Kennedy's death in order to support his own conspiracy theories about the assassination.

In 1994 Stone released *Natural Born Killers,* an extremely violent movie about a murderous young couple who become celebrities after a long killing spree. Some people viewed the film as an insightful commentary on American popular culture. But many reviewers, politicians, and ordinary Americans strongly criticized the movie for its twisted characters and bloody storyline.

Stone's next film examined the life of President Richard Nixon (see entry), who served from 1969 to 1974 before resigning as a result of the Watergate scandal. *Nixon* drew praise from many critics for its intelligent and sensitive portrait of the disgraced president, but the 1995 film performed poorly at the box office.

Examines the war from Vietnamese perspective

Stone made his third film about the Vietnam War in the mid-1990s. This work, called *Heaven and Earth,* is based on the memoirs of Le Ly Hayslip (see entry), a Vietnamese woman who came of age as war raged across her country. Released in 1994, *Heaven and Earth* failed to generate much excitement among American moviegoers. It also received poor marks from reviewers, although they gave the director credit for examining the war from the perspective of a Vietnamese woman.

Sources

Ansen, David, with Peter McAlevey. "A Ferocious Vietnam Elegy." *Newsweek,* January 5, 1987.

Appy, Christian. "Vietnam According to Oliver Stone." *Commonweal,* March 23, 1990.

Breskin, David. "The Rolling Stone Interview: Oliver Stone." *Rolling Stone,* April 4, 1991.

Corliss, Richard. "Platoon: Viet Nam, the Way It Really Was, on Film." *Time,* January 26, 1987.

Halberstam, David, and Bernard E. Trainor. "Two Who Were There View 'Platoon.'" *New York Times,* March 8, 1987.

Kagan, Norman. *The Cinema of Oliver Stone.* New York: Continuum, 1995.

Riordan, James. *Stone: The Controversies, Excesses, and Exploits of a Radical Filmmaker.* New York: Hyperion, 1995.

Stone, Oliver. "One from the Heart." *American Film,* January-February 1987.

Maxwell Taylor

Born August 26, 1901
Keytesville, Missouri
Died April 19, 1987
Washington, D.C.

American general; ambassador to
South Vietnam, 1964–1965

"The ability of the Viet Cong continuously to rebuild their units and to make good their losses is one of the mysteries of this guerrilla war . . . ."

Maxwell Taylor.
Reproduced by permission of Corbis Corporation.

General Maxwell Taylor was one of America's leading military figures of the twentieth century. He served in the United States military for nearly five decades, from the early 1920s through the late 1960s. During that time he became known as a top military general, scholar, and administrator. In 1962 he was named chairman of the nation's Joint Chiefs of Staff (JCS), a military advisory group to the president that includes the top officers from each branch of the American armed forces. As chairman of the JCS from 1962 to 1964, he advocated extensive bombing campaigns against North Vietnam but warned against introducing U.S. ground troops into the conflict. When U.S. involvement in the war deepened, he also helped shape Vietnam policies as American ambassador to South Vietnam (1964–1965) and special military advisor to President Lyndon B. Johnson (1965–1969). During this period, he repeatedly expressed his belief that America needed to stay in Vietnam until the Communists were defeated.

Early military career

Maxwell Davenport Taylor was born August 26, 1901, in Keytesville, Missouri. He was the only child of John E.

Maxwell, an attorney, and Pearle (Davenport) Taylor. As a child, young Taylor became known as a bright boy with a strong interest in the military (at age five, he announced that he planned to attend the prestigious West Point Military Academy when he grew up). He attended high school in Kansas City, and in 1918 his application for admittance into West Point was accepted.

Taylor excelled at West Point, graduating fourth in his class in 1922. He then entered the Army, where he worked for the next several years as an engineer and artillery specialist in the United States, France, China, and Japan. In 1925 he married Lydia Gardner Happer, with whom he eventually had two sons. In 1932 Taylor returned to West Point, where he worked as a language instructor. He also continued his military education during this period, graduating from the Army's Command and Staff School in 1935 and the Army War College in 1940.

By the time the United States entered World War II in 1941, Taylor had achieved the rank of lieutenant colonel and was regarded as one of the Army's bright young officers. During the first two years of the war, his assignments kept him in the United States. But in March 1943 he was sent to the battlefields of Europe as an artillery commander with the Army's 82nd Airborne Division.

World War II hero

Taylor performed brilliantly over the next two years in Europe. During the summer of 1943 he commanded the division's artillery in two major victories in Italy. A short time later, he volunteered to go on a dangerous information-gathering mission behind enemy lines. After he successfully completed the mission, U.S. military commander (and later president) Dwight Eisenhower offered high praise: "The risks he ran were greater than I asked any other agent . . . to undertake during the war. He carried weighty responsibilities and discharged them with unerring judgement [despite being in constant] danger of discovery or death."

In March 1944 Taylor took command of the Army's 101st Airborne Division. On June 6, 1944, he participated in the crucial Allied invasion of Normandy, France (the "Allies" included the United States, England, Soviet Union, and other nations that fought against Germany, Italy, and Japan during the war). During the course of this battle, which was one of the biggest Allied victories of the entire war, Taylor parachuted into battle with his division. A few months later, he was wounded when Allied forces tried to liberate Holland from German occupation. But Taylor recovered from his injury in time to command his division in the December 1944–January 1945 "Battle of the Bulge." Over the course of this famous battle, Allied forces turned back the last major German offensive of the war.

After World War II ended in May 1945, Taylor continued his rise through the ranks. In 1945 he began a four-year term as superintendent of the West Point Academy. He was then appointed Chief of Staff of U.S. forces in Europe. He served in that capacity for two years before being promoted to deputy chief of staff of the Army in 1951.

Taylor returned to the battlefield two years later. He commanded U.S. forces in the Korean War from January to July of 1953, when a truce ending the war was signed. In 1955 he was promoted to four-star general and given command over all United States forces in the Far East. But this assignment lasted only a few months before he was promoted to chief of staff, the top-ranked position in the entire U.S. Army.

As army chief of staff, Taylor repeatedly clashed with President Dwight Eisenhower. He strongly opposed the president's strategic emphasis on nuclear weaponry. Instead, the general favored building a large but flexible military that could react effectively to a wide range of situations. Taylor served as army chief of staff until 1959, when he retired from active military duty. Upon retiring, he published a detailed explanation of his military philosophy in a book called *The Uncertain Trumpet* (1959).

Special advisor to Kennedy

In January 1961 John F. Kennedy (see entry) succeeded Eisenhower as president of the United States. Unlike Eisenhower, Kennedy agreed with Taylor's views on military issues and strategy. As a result, he asked Taylor to serve as a special advisor to the president on military matters. When Taylor accepted the invitation, Kennedy immediately asked him to study the growing bloodshed in South Vietnam.

South Vietnam had been formed only seven years earlier, when Vietnam defeated French colonial rulers to gain independence. But the 1954 Geneva Peace Accords that ended the French-Vietnamese conflict created two countries within Vietnam. North Vietnam was headed by a Communist government under revolutionary leader Ho Chi Minh (see entry). South Vietnam, meanwhile, was led by a U.S.-supported government under President Ngo Dinh Diem (see entry).

The Geneva Accords provided for nationwide free elections to be held in 1956 so that the two sections of Vietnam could be united under one government. But U.S. and South Vietnamese officials refused to hold the elections because they feared that the results would give the Communists control over the entire country. When the South refused to hold elections, North Vietnam and their allies in the South—known as the Viet Cong—launched a guerrilla war against Diem's government. The United States responded by sending money, weapons, and advisors to aid in South Vietnam's defense. Despite this assistance, however, some American analysts expressed concern that Diem's government might soon fall to the Communists.

Taylor paid his first visit to South Vietnam in the fall of 1961. After completing his two-week tour of the country, he and fellow military advisor Walt Rostow urged Kennedy to increase U.S. aid to Diem. This advice was based on their deep belief that "if Vietnam goes, it will be exceedingly difficult if not impossible to hold Southeast Asia" from other Communist aggressors. Taylor believed that "the weakness of Diem's regime could be overcome if enough Americans—civilian and military alike—took an active role in showing the Vietnamese how to win the war," explained Sanford Wexler in *The Vietnam War: An Eyewitness History.* A few months later, Taylor returned to active military service when Kennedy appointed him chairman of the JCS in 1962. As chairman, he repeatedly recommended air attacks against North Vietnam but expressed deep reservations about using American combat troops in the war.

Changing views on Vietnam

The Kennedy administration dramatically increased U.S. military and financial assistance to South Vietnam during the early 1960s. But Diem's government continued to lose

Maxwell Taylor, left, and Robert McNamara, third from left, listen to a briefing by a captain of the South Vietnamese army's special forces in September 1963.
Reproduced by permission of AP/Wide World Photos.

ground to the Viet Cong. In September 1963 Kennedy sent Taylor and Secretary of Defense Robert McNamara (see entry) to Vietnam to conduct a study of the situation. When they returned, Taylor and McNamara reported "great progress" against the Viet Cong but criticized the Diem government for corruption and ineffectiveness. They speculated that South Vietnam might be better off with new political leadership. A short time later, South Vietnamese military officials overthrew Diem's government with America's approval.

In November 1963 Kennedy was assassinated, and Vice President Lyndon B. Johnson (see entry) was sworn in as president. The following year Johnson sent Taylor to South Vietnam to serve as U.S. ambassador. When Taylor arrived in Saigon, South Vietnam's capital, he took over primary responsibility for coordinating the American war effort and advising the South's political leadership.

During his year as ambassador, Taylor's confidence in an eventual Communist defeat began to fade. In November

1964, for example, he reported that "the ability of the Viet Cong continuously to rebuild their units and to make good their losses is one of the mysteries of this guerrilla war. . . . Not only do the Viet Cong units have recuperative powers of the phoenix [a mythical bird that came back to life after burning to ashes], but they have an amazing ability to maintain morale." He also had a very low opinion of South Vietnam's political leaders, with whom he continuously feuded.

By January 1965 Taylor was warning Johnson that "we are presently on a losing track" in Vietnam. Taylor urged Johnson to order a major bombing campaign against North Vietnam, stating that "to take no positive action now is to accept defeat in the fairly near future." But he continued to oppose the introduction of American ground troops into the conflict. He worried that once the United States started sending soldiers to Vietnam, it would have a hard time cutting off the flow. Taylor also believed that Vietnam's hot climate and jungle terrain would be a problem for American foot soldiers, and he warned that U.S. soldiers stationed in Vietnam would have a great deal of difficulty "distinguish[ing] between a VC [Viet Cong] and friendly Vietnamese farmer." Taylor's concerns eventually proved to be well-founded. When Johnson began sending U.S. combat troops to Vietnam later in 1965, all of these factors emerged as major problems for American soldiers.

Taylor remains a "hawk" on Vietnam

In 1965 Taylor returned to Washington, D.C., to serve as a special consultant to President Johnson. Over the next three years, he remained a dedicated "hawk" (supporter of U.S. military involvement) on the issue of Vietnam. During this time, he expressed frustration about America's inability to defeat North Vietnam and the Viet Cong. But in Taylor's view, the strategic importance of keeping South Vietnam out of Communist hands outweighed all other considerations.

In 1968 Johnson asked Taylor and other close political advisors—collectively known as the "Wise Men"—for advice about how to proceed in Vietnam. By this time the war had become a bloody stalemate despite the presence of more than 500,000 U.S. troops in the South. In addition, the war had become a source of great unrest in communities all across the United States. During the meeting, nearly all of the so-called

Wise Men told Johnson that he should begin withdrawing U.S. forces from Vietnam. Taylor supported continued American military involvement in the war, but his advice was drowned out by the others. After the meeting, Johnson reluctantly began taking steps to end the U.S. role in Vietnam.

In 1969 Taylor retired again from public life. He spent the next several years writing about military strategy and international affairs in such books as *Swords and Plowshares* (1972) and *Precarious Security* (1976). He died in 1987 in Washington, D.C.

Sources

Berman, Larry. *Planning a Tragedy: The Americanization of the War in Vietnam.* New York: W. W. Norton, 1982.

Halberstam, David. *The Making of a Quagmire: America and Vietnam during the Kennedy Era.* Rev. ed. New York: Knopf, 1988.

Herring, George C. *America's Longest War: The United States and Vietnam, 1950–1975.* 3rd ed. New York: McGraw Hill, 1996.

Kinnard, Douglas. *The Certain Trumpet: Maxwell Taylor and the American Experience in Vietnam.*1991.

Taylor, John M. *General Maxwell Taylor: The Sword and the Pen.* New York: Doubleday, 1989.

Taylor, Maxwell D. *Swords and Plowshares.* 1972.

Lynda Van Devanter

Born May 27, 1947
Washington, D.C.

U.S. Army nurse; activist for women veterans

> "When each new woman tells me she's made her peace with Vietnam, I know I've helped in some small way."

Lynda Van Devanter was one of thousands of American women who served as nurses in Vietnam during the war. Like many of these other women, she worked grueling shifts in a poorly equipped hospital and treated horrible wounds. Upon returning to the United States, she struggled with feelings of anger, depression, and hopelessness with little support from either the U.S. government or American society. In fact, she found that women veterans were even more isolated than their male peers. Determined to help other women in the same situation, Van Devanter founded the Vietnam Veterans of America Women's Project in 1980. She also wrote a book about her experiences, *Home before Morning,* which brought national attention to the contributions of women veterans.

Becomes a nurse

Lynda Van Devanter was born in 1947 in Washington, D.C., and grew up in a close-knit Catholic family with four sisters. Her parents always encouraged her to find a way to contribute to society. "As we were growing up, both [my father] and my mother emphasized the obligation we all had

Lynda Van Devanter.
Reproduced by permission of AP/Wide World Photos.

to be of service not only to our family, community, church, and country, but to all of mankind," she recalled in *Home before Morning*.

From the time she was a little girl, Van Devanter dreamed of being a nurse. She read books about famous nurses, bandaged people's cuts, nursed injured animals back to health, and worked at a nursing home during high school. So it was no surprise when she enrolled in the Mercy Hospital School of Nursing in Baltimore following high school graduation in 1965. "Nursing was the way I was going to make my contribution to society," she explained in her memoir. "I was part of a generation of Americans who were 'chosen' to change the world. We were sure of that. It was only a matter of waiting until we all grew up."

Shortly before Van Devanter graduated from nursing school in 1968, she went to a presentation given by a U.S. Army recruiter. He asked the nursing students to consider joining the army and serve their country in the Vietnam War. At this time, the United States was rapidly increasing its military support for the nation of South Vietnam. The Communist nation of North Vietnam wanted to overthrow the South Vietnamese government and reunite the two countries under one Communist government.

But U.S. government officials felt that a Communist government in Vietnam would increase the power of China and the Soviet Union and threaten the security of the United States. In the late 1950s and early 1960s the U.S. government sent money, weapons, and military advisors to help South Vietnam defend itself. In 1965 President Lyndon Johnson (see entry) sent American combat troops to join the fight on the side of South Vietnam. After listening to the army recruiters, Van Devanter decided that she could best contribute to society by working as a nurse in Vietnam.

"I eagerly anticipated my work as an Army nurse. I saw it as one of the best ways to help those in need," Van Devanter recalled in her book. "There were brave boys fighting and dying for democracy, I thought. And if our boys were being blown apart, then somebody better be over there putting them back together again. I started to think that maybe that somebody should be me."

Serves in Vietnam

After completing six weeks of basic training at an army base in Texas, Van Devanter flew to Vietnam in June 1969. She was assigned to the 71st Evacuation Hospital in Pleiku province, located in the mountains near the Cambodian border. "One thing everybody agreed on was that assignments to certain medical facilities should be avoided at all costs, because of their unreasonable workloads and constant danger. One unit that was near the head of this list was the 71st Evacuation Hospital," she noted. "Pleiku was an area of heavy combat and the casualties were supposedly unending."

Within the first few weeks after she arrived, Van Devanter found out that the hospital deserved its reputation. She worked exhausting, twelve-hour shifts in poorly equipped operating rooms. She treated young soldiers with missing limbs, terrible burns, and huge blast wounds on a regular basis. "No amount of warning could have ever prepared me for the sheer numbers of mutilated young bodies that helicopters kept bringing to the 71st," she recalled. "The emergency room floor was practically covered with blood. Dozens of gurneys were tightly packed into the ER [emergency room], with barely enough space for medical people to move between them. And the helicopters were still bringing more." To make matters worse, explosions and sniper fire often occurred just outside the hospital compound.

Over time, the constant exposure to death and danger took a toll on Van Devanter. She began to lose her faith in what the U.S. forces were trying to accomplish in Vietnam. "I still tried to remind myself that we were in Vietnam to save people who were threatened by tyranny [a government that denies people their basic rights]," she stated. "But that became more and more difficult to believe as I heard stories of corrupt South Vietnamese officials, U.S. Army atrocities [extremely cruel or brutal acts], and a [Vietnamese] population who wanted nothing more than to be left alone so they could return to farming their land."

A bitter homecoming

After completing her one-year tour of duty in Vietnam, Van Devanter returned to the United States. But her home-

Anticipation of Coming Home

Like most other American military personnel, Lynda Van Devanter eagerly anticipated her return to the United States. A short time before she went home, she sent the following form letter to her family. (Van Devanter did not write this letter; it was available to all U.S. personnel returning home.) It was intended to prepare them for some of the changes they might notice in her behavior, but in a light and funny way. However, it also shows some of the dangers and hardships she endured during her tour of duty in Vietnam.

The above-named individual is very shortly returning to the WORLD after spending one year in the combat zone of Vietnam. In order that you may be adequately prepared to communicate with the named individual, it is highly suggested you thoroughly read and digest the following:

Her language will be totally Army-oriented. Please smile appropriately when she utters such terms as latrine, hooch, flak jacket, boonies, grunt, DEROS [Date of Expected Return from Overseas], Victor Charlie, incoming, Medicap, roger that, and negative.

You must realize she has worn combat boots and fatigues for a year. Please gently remind her of correct ladylike manners. Please do not get hysterical if she continually throws her feet up on the furniture or on the walls.

The first few times she should ride in a vehicle, please remind her to close the car door. Jeeps do not have doors. Do not allow her to throw her feet up on the dashboard.

coming was not the happy occasion she had hoped for. As the Vietnam War dragged on, the American people became bitterly divided over U.S. involvement. Antiwar demonstrations took place across the country. Some people viewed Vietnam veterans, or anyone in a military uniform, as symbols of an increasingly unpopular war. Like many male veterans, Van Devanter found that many Americans seemed to treat her with disinterest or even hostility. In fact, her homecoming experience was even worse than those of some male veterans because few people seemed to realize that women had served in the Vietnam War. Even the U.S. government did not provide support programs for women veterans.

"When I returned to my country in June of 1970, I began to learn a very bitter lesson," Van Devanter noted in *Home before Morning.* "The values with which I had been raised

If she should ask you which unit you are with, or when your DEROS date is, make something up.

If she should turn the shower on and then let the water run for thirty minutes, don't yell about the water bill. She is merely waiting for the water to warm up. When she discovers hot water is a standard item in your house, don't be surprised if she insists everyone take a shower before the hot water system breaks down.

If she insists on putting blankets, flashlights, books, helmet, and flak jacket under her bed, please do not remove these items until she is thoroughly convinced incoming rockets and mortars are not likely in your neighborhood . . . .

Never, under any circumstances, mention the word HELICOPTER.

Please allow her to open the refrigerator at least twenty-six times a day. If she insists on standing in line for meals, gently guide her toward the table. Assure her she does not have to sign for meals . . . .

If you have any green objects in the house, remove them. Never wear any green clothes in her presence.

Never serve meals on a tray of any type. A plate will bring her total happiness . . . .

Do not allow her to go shopping alone. She is accustomed to the small PX [post exchange, or military store]. She may well buy six bottles of shampoo, twelve bars of soap, and four toothbrushes because you can never tell when the PX will be resupplied.

And NEVER make any loud, sudden noises unless you are prepared to pick her up off the floor.

had changed; in the eyes of most Americans, the military services had no more heroes, merely babykillers, misfits, and fools. I was certain that I was neither a babykiller nor a misfit. Maybe I was a fool. . . . I was as popular as a disease and as untouchable as a piece of [garbage]. . . . I almost wished I was back in 'Nam. At least there you expected people to hate you. That was a war. But here, in the United States, I guess I wanted everything to be wonderful."

Van Devanter's memories of Vietnam, combined with the lack of recognition and support she received upon returning home, took a heavy emotional toll on her. She felt angry and isolated from other people. For many years, she suffered from depression, nightmares, flashbacks, crying spells, and angry outbursts. Unable to put her memories of Vietnam behind her, she drank and smoked heavily, and she even considered suicide. She had trouble keeping a job as a nurse because being in hospitals reminded her of terrible things from the war. "For years I tried to talk about it," she noted. "Nobody listened. Who would have wanted to listen? Mine were not nice, neat stories. . . . The stories, even the funny ones, were all dirty. They were rotten and they stank."

For Van Devanter, the turning point came when she met Bobby Muller (see entry), a disabled veteran who founded Vietnam Veterans of America (VVA). This organization was designed to help American veterans deal with their painful memories and physical wounds from the Vietnam War. "I began spending my days at the VVA headquarters in lower Manhattan, where I met dozens of other veterans—all men—who talked about the kinds of experiences that I had been having since my return from Vietnam," Van Devanter recalled. "Suddenly, I didn't feel so alone anymore. These people were telling me that I could be proud of my service. The organization was trying to instill pride into all Vietnam vets. We had answered our country's call. It wasn't our fault that we were called for the wrong war."

Helps other Vietnam veterans

Encouraged by the support she received from VVA, Van Devanter decided that she wanted to help other veterans—especially women veterans—who might be struggling with the same problems she had experienced. She began studying for a bachelor's degree in psychology at Antioch University in Los Angeles in order to become a counselor for veterans.

During her studies, Van Devanter learned about Post-Traumatic Stress Disorder (PTSD). PTSD is the medical name for a set of psychological problems that are caused by exposure to a dangerous or disturbing situation, such as combat. People who suffer from PTSD often have the symptoms that Van Devanter experienced, such as depression, flashbacks, and angry outbursts. "It sounded like I was reading my own psychological profile," she noted. "I began thinking that . . . there must be plenty of other women in similar circumstances. There could be thousands of women vets experiencing PTSD who thought they were alone. My job would be to reach them before it was too late."

In 1980 Van Devanter founded the Vietnam Veterans of America Women's Project. The idea behind this project was to bring recognition to female nurses and other women veterans and to provide them with support. Through the VVA Women's Project, Van Devanter began counseling women veterans and conducting seminars about PTSD. "Since November of 1980, the Vietnam Veterans of America Women's Project has been my entire life," she explained. "I've done hundreds of interviews, spoken to thousands of people, and lobbied hard in Congress to get recognition for women who served in Vietnam."

Perhaps Van Devanter's most effective tool in reaching women veterans was her memoir *Home before Morning: The Story of an Army Nurse in Vietnam.* She started writing the book in the late 1970s as a way to gain a better understanding and acceptance of her own experiences. When it was published in 1983, however, it also helped large numbers of women veterans feel less isolated and alone. "My story is only my own, but many other women and men shared similar experiences both during and after the war," Van Devanter wrote in the book. "I hope to let them know that they are not alone, and that they, too, can find the way back home." Critics praised *Home Before Morning* for providing a woman's perspective on the horrors of war.

"These days, in spite of my work with others who are in pain, I can say that I am no longer unhappy," Van Devanter stated. "I can see, little by little, that progress is being made. I am optimistic. Other women vets are beginning to learn that they are not alone. They are forming groups, getting counseling and, in some small measure, being recognized for the contributions they have made. When each new woman tells me she's made her peace with Vietnam, I know I've helped in some small way."

Sources

Marshall, Kathryn. *In the Combat Zone: An Oral History of American Women in Vietnam.* Boston: Little, Brown, 1987.

Norman, Elizabeth M. *Women at War: The Story of Fifty Military Nurses Who Served in Vietnam.* Philadelphia: University of Pennsylvania Press, 1990.

Palmer, Laura. "The Nurses of Vietnam, Still Wounded: Only Now Are They Healing Themselves." *New York Times Magazine,* November 7, 1993.

Van Devanter, Lynda, with Christopher Morgan. *Home before Morning: The Story of an Army Nurse in Vietnam.* New York: Beaufort Books, 1983.

Van Devanter, Lynda, and Joan Furey, eds. *Visions of War, Dreams of Peace: Writings of Women in the Vietnam War.* New York: Warner Books, 1991.

Vo Nguyen Giap

Born August 28, 1911
Quang Binh Province, Vietnam

North Vietnamese military leader

G eneral Vo Nguyen Giap was the leader of the North Vietnamese military forces for over thirty years. He began his career by fighting against French colonial forces during the Indochina War. One of his greatest achievements came in the decisive battle of Dien Bien Phu, which ended that war in 1954. Giap also oversaw the North Vietnamese military strategy during the Vietnam War. Under his guidance, the Communist forces frustrated the U.S. military by using tactics of guerilla warfare. Over time, they gradually advanced to conventional warfare and launched all-out offensive attacks. Giap's strategy helped North Vietnam win the war and reunite Vietnam under a Communist government in 1975.

Thanks to his victories over France and the United States, some historians have ranked Giap among the top military leaders of the twentieth century. "That the army of a small, poverty-stricken, industrially backward nation could defeat two world powers was remarkable, but then the man who played such a large part in it is himself remarkable," Peter Macdonald wrote in the biography *Giap: The Victor in Vietnam*. "Starting

Vo Nguyen Giap.
Reproduced by permission of Archive Photos.

421

with thirty-four soldiers, he ended up commanding nearly a million. And at the end of it all he remained undefeated."

A young revolutionary

Vo Nguyen Giap was born August 28, 1911, in the small village of An Xa in Quang Binh province in central Vietnam. He was one of five children in a family of poor farmers. At the time of Giap's birth, Vietnam was a colony of France. His father strongly opposed French colonial rule and often took part in demonstrations demanding Vietnamese independence. By the time Giap was a teenager, he had joined the Vietnamese Communist Party—a secret organization of people who wanted to fight against French rule. He was influenced by the writings of Ho Chi Minh (see entry), a Vietnamese nationalist who was then living in France.

Throughout his youth, Giap worked in his family's rice fields in order to earn enough money for an education. When he was eighteen, he was sent to prison for three years for his anti-French political activities. Upon his release, he attended the prestigious Vietnamese National Academy in Hanoi. Giap proved to be an excellent student and earned a bachelor's degree in law. Both during and after college he wrote books, articles, and pamphlets expressing his political ideas. In one of these works, a book called *The Question of a National Liberation in Indochina,* Giap argued that Vietnam's only hope for defeating a major foreign power like France was through a long, drawn-out war.

In the late 1930s Giap fled to China in order to escape a French crackdown against its political enemies in Vietnam. Unfortunately, Giap's young wife was arrested by the French colonial forces and died in prison. Feeling more bitter than ever toward the French, Giap joined a group of Vietnamese Communist revolutionaries in China led by Ho Chi Minh. He soon became one of Ho's most trusted advisors. In 1941 Ho and his supporters returned to Vietnam and formed the Vietnam Doc Lap Dong Minh Hoa (League for the Independence of Vietnam). This Communist-led nationalist group, usually known by the shortened name Viet Minh, was determined to fight for Vietnamese independence.

Leads Viet Minh forces against the French

During World War II (1939–45), France suffered a series of military defeats and surrendered to Germany. Unable to protect its colonies in Indochina, the French government allowed Japan to occupy Vietnam and set up military bases there in the 1940s. The Viet Minh viewed the Japanese occupation as an opportunity to gain control of the country. Giap took command of the Viet Minh guerrilla fighters and began helping the American forces that were fighting against the Japanese. The Viet Minh leaders hoped that the U.S. government would reward their efforts by supporting their bid for independence.

In 1945 the Allied forces (which mainly consisted of the United States, Great Britain, and the Soviet Union) defeated both Germany and Japan to win World War II. As soon as Japan was defeated, the Viet Minh launched a revolution to take control of Vietnam. This so-called August Revolution was successful, as the Viet Minh captured large areas of the country. In September 1945 Ho Chi Minh formally declared Vietnam's independence from both the French and the Japanese. Giap became a top official in the government of the new nation, known as the Democratic Republic of Vietnam.

But it soon became clear that France—which had suffered a great deal of damage to its land, economy, and reputation as a world leader during World War II—was not willing to give up its former colony. After a year of negotiations, war erupted between the French and the Viet Minh in

North Vietnamese Political and Military Leaders in Prison

During the period when Vietnam was a colony of France, the colonial government often arrested Vietnamese people considered dangerous to French rule. For example, French authorities routinely detained people who joined rival political parties, participated in demonstrations against the government, or spoke out in favor of Vietnamese independence.

Most of the people who went on to become political and military leaders in North Vietnam during the Vietnam War went to prison during this time. At one point, North Vietnamese President Ho Chi Minh calculated that the thirty-one top officials in his government had spent a total of 222 years in prison—an average of more than seven years per person.

Like most other North Vietnamese leaders, General Vo Nguyen Giap spent several years in prison under the French. In addition, his wife received a life sentence and died in a French prison in 1941. Many sources claim that these experiences hardened Giap and made him determined to continue fighting until Vietnam gained its late 1946. As the war got under way, Giap organized a formal military force for his nation, which became known as the People's Army of Vietnam (PAVN). As commander of the PAVN, Giap created a military system that consisted of regular army troops as well as regional and local forces. By 1952 he had recruited more than 250,000 PAVN troops and two million regional and local militia forces to fight for Vietnam's independence from France.

Victory at Dien Bien Phu

Giap always characterized the Vietnamese struggle for independence as a "people's war." He claimed that the Vietnamese people wanted freedom from foreign control and were willing to make whatever sacrifices were necessary to achieve that goal. Within the Communist government, Giap argued that it would take all of the resources of the nation to defeat the French, including the full emotional commitment of the people. "To educate, mobilize, organize, and arm the whole people in order that they might take part in the resistance was a crucial question," he explained. As a military leader, Giap fought to win regardless of the cost. "Every minute, hundreds of thousands of people die on this earth," he once said. "The life or death of a hundred, a thousand, tens of thousands of human beings, even our compatriots, means little."

Giap recognized that France had better military training and equipment than the PAVN. To overcome his opponent's advantages, he relied on Communist principles that divided a revolution into three stages: first, using tactics of guerrilla warfare while building political support for the revolution among the people; second, gradually advancing from tactics of guerrilla warfare to those of conventional warfare; and third, launching a large-scale offensive attack that leads to political revolution. Giap believed that patience was key to the success of this plan. He told the Vietnamese people that they must continue fighting for many years to achieve a total victory.

The Vietnamese Communists finally achieved a major victory against France after nine years of war. Under Giap's leadership, the PAVN defeated the French in the battle of Dien Bien Phu in May 1954. First Giap convinced the French to position 14,000 men in a remote outpost near the border of Laos. Then he surrounded the fort with 50,000 PAVN soldiers, pounded it with artillery fire, and eventually forced the French to surrender. This battle marked the end of the Indochina War. In July 1954 the two sides signed a peace agreement that provided for France to withdraw from Indochina.

But the Geneva Accords of 1954 also divided Vietnam into two sections—Communist North Vietnam and U.S.-supported South Vietnam. Under the terms of the agreement, the two parts of Vietnam were supposed to hold nationwide free elections in 1956 in order to reunite the country under one government. But U.S. government officials worried that holding free elections in Vietnam would bring power to the Communists who had led the nation's war for independence from France. They felt that a Communist government in Vietnam would increase the power of China and the Soviet Union and threaten the security of the United States. As a result, the South Vietnamese government and its American advisors refused to hold the elections.

North Vietnam's main military strategist

Giap and the other North Vietnamese leaders grew very angry when the elections did not take place as scheduled. They remained determined to reunite the two parts of the country under a Communist government, by force if necessary. Despite his position as head of the military, Giap initially hoped to reunite Vietnam through peaceful negotiations. But more militant members of the Communist government convinced Ho Chi Minh to resume fighting. Within a short time, a new war began between the two sections of Vietnam.

During the early years of the Vietnam War, North Vietnam followed Giap's overall plan for the three stages of revolution. One of the North's main weapons was a group of South Vietnamese Communist rebels called the Viet Cong. Using tactics of guerrilla warfare, the Viet Cong gradually gained control of large areas of the South Vietnamese countryside. In the late 1950s and early 1960s the U.S. government sent money, weapons, and military advisors to help South Vietnam defend itself against North Vietnam and the Viet Cong. In 1965 President Lyndon Johnson (see entry) authorized U.S. bombing missions over North Vietnam and sent American combat troops to South Vietnam.

But deepening U.S. involvement failed to defeat the Communists. Instead, the Vietnam War turned into a bloody stalemate. The Viet Cong guerrillas frustrated the American forces and reduced the advantage of their superior firepower. In the meantime, Giap continued building up his military forces, which became known as the North Vietnamese Army (NVA). In January 1968 North Vietnamese government leaders decided that the time had come to put the final stage of the revolution into motion. Giap launched a coordinated series of attacks on major South Vietnamese cities, which was known as the Tet Offensive.

In designing the Tet Offensive, Giap assumed that the large-scale attack would encourage South Vietnamese citizens and soldiers to join the Communist forces and overthrow the South Vietnamese government. But the offensive failed to spark a revolt among the people, and American forces rallied to turn back the attack. The Tet Offensive ended up being a serious military defeat for North Vietnam, but it also shocked the American people and helped turn public opinion against the war.

Victory for the Communists

Between 1968 and 1972 Giap and the North Vietnamese military returned to the guerrilla warfare tactics that had frustrated the U.S. and South Vietnamese armies. In the meantime, the U.S. government began withdrawing American troops from the conflict while also strengthening the South Vietnamese Army to continue the fight. In March 1972 Giap tried to take advantage of this situation by launching another attack, known as the Easter Offensive. But the South Vietnamese military managed to fight off the attack with the help of U.S. air power.

In 1973 Giap stepped down from his position as commander of the NVA. According to some reports, his health had begun to fail. But other sources claimed that he had disagreed with Communist Party leaders over military strategy. Two years later, North Vietnamese forces captured the South Vietnamese capital city of Saigon to win the Vietnam War. After decades of fighting, they finally achieved Giap's dream of an independent Vietnam under a Communist government.

After the war ended, Giap continued to fall from power within the government. He resigned as minister of defense in

Giap's Military Strategy

Since the Vietnam War ended in a North Vietnamese victory in 1975, General Vo Nguyen Giap has written a great deal about his successful military strategy. The following excerpt from one of his books explains his method of defeating a powerful foreign enemy:

> The war of liberation is a protracted war and a hard war in which we must rely mainly on ourselves—for we are strong politically but weak materially, while the enemy is very weak politically but stronger materially.
>
> Guerrilla warfare is a means of fighting a revolutionary war that relies on

the heroic spirit to triumph over modern weapons. It is the means whereby the people of a weak, badly equipped country can stand up against an aggressive army possessing better equipment and techniques.

> The correct tactics for a protracted revolutionary war are to wage guerrilla warfare, to advance from guerrilla warfare to regular warfare and then closely combine these two forms of war; to develop from guerrilla to mobile and then to siege warfare.
>
> Accumulate a thousand small victories to turn into one great success.

1980, and he lost his position within the Communist Party leadership two years later. Nevertheless, he remained very popular among the Vietnamese people. Many people viewed him as the man who had won the war for independence. In 1992 Giap received the highest honor given by the Vietnamese government, the Gold Star Order, "for his services to the revolutionary cause of party and nation."

In 2000, on the 25th anniversary of the North Vietnamese victory in the Vietnam War, Giap told an interviewer that Americans had a responsibility to help Vietnam recover from the war. "We can put the past behind, but we cannot completely forget it," he stated. "As we help in finding missing U.S. soldiers, the United States should also help Vietnam overcome the extremely enormous consequences of the war."

Sources

Giap, Vo Nguyen. *The People's War for the Defense of the Homeland in the New Era.* Hanoi: Foreign Languages Publishing House, 1981.

Giap, Vo Nguyen. *Unforgettable Days.* Hanoi: Foreign Languages Publishing House, 1974.

Karnow, Stanley. "Giap Remembers." *New York Times Magazine,* June 24, 1990.

Macdonald, Peter. *Giap: The Victor in Vietnam.* New York: W. W. Norton, 1993.

McNamara, Robert S. *Argument without End: In Search of Answers to the Vietnam Tragedy.* Public Affairs, 1999.

Myre, Greg. "Vietnam Nemesis Reaches Out to U.S." *Detroit Free Press,* April 9, 2000.

William C. Westmoreland

Born March 26, 1914
Spartanburg, South Carolina

U.S. Army general and member of the Joint Chiefs of Staff; commander of the American troops in Vietnam, 1964–68

General William C. Westmoreland served as the commander of the U.S. military forces in Vietnam during the first four years of direct American involvement, from 1964 to 1968. In this position he helped determine American military strategy and presided over a steady increase in U.S. troop levels. As more American people turned against the war in the late 1960s, Westmoreland spoke out in defense of both the U.S. mission and his own performance. Relieved of his command following the Tet Offensive in 1968, he served as a military advisor to the president with the Joint Chiefs of Staff until his retirement.

"In short we [the U.S.] abandoned the South Vietnamese government. The American military was not defeated in Vietnam."

A born military leader

William Childs Westmoreland was born on March 26, 1914, in Spartanburg, South Carolina. His father was a successful businessman. From the early years of his life, Westmoreland demonstrated strong leadership qualities, becoming an Eagle Scout and serving as president of his high school class. Upon graduating in 1931, he attended the Citadel military school in Charleston, South Carolina. The following year he transferred

William Westmoreland.
Reproduced by permission of Archive Photos.

to the U.S. Military Academy at West Point. Westmoreland continued to show leadership abilities as a West Point cadet. He became captain of his class during his senior year, and he won the prestigious Pershing Award for leadership.

After graduating from West Point in 1936, Westmoreland received the rank of second lieutenant in the artillery. At the beginning of World War II (1939–45), he was promoted to major and sent into battle in North Africa and Sicily. In 1944 he fought bravely during the invasion of Normandy, when the United States and its allies pushed the German army out of France. Westmoreland continued rising through the military ranks after World War II, earning promotions to colonel and then division commander. In 1947 he married Katherine Stevens Van Dusen, the daughter of one of his commanding officers. They eventually had three children together.

In 1952 Westmoreland took command of the 187th Airborne Regimental Combat Team in the Korean War. The following year he was assigned the position of secretary to U.S. Army Chief of Staff Maxwell D. Taylor (see entry). In 1956 Westmoreland was promoted again and became the youngest major general in the U.S. Army. A short time later he took command of the 101st Airborne Division, a group of paratroopers sometimes known as the Screaming Eagles. On one training jump, five of his men were killed when their parachutes were caught in high winds. After that incident, Westmoreland always jumped before his men in order to test the wind conditions.

In 1960 Westmoreland became superintendent of West Point. This job gave him an opportunity to train future military officers. In 1963 he returned to the military and was promoted to lieutenant general. By this time Westmoreland was widely considered to be one of the most promising young officers in the American armed forces. He had taken on a variety of challenges and succeeded in meeting each one. In 1964 he was asked to take on what became the greatest challenge of his career. President Lyndon Johnson (see entry) placed Westmoreland in charge of the growing U.S. military presence in Vietnam.

Takes charge of U.S. forces in Vietnam

The Vietnam War was a conflict between the Communist nation of North Vietnam and the U.S.-supported nation of

South Vietnam. North Vietnam wanted to overthrow the South Vietnamese government and reunite the two countries under one Communist government. But U.S. government officials felt that a Communist government in Vietnam would increase the power of the Soviet Union and threaten the security of the United States. In the late 1950s and early 1960s the U.S. government sent money, weapons, and military advisors to help the South Vietnamese Army fight the Communists.

North Vietnam's main weapon during this phase of the Vietnam War was a guerrilla army known as the Viet Cong that operated in the South Vietnamese countryside. The Viet Cong mingled with the villagers and tried to convince them to support the Communist efforts to overthrow the government. At the time Westmoreland became head of the U.S. Military Assistance Command in South Vietnam, there were 15,000 American military advisors stationed in Vietnam. Despite the U.S. assistance, however, the South Vietnamese Army was losing ground to the Viet Cong. Westmoreland immediately began pressuring Johnson to send U.S. combat troops to Vietnam in order to prevent a Communist takeover.

Once the president committed the first American combat troops to Vietnam in 1965, Westmoreland became one of the guiding forces behind the U.S. military strategy. Like some other prominent officials, he viewed the Vietnam War as a war of attrition. "As a military strategy, attrition meant wearing down or grinding down the enemy until the enemy lost its will to fight or the capacity to sustain its military effort," Larry Berman explained in *Lyndon Johnson's War*. Westmoreland planned to increase the number of American troops steadily, and then use them to conduct "search and destroy" missions against North Vietnamese and Viet Cong bases. In the meantime, the U.S. planes would also launch bombing raids against the Communists. Westmoreland believed that, over time, the superior U.S. weapons and equipment would wear down the enemy and force them to negotiate a settlement.

Over the next few years, the number of U.S. troops in Vietnam increased to over 500,000. On the occasions when they faced the Communist forces in battle, they usually came out on top. But the North Vietnamese Army and their Viet Cong allies rarely engaged the American troops directly. Instead, they used tactics of guerrilla warfare—such as sneak

A North Vietnamese General Explains Why the U.S. Strategy Failed

The man in charge of the North Vietnamese Army during the early years of the Vietnam War was Vo Nguyen Giap (see entry). In the following statement, which was published in the *New York Times* on June 24, 1990, Giap tells reporter Stanley Karnow why he believes that the U.S. military strategy failed to defeat his forces:

> Westmoreland was wrong to expect that his superior firepower would grind us down. If we had focused on the balance of forces, we would have been defeated in two hours. We were waging a people's war. . . . America's sophisticated arms, electronic devices and all the rest were to no avail in the end. In war there are two factors—human beings and weapons. Ultimately, though, human beings are the decisive factor.

attacks and booby traps—in order to reduce the American advantages in resources and firepower. The North Vietnamese seemed willing to engage the United States in a war of attrition. In fact, they appeared determined to continue fighting until the Americans withdrew. "The enemy is relying on his greater staying power," Westmoreland admitted in a report to Johnson. "It is only his will and resolve that are sustaining him now, and his faith that his will is stronger than ours."

Strategy comes under criticism at home

Despite the steady increase in U.S. military involvement in Vietnam, the war soon turned into a bloody stalemate. As a result, some people began to question Westmoreland's strategy. But the general believed that the problem was not his strategy, but the U.S. government's lack of commitment to it. "A major problem in those early days," he wrote in his memoir *A Soldier Reports,* "as through the entire war, was that Washington policy decisions forced us to fight with but one hand."

One major problem, in Westmoreland's view, was that Johnson would not allow U.S. troops or bombers to operate in the neighboring countries of Cambodia or Laos. Westmoreland argued that the North Vietnamese Army and Viet Cong guerrillas maintained bases in these countries. He noted that the enemy forces used these bases to launch their guerrilla attacks against the U.S. troops. But the president worried that this action would be considered an escalation of the war and would increase public opposition to his policies. In addition, he thought that attacking Cambodia or Laos might provoke China into joining the fight on the side of the Communists.

As the war dragged on, the American people became bitterly divided over the government's policies. Antiwar demonstrations took place across the country. In November 1967 Johnson called Westmoreland home to reassure the U.S. Congress and the American people about his progress against the Communists. In a series of speeches the general said that his strategy was working. He also asked for continued support. "We have reached an important point when the end begins to come into view," he told the National Press Club. "Backed at home by resolve, confidence, patience, determination, and continued support, we will prevail in Vietnam over the communist aggressor."

Privately, however, Westmoreland continued pressing Johnson to increase the number of U.S. troops in Vietnam. In his memoir he recalled telling the president that "Unless the will of the enemy was broken or unless there was unraveling of the VC [Viet Cong] structure, the war could go on for five years."

Removed from command after the Tet Offensive

In January 1968—just two months after Westmoreland said that the end of the war was in sight—the Communist forces launched a major attack on the cities of South Vietnam. This attack, which took place during Vietnam's Tet holiday, became known as the Tet Offensive. The attack took Westmoreland and other U.S. military leaders by surprise. But the American forces recovered quickly and turned back the offensive. In fact, they did a great deal of damage to the North Vietnamese and Viet Cong forces in the process.

Afterward, Westmoreland proclaimed that Tet had resulted in a major defeat for the enemy. However, he admitted that the Communists still showed few signs of backing down. "Enemy losses have been heavy; he has failed to achieve his prime objectives of mass uprisings and capture of a large number of the capital cities and towns. Morale in enemy units which were badly mauled or where the men were oversold the idea of a decisive victory at Tet probably has suffered severely," Westmoreland wrote in an official report. "However, with replacements, his [the Communists'] indoctrination [training] system would seem capable of maintaining morale at a generally adequate level. His determination appears to be unshaken."

Creighton W. Abrams (1914–1974)

General Creighton Abrams replaced William Westmoreland as the commander of U.S. military forces in Vietnam in 1968. Creighton Williams Abrams was born on September 15, 1914, in Springfield, Massachusetts. After graduating from the U.S. Military Academy at West Point in 1940, he took command of the 37th Tank Battalion during World War II. Abrams proved to be a brave and daring fighter in numerous battles across Europe. In fact, he wore out seven tanks, won several medals for distinguished service, and earned the praise of his commanding officer, General George S. Patton.

After World War II ended, Abrams continued moving up through the military ranks. In 1962, he was asked to handle an extremely tense situation within the United States. At this time in American history, there were laws that segregated (separated) people by race. These laws— which required white people and "colored" people to use different restrooms, schools, and restaurants— discriminated against blacks and placed them in an inferior position in society.

When the Supreme Court ruled that such laws were unconstitutional (not allowed under the U.S. Constitution), violent protests took place in some areas of the South. Abrams led the U.S. troops that calmed the protests and enforced the Supreme Court's ruling in Mississippi and Alabama. He was widely praised for his sensitive handling of the situation.

In 1964, Abrams was promoted to full general in the U.S. Army. Three years later, he went to Vietnam, where he became deputy commander of the U.S. forces under William Westmoreland. In this position, Abrams was responsible for training and preparing the South Vietnamese Army. During the Tet Offensive of 1968, when North Vietnam launched surprise attacks against several major cities, Abrams led the recapture of Hue. The South Vietnamese forces he had trained fought well during this time.

In June 1968, Abrams replaced Westmoreland as head of the U.S. military forces in Vietnam. Beginning the following year, he oversaw the implementation of President Richard Nixon's "Vietnamization" policy, which involved withdrawing

Even though the Communists failed to achieve their military goals in the Tet Offensive, they did succeed in turning public opinion in the United States against the war. The large-scale, coordinated attack shocked many U.S. government officials and the American public. After all, Westmore-

Creighton Abrams. *Courtesy of the Library of Congress.*

American troops gradually while also strengthening the South Vietnamese forces. As U.S. involvement wound down, Abrams also established programs to help the South Vietnamese people. By improving education, medical care, transportation, and farming methods, these programs were designed to keep the people loyal to the South Vietnamese government rather than the Communists. Abrams received praise from international observers for his efforts to reduce the

suffering and improve the lives of the South Vietnamese people.

In 1972, Abrams returned to the United States and became a member of the Joint Chiefs of Staff, a group of military leaders that acts as advisors to the president. In this position, he worked to correct some of the problems that had developed in the U.S. armed forces during the Vietnam War, such as low morale, drug use, and poor race relations. Once the military draft ended, he also oversaw the transition to a volunteer-based army.

Abrams died of cancer on September 4, 1974. Throughout his long career, he gained the respect of many soldiers and government officials with his bravery, integrity, analytical ability, and sensitivity. Although he took command of U.S. forces in Vietnam when the war was extremely unpopular among the American people, Abrams always maintained a good relationship with the media. In fact, one admiring reporter called him "a general who deserves a better war." After his death, the U.S. Army named a new, turbine-powered tank the M-1 *Abrams* in his honor.

land had just assured them that the U.S. forces were close to victory. The media became highly critical of the general afterward, and several of his main supporters within the government began to doubt him as well. In March Johnson refused to grant Westmoreland's request for an additional 200,000

U.S. combat troops. Instead, the president opened peace negotiations with North Vietnam. In June 1968 Johnson sent General Creighton W. Abrams to replace Westmoreland as head of the American forces in Vietnam.

Remains a central figure in debate over the war

Upon returning to the United States, Westmoreland became a member of the Joint Chiefs of Staff. This group of military leaders—which includes the head of each branch of the U.S. armed forces—advises the president on military matters. In this position Westmoreland oversaw the withdrawal of U.S. combat troops from Vietnam, which was completed in 1973. He also took steps to restore the morale of the American armed forces and prepare them to fight in future conflicts.

In June 1972 Westmoreland retired from the military. Two years later, he made an unsuccessful run for governor of South Carolina. In 1975 North Vietnamese troops captured the South Vietnamese capital of Saigon to end the Vietnam War. The following year, Westmoreland published a book about his experiences in Vietnam, *A Soldier Reports*. In this controversial book he argued that the U.S. government, rather than the military, was responsible for the Communist victory in Vietnam.

"It is perplexing to me that one often reads that the American military lost the war in Vietnam when it is a fact that: the American military did not lose a battle of consequence; the Nixon administration withdrew our ground forces and they were out of the country by early 1973; . . . and it was two years after our withdrawal that the North Vietnamese Army came down en masse [as a whole] and seized the South," Westmoreland told Sanford Wexler in *The Vietnam War: An Eyewitness History*. "In short we abandoned the South Vietnamese government. The American military was not defeated in Vietnam."

In the years since the Communist victory, Westmoreland has remained a central figure in the debate over American involvement in the Vietnam War. Military historians continue to question the appropriateness of his strategy. "Whether Westmoreland's strategy could ever have won the war will never be known," K. E. Hamburger wrote in *Encyclopedia of the*

Vietnam War. "Certainly victory would probably have required many things he did not have—more troops, more time, more political will, and reform of the [South Vietnamese Army], to name a few."

In 1982 Westmoreland's performance in Vietnam became the topic of news once again. A television documentary shown on the CBS network, called *The Uncounted Enemy*, charged that the general had lied about the level of enemy troops in South Vietnam in order to make his policies seem more effective. The report was based on enemy documents uncovered by the Central Intelligence Agency (CIA), which indicated that there were twice as many enemy forces as Westmoreland had claimed. Westmoreland denied the accusations and sued CBS for libel (intentionally making false statements about him). In 1984 Westmoreland agreed to drop the lawsuit when CBS admitted that the documentary had contained factual errors.

Sources

Berman, Larry. *Lyndon Johnson's War.* New York: Norton, 1989.

Furguson, Ernest B. *Westmoreland: The Inevitable General.* Boston: Little, Brown, 1968.

Where to Learn More

Against the Vietnam War: Writings by Activists. New York: Syracuse University Press, 1999.

Agnew, Spiro. *Go Quietly . . . or Else*. New York: William Morrow, 1980.

Ambrose, Stephen E. *Nixon*. 3 vols. New York: Simon and Schuster, 1987, 1989, 1991.

American Writers of the Vietnam War, Vol. 9 of *Dictionary of Literary Biography Documentary Series*. Detroit: Gale Research, 1991.

Anderson, David L., ed. *Shadow on the White House: Presidents and the Vietnam War, 1945-1975*. Lawrence, KS: University Press of Kansas, 1993.

Andrews, Owen, et al. *Vietnam: Images from Combat Photographers*. Washington: Starwood, 1991.

Anson, Robert S. *McGovern: A Biography*. New York: Holt, Rinehart and Winston, 1972.

Baez, Joan. *And a Voice to Sing With*. New York: Summit Books, 1978.

Beidler, Philip D. *Re-Writing America: Vietnam Authors in Their Generation*. Athens: University of Georgia Press, 1991.

Berman, Larry. *Lyndon Johnson's War*. New York: W.W. Norton, 1989.

Berman, Larry. *Planning a Tragedy: The Americanization of the War in Vietnam*. New York: W.W. Norton, 1982.

Bernstein, Irving. *Guns or Butter: The Presidency of Lyndon Johnson.* New York: Oxford University Press, 1996.

Berrigan, Daniel. *Night Flight to Hanoi.* New York: Macmillan, 1968.

Berrigan, Daniel. *To Dwell in Peace: An Autobiography.* New York: Harper, 1987.

Bird, Kai. *The Color of Truth: McGeorge Bundy and William Bundy, Brothers in Arms: A Biography.* New York: Simon and Schuster, 1998.

Blair, Anne E. *Lodge in Vietnam: A Patriot Abroad.* New Haven, CT: Yale University Press, 1995.

Boetcher, Thomas D. *Vietnam: The Valor and the Sorrow.* Boston: Little, Brown, 1985.

Calley, William L., as told to John Sack. *Lieutenant Calley: His Own Story.* New York: Viking Press, 1971.

Chandler, David P. *Brother Number One: A Political Biography of Pol Pot.* Boulder, CO: Westview Press, 1992.

Chong, Denise. *The Girl in the Picture: The Story of Kim Phuc, The Photograph, and the Vietnam War.* New York: Viking, 2000.

Cohen, Warren I. *Dean Rusk.* Totowa, NJ: Cooper Square, 1980.

Conkin, Paul K. *Big Daddy from the Pedernales: Lyndon Baines Johnson.* Boston: Twayne Publishers, 1986.

Currey, Cecil B. *Edward Lansdale: The Unquiet American.* Boston: Houghton Mifflin, 1988.

Dear, John, ed. *Apostle of Peace: Essays in Honor of Daniel Berrigan.* Maryknoll, New York: Orbis, 1996.

DeBenedetti, Charles, and Charles Chatfield. *An American Ordeal: The Antiwar Movement of the Vietnam Era.* New York: Syracuse University Press, 1990.

Dellinger, David. *From Yale to Jail: The Life Story of a Moral Dissenter.* New York: Pantheon, 1993.

Denton, Jeremiah A., Jr., with Edwin H. Broadt. *When Hell Was in Session.* Clover, South Carolina: Commission Press, 1976.

Duiker, William J. *Ho Chi Minh.* New York: Hyperion, 2000.

Dyson, Michael Eric. *I May Not Get There with You: The True Martin Luther King Jr.* New York: Free Press, 2000.

Eisen, Arlene. *Women and Revolution in Vietnam.* London: Zed Books, 1984.

Elliff, John T. *Crime, Dissent, and the Attorney General: The Justice Department in the 1960s.* 1971.

Ellsberg, Daniel. *Papers on the War.* New York: Simon and Schuster, 1972.

Elwood-Akers, Virginia. *Women Correspondents in the Vietnam War, 1961–1975.* Metuchen, NJ: Scarecrow Press, 1988.

Encyclopedia of World Biography. Detroit: Gale Research, 1999.

Engelmann, Larry. *Tears Before the Rain: An Oral History of the Fall of South Vietnam.* New York: Oxford University Press, 1990.

Fall, Bernard B. *Hell in a Very Small Place: The Siege of Dien Bien Phu.* Philadelphia: Lippincott, 1967.

Fall, Bernard B. *Last Reflections on a War.* New York: Doubleday, 1968.

Fall, Bernard B. *Viet-Nam Witness, 1953–1966.* New York: Praeger, 1967.

Farber, David, ed. *The Sixties: From Memory to History.* Chapel Hill, NC: University of North Carolina Press, 1994.

Farber, David. *Chicago '68.* Chicago: University of Chicago Press, 1988.

Fenn, Charles. *Ho Chi Minh: A Biographical Introduction.* New York: Scribner's, 1973.

Figley, Charles R., and Seymour Leventman, eds. *Strangers at Home: Vietnam Veterans Since the War.* New York: Praeger, 1980.

FitzGerald, Frances. *Fire in the Lake: The Vietnamese and the Americans in Vietnam.* Boston: Little, Brown, 1987.

Freedland, Michael. *Jane Fonda: A Biography.* London: Weidenfeld and Nicolson, 1988.

Fulbright, J. William. *The Arrogance of Power.* New York: Random House, 1967.

Furguson, Ernest B. *Westmoreland: The Inevitable General.* Boston: Little, Brown, 1968.

Garfinkle, Adam. *Telltale Hearts: The Origins and Impact of the Vietnam Antiwar Movement.* New York: St. Martin's Press, 1995.

Garrow, David J. *Bearing the Cross: Martin Luther King, Jr. and the Southern Christian Leadership Conference.* New York: Random House, 1986.

Giap, Vo Nguyen. *The People's War for the Defense of the Homeland in the New Era.* Hanoi: Foreign Languages Publishing House, 1981.

Giap, Vo Nguyen. *Unforgettable Days.* Hanoi: Foreign Languages Publishing House, 1974.

Gitlin, Todd. *The Sixties: Years of Hope, Days of Rage.* New York: Bantam Books, 1987.

Goldberg, Robert Alan. *Barry Goldwater.* New Haven, CT: Yale University Press, 1995.

Goldwater, Barry, with Jack Casserly. *Goldwater*. New York: Doubleday, 1988.

Halberstam, David. *Ho*. New York: Random House, 1971.

Halberstam, David. *The Best and the Brightest*. New York: Random House, 1972.

Halberstam, David. *The Making of a Quagmire: America and Vietnam During the Kennedy Era*. Rev. ed. New York: Knopf, 1988.

Halberstam, David. *The Unfinished Odyssey of Robert Kennedy*. New York: Random House, 1969.

Hall, Mitchell K. *Because of Their Faith: CALCAV and Religious Opposition to the Vietnam War*. New York: Columbia University Press, 1990.

Hammer, Ellen J. *A Death in November: America in Vietnam, 1963*. New York: Dutton, 1987.

Harrison, James Pincklney. *The Endless War: Vietnam's Struggle for Independence*. New York: McGraw-Hill, 1982.

Hayden, Tom. *Reunion: A Memoir*. New York: Random House, 1988.

Hayslip, Le Ly, with James Hayslip. *Child of War, Woman of Peace*. New York: Anchor Books, 1993.

Hayslip, Le Ly, with Jay Wurts. *When Heaven and Earth Changed Places: A Vietnamese Woman's Journey from War to Peace*. New York: Doubleday, 1989.

Heath, Jim F. *Decade of Disillusionment: The Kennedy–Johnson Years*. Bloomington: Indiana University Press, 1975.

Heller, Jeffrey. *Joan Baez: Singer with a Cause*. Chicago: Children's Press, 1991.

Hellman, John. *American Myth and the Legacy of Vietnam*. New York: Columbia University Press, 1986.

Hendrickson, Paul. *The Living and the Dead: Robert McNamara and Five Lives of a Lost War*. New York: Knopf, 1996.

Herr, Michael. *Dispatches*. New York: Knopf, 1977.

Herring, George C. *LBJ and Vietnam: A Different Kind of War*. Austin: University of Texas Press, 1994.

Herring, George. *The Secret Diplomacy of the Vietnam War: The Negotiating Volumes of the Pentagon Papers*. Austin: University of Texas Press, 1983.

Hersh, Seymour M. *My Lai 4: A Report on the Massacre and Its Aftermath*. New York: Random House, 1970.

Hersh, Seymour M. *The Price of Power: Kissinger in the Nixon White House*. New York: Summit Books, 1983.

Hilty, James W. *Robert Kennedy, Brother Protector*. Philadelphia: Temple University Press, 1997.

Ho Chi Minh. *Against U.S. Aggression, for National Salvation*. Hanoi, Vietnam: Foreign Languages Publishing House, 1967.

Hoffman, Abbie. *The Best of Abbie Hoffman*. New York: Four Walls, Eight Windows, 1990.

Howes, Craig. *Voices of the Vietnam POWs: Witnesses to Their Fight*. 1993.

Hubbell, John, with Andrew Jones and Kenneth Y. Tomlinson. *P.O.W.: A Definitive History of the American Prisoner-of-War Experience in Vietnam, 1964–1973*. New York: Reader's Digest Press, 1976.

Isaacs, Arnold R. *Vietnam Shadows: The War, Its Ghosts, and Its Legacy*. Baltimore: Johns Hopkins University Press, 1997.

Isaacs, Arnold R. *Without Honor: Defeat in Vietnam and Cambodia*. Baltimore: Johns Hopkins University Press, 1983.

Johnson, Lady Bird. *A White House Diary*. New York: Holt, Rinehart and Winston, 1970.

Johnson, Lyndon B. *The Vantage Point: Perspectives of the Presidency, 1963–1969*. New York: Holt, Rinehart and Winston, 1971.

Kamm, Henry. *Cambodia: Report from a Stricken Land*. New York: Arcade Publishing, 1998.

Kaplan, Steven. *Understanding Tim O'Brien*. Columbia, SC: University of South Carolina Press, 1994.

Karnow, Stanley. *Vietnam: A History*. New York: Viking, 1983.

Katakis, Michael. *The Vietnam Veterans Memorial*. New York: Crown, 1988.

Kaye, Tony. *Lyndon B. Johnson*. New York: Chelsea House, 1987.

Kearns, Doris. *Lyndon Johnson and the American Dream*. New York: Signet Books, 1976.

Kennedy, Robert F. *To Seek a Newer World*. Garden City, NY: Doubleday, 1967.

Kimball, Jeffrey. *Nixon's Vietnam War*. Lawrence: University Press of Kansas, 1998.

King, Martin Luther, Jr. *Autobiography of Martin Luther King, Jr.* Edited by Clayborne Carson. New York: Warner Books, 1998.

King, Martin Luther, Jr. *I Have a Dream: Writings and Speeches That Changed the World*. New York: HarperCollins, 1986.

Kinnard, Douglas. *The Certain Trumpet: Maxwell Taylor and the American Experience in Vietnam*. 1991.

Kirk, Donald. *Wider War: The Struggle for Cambodia, Thailand, and Laos*. New York: Praeger, 1971.

Kissinger, Henry. *White House Years*. Boston: Little, Brown, 1979.

Kovic, Ron. *Born on the Fourth of July*. New York: McGraw Hill, 1976.

Lansdale, Edward G. *In the Midst of Wars: An American's Mission to Southeast Asia*. New York: Harper and Row, 1972.

Le Duan. *The October Revolution and the Vietnamese Revolution*. Hanoi: Foreign Languages Publishing House, 1978.

Lodge, Henry Cabot. *The Storm Has Many Eyes: A Personal Narrative*. New York: Norton, 1973.

Lukas, Anthony J. *Nightmare: The Underside of the Nixon Years*. New York: Viking Press, 1976.

Macdonald, Peter. *Giap: The Victor in Vietnam*. New York: W.W. Norton, 1993.

Maclear, Michael. *The Ten Thousand Day War: Vietnam, 1945–1975*. New York: St. Martin's Press, 1979.

MacPherson, Myra. *Long Time Passing: Vietnam and the Haunted Generation*. Garden City, NY: Doubleday, 1984.

Mailer, Norman. *Armies of the Night*. New York: New American Library, 1968.

Malone, Mary. *Maya Lin: Architect and Artist*. Springfield, NJ: Enslow, 1995.

Manchester, William. *Portrait of a President: JFK in Profile*. Boston: Little, Brown, 1967.

Marshall, Kathryn. *In the Combat Zone: An Oral History of American Women in Vietnam*. Boston: Little, Brown, 1987.

McCain, John, with Mark Salter. *Faith of My Fathers: A Family Memoir*. New York: Random House, 1999.

McGovern, George. *Grassroots: The Autobiography of George McGovern*. New York: Random House, 1977.

McGovern, George. *Vietnam, Four American Perspectives: Lectures*. West Lafayette, IN: Purdue University Press, 1990.

McNamara, Robert S., and others. *Argument Without End: In Search of Answers to the Vietnam Tragedy*. Public Affairs, 1999.

McNamara, Robert S., with Brian VanDeMark. *In Retrospect: The Tragedy and Lessons of Vietnam*. New York: Times Books, 1995.

Moss, Nathaniel. *Ron Kovic: Antiwar Activist*. New York: Chelsea House, 1994.

Myers, Thomas. *Walking Point: American Narratives of Vietnam*. Oxford University Press, 1988.

Newman, John M. *JFK and Vietnam: Deception, Intrigue, and the Struggle for Power*. New York: Warner Books, 1992

Nguyen Cao Ky. *Twenty Years and Twenty Days.* New York: Stein and Day, 1976.

Nguyen Thi Dinh. *No Other Road to Take: Memoir of Mrs. Nguyen Thi Dinh.* Translated by Mai V. Elliott. New York: Cornell University Southeast Asian Studies Program, 1976.

Nixon, Richard M. *No More Vietnams.* New York: Arbor House, 1985.

Nixon, Richard M. *The Memoirs of Richard Nixon.* New York: Grosset and Dunlap, 1978.

Norman, Elizabeth M. *Women at War: The Story of Fifty Military Nurses Who Served in Vietnam.* Philadelphia: University of Pennsylvania Press, 1990.

Oates, Stephen B. *Let the Trumpet Sound: The Life of Martin Luther King, Jr.* New York: Harper and Row, 1982.

Osborne, Milton E. *Sihanouk: Prince of Light, Prince of Darkness.* Honolulu: University of Hawaii Press, 1994.

O'Brien, Tim. *If I Die in a Combat Zone, Box Me Up and Ship Me Home.* New York: Delacorte, 1973.

O'Brien, Tim. *The Things They Carried.* Boston: Seymour Lawrence/Houghton Mifflin, 1990.

O'Grady, Jim, and Murray Polner. *Disarmed and Dangerous: The Radical Lives and Times of Daniel and Philip Berrigan.* New York: Basic Books, 1997.

Page, Tim. *Derailed in Uncle Ho's Victory Garden: Return to Vietnam and Cambodia.* New York: Touchstone, 1995.

Page, Tim. *Page after Page: Memoirs of a War-Torn Photographer.* New York: Atheneum, 1989.

Pham Van Dong. *Selected Writings.* Hanoi: Foreign Language Publishing House, 1977.

Ponchaud, Francois. *Cambodia: Year Zero.* New York: Holt, Rinehart, and Winston, 1977.

Porter, Gareth. *A Peace Denied: The United States, Vietnam, and the Paris Agreement.* Bloomington: Indiana University Press, 1975.

Prochnau, William W. *Once Upon a Distant War: David Halberstam, Neil Sheehan, Peter Arnett—Young War Correspondents and Their Early Vietnam Battles.* New York: Times Books, 1995.

Rokyo, Mike. *Boss: Richard J. Daley of Chicago.* New York: New American Library, 1970.

Rusk, Dean, as told to Richard Rusk. *As I Saw It.* New York: Norton, 1990.

Sainteny, Jean. *Ho Chi Minh and His Vietnam: A Personal Memoir.* Chicago: Cowles, 1972.

Schanberg, Sydney H. *The Death and Life of Dith Pran*. New York: Viking Penguin, 1980.

Schlesinger, Arthur, Jr. *A Thousand Days: John F. Kennedy in the White House*. Boston: Houghton Mifflin, 1965.

Schlesinger, Arthur, Jr. *Robert Kennedy and His Times*. Boston: Houghton Mifflin, 1978.

Schrag, Peter. *Test of Loyalty: Daniel Ellsberg and the Rituals of Secret Government*. New York: Simon and Schuster, 1974.

Schroeder, Eric James. *Vietnam, We've All Been There: Interviews with American Writers*. Westport, CT: Praeger, 1992.

Schulzinger, Robert D. *A Time for War: The United States and Vietnam, 1941–1975*. New York: Oxford University Press, 1997.

Scruggs, Jan C., and Joel L. Swerdlow. *To Heal a Nation: The Vietnam Veterans Memorial*. New York: Harper and Row, 1985.

Scruggs, Jan C., ed. *Why Vietnam Still Matters: The War and the Wall*. Vietnam Veterans Memorial Fund, 1996.

Shapley, Deborah. *Promise and Power: The Life and Times of Robert McNamara*. Boston: Little, Brown, 1993.

Sheehan, Neil. *A Bright Shining Lie: John Paul Vann and America in Vietnam*. New York: Random House, 1988.

Sihanouk, Norodom, with Wilfred Burchett. *My War with the CIA: The Memoirs of Prince Norodom Sihanouk*. New York: Pantheon, 1973.

Small, Melvin. *Johnson, Nixon, and the Doves*. New Brunswick, NJ: Rutgers University Press, 1988.

Snepp, Frank. *Decent Interval: An Insider's Account of Saigon's Indecent End*. New York: Random House, 1977.

Sorenson, Theodore. *The Kennedy Legacy*. New York: Macmillan, 1969.

Steel, Ronald. *In Love with Night: The American Romance with Robert Kennedy*. New York: Simon and Shuster, 2000.

Stieglitz, Perry. *In a Little Kingdom: The Tragedy of Laos, 1960–1980*. Armonk, NY: M.E. Sharpe, 1990.

Taylor, John M. *General Maxwell Taylor: The Sword and the Pen*. New York: Doubleday, 1989.

Timberg, Robert. *John McCain: An American Odyssey*. New York: Simon and Schuster, 1999.

Vanden Heuvel, William J. *On His Own: Robert F. Kennedy, 1964–1968*. Garden City, NY: Doubleday, 1970.

Van Devanter, Lynda, and Joan Furey, eds. *Visions of War, Dreams of Peace: Writings of Women in the Vietnam War*. New York: Warner Books, 1991.

Van Devanter, Lynda, with Christopher Morgan. *Home before Morning: The Story of an Army Nurse in Vietnam.* New York: Beaufort Books, 1983.

The Vietnam Hearings. Introduction by J. William Fulbright. New York: Random House, 1966.

Wells, Tom. *The War Within: America's Battle Over Vietnam.* Berkeley: University of California Press, 1994.

Werner, Jayne, and Luu Doan Huynh, eds. *The Vietnam War: Vietnamese and American Perspectives.* Armonk, NY: M.E. Sharpe, 1993.

Westmoreland, William C. *A Soldier Reports.* New York: Doubleday, 1976.

White, Theodore H. *The Making of the President, 1972.* New York: Atheneum, 1973.

Wicker, Tom. *One of Us: Richard Nixon and the American Dream.* New York: Random House, 1991.

Willenson, Kim. *The Bad War: An Oral History of the Vietnam War.* New York: New American Library, 1987.

Woods, Randall Bennett. *Fulbright: A Biography.* New York: Cambridge University Press, 1995.

Wyatt, Clarence. *Paper Soldiers: The American Press and the Vietnam War.* New York: W.W. Norton, 1993.

Zafiri, Samule. *Westmoreland: A Biography.* New York: Morrow, 1994.

Zaroulis, Nancy, and Gerald Sullivan. *Who Spoke Up? American Protest Against the War in Vietnam, 1963–1975.* Garden City, NY: Doubleday, 1984.

Index